CNC Programming product family.....

CW01432024

"CNC Programming: Basics & Tutorial Textbook"

"CNC Programming: Reference Book"

"CNC Programming: Workbook"

"CNC Programming: Workbook - Instructor Edition"

"CNC Programming: Basics & Tutorial"

"CNC Programming: Basics & Tutorial Textbook"

This book is an introduction to G-Code CNC programming. This book starts out explaining the basics in CNC programming along with practical information and explanation of code. Included in this book are four part tutorials with G-Code explanations for milling and lathes.

"CNC Programming: Reference Book"

This book has sections taken from *"CNC Programming: Basics & Tutorial Textbook"* as a refresher to programming. This book has reference information that the CNC Programmer will need on day to day work in the CNC programming area. This book has simple charts and formulas that will be the most valuable reference book in your toolbox.

"CNC Programming: Workbook"

This book has study questions, G-Code applications, and projects that aide in the understanding of CNC Programming. This workbook ties in parts from the *"CNC Programming: Basics & Tutorial Textbook"* & *"CNC Programming: Reference Book"*.

"CNC Programming: Basics & Tutorial"

This book is the original work by the author which has basic CNC Programming concepts of only milling applications. The book is has been replaced by the *"CNC Programming: Reference Book"* and will no longer be updated. This book has basic information about milling programming.

Thank you for your interest in my products.

Sincerely,

Michael J Peterson

CNC Programming: Basics & Tutorial Textbook
Edition 1

Written by Michael J Peterson
Published by CreateSpace
Copyright Pending 2008

Purchase another copy of this book via the internet at:

www.cncbasics.com

To Receive Quantity Discounts Please Contact the Author at:

Michael J Peterson
PO Box 713
Gilbert, MN 55741
mike@dimensionalexperts.com

About the Author…

The author started out machining by accident 15 years ago. He moved to go to school and his college roommate was in a machining program and worked in a machine shop. He looked for work and ended up working in the assembly department at the shop that his roommate worked in. One night a guy called in sick and they pulled him out of assembly and put him on a load and go machine.

From that day forward he soaked up everything. He asked questions about how the machines worked and what the overwhelming codes meant. 3 months later he was "The Man" on the swing-shift that he worked on, he was his roommates lead.

From there the shop foreman took him under his wing and within a couple months, he was setting up repeat parts. Within the first 2 years he double his hourly rate and graduated in the company to work on prototype parts, which did not entail programming, but extensive editing unproven programs.

He left that company and went to another machine shop that was far less structured and had to self teach himself in order to survive. He started programming everything with a calculator and a print, eventually working on the night shift, he took everything they threw at him and made it work, which ended up learning CAD/CAM.

Today, he has programmed up to 5 axis indexable milling machines, user defined variable macros, multiple sub programming, and complex surfacing. He has programmed everything in the milling area of shops, short of Custom Macro B.

CNC Programming

Beginning Basics of G-Code

Textbook

Table of Contents

Introduction to CNC

CNC

From Wikipedia, the free encyclopedia

The abbreviation **CNC** stands for **computer numerical control**, and refers specifically to a computer "controller" that reads G-code instructions and drives a machine tool, a powered mechanical device typically used to fabricate components by the selective removal of material. CNC does numerically directed interpolation of a cutting tool in the work envelope of a machine. The operating parameters of the CNC can be altered via software load program.

CNC was preceded by NC (Numerically Controlled) machines, which were hard wired and their operating parameters could not be changed. NC was developed in the late 1940s and early 1950s by John T. Parsons in collaboration with the MIT Servomechanisms Laboratory. The first CNC systems used NC style hardware, and the computer was used for the tool compensation calculations and sometimes for editing.

Punched tape continued to be used as a medium for transferring G-codes into the controller for many decades after 1950, until it was eventually superseded by RS232 cables, floppy disks, and now is commonly tied directly into plant networks. The files containing the G-codes to be interpreted by the controller are usually saved under the .NC extension. Most shops have their own saving format that matches their ISO certification requirements.

The introduction of CNC machines radically changed the manufacturing industry. Curves are as easy to cut as straight lines, complex 3-D structures are relatively easy to produce, and the number of machining steps that required human action has been dramatically reduced.

With the increased automation of manufacturing processes with CNC machining, considerable improvements in consistency and quality have been achieved with no strain on the operator. CNC automation reduced the frequency of errors and provided CNC operators with time to perform additional tasks. CNC automation also allows for more flexibility in the way parts are held in the manufacturing process and the time required to change the machine to produce different components.

In a production environment, a series of CNC machines may be combined into one station, commonly called a "cell", to progressively machine a part requiring several operations. CNC machines today are controlled directly from files created by CAM software packages, so that a part or assembly can go directly from design to manufacturing without the need of producing a drafted paper drawing of the manufactured component. In a sense, the CNC machines represent a special segment of industrial robot systems, as they are programmable to perform many kinds of machining operations (within their designed physical limits, like other robotic systems). CNC machines can run over night and over weekends without operator intervention. Error detection features have been developed, giving CNC machines the ability to call the operator's mobile phone if it detects that a tool has broken. While the machine is awaiting replacement on the tool, it would run other parts it is already loaded with up to that tool and wait for the operator. The ever changing intelligence of CNC controllers has dramatically increased job shop cell production. Some machines might even make 1000 parts on a weekend with no operator, checking each part with lasers and sensors.

Types of instruction

A line in a G-code file can instruct the machine tool to do one of several things.

Movements

The most basic motion for a controller is to move the machine tool along a linear path from one point to another. Some machine tools can only do this in XY, and have to accept changes in Z separately. Some have two further axes of rotation to control the orientation of the cutter, and can move them simultaneously with the XYZ motion. Lately 4 and 5 axis machines have become popular. The 2 additional axis allow for the work surface or medium to be rotated around X and Y. For example, a 4-axis machine can move the tool head in XY and Z directions, and also rotate the medium around the X or Y axis, similar to a lathe. This is called the A or B axis in most cases.

All motions can be built from linear motions if they are short and there are enough of them. But most controllers can interpolate horizontal circular arcs in XY.

Lately, some controllers have implemented the ability to follow an arbitrary curve (NURBS), but these efforts have been met with skepticism since, unlike circular arcs, their definitions are not natural and are too complicated to set up by hand, and CAM software can already generate any motion using many short linear segments.

With the advent of the vortech router cnc quad drive system which utilizes four (bidirectional) motors and drive, users are able to achieve greater speeds and accuracy.

Drilling

A tool can be used to drill holes by pecking to let the swarf out. Using an internal thread cutting tool and the ability to control the exact rotational position of the tool with the depth of cut, it can be used to cut screw threads.

Drilling cycles

A drilling cycle is used to repeat drilling or tapping operations on a workpiece. The drilling cycle accepts a list of parameters about the operation, such as depth and feed rate. To begin drilling any number of holes to the specifications configured in the cycle, the only input required is a set of coordinates for hole location. The cycle takes care of depth, feed rate, retraction, and other parameters that appear in more complex cycles. After the holes are completed, the machine is given another command to cancel the cycle, and resumes operation.

Parametric programming

A more recent advancement in CNC interpreters is support of logical commands, known as parametric programming. Parametric programs incorporate both G-code and these logical constructs to create a programming language and syntax similar to BASIC. Various manufacturers refer to parametric programming in brand-specific ways. For instance, Haas refers to parametric programs as macros. GE Fanuc refers to it as Custom Macro A & B, while Okuma refers to it as User Task 2. The programmer can make if/then/else statements, loops, subprogram calls, perform various arithmetic, and manipulate variables to create a large degree of freedom within one program. An entire product line of different sizes can be programmed using logic and simple math to create and scale an entire range of parts, or create a stock part that can be scaled to any size a customer demands.

Parametric programming also enables custom machining cycles, such as fixture creation and bolt circles. If a user wishes to create additional fixture locations on a work holding device, the machine can be manually guided to the new location and the fixture subroutine called. The machine will then drill and form the patterns required to mount additional vises or clamps at that location. Parametric programs are also used to shorten long programs with incremental or stepped passes. A loop can be created with variables for step values and other parameters, and in doing so remove a large amount of repetition in the program body.

Because of these features, a parametric program is more efficient than using CAD/CAM software for large part runs. The brevity of the program allows the CNC programmer to rapidly make performance adjustments to looped commands, and tailor the program to the machine it is running on. Tool wear, breakage, and other system parameters can be accessed and changed directly in the program, allowing extensions and modifications to the functionality of a machine beyond what a manufacturer envisioned.

There are three types of variables used in CNC systems: Local variable, Common variable, and System variable. Local variable is used to hold data after machine off preset value. Common variable is used to hold data if machine switch off does not erase form data. The System variable this variable used system parameter this cannot use direct to convert the common variable for example Tool radius, Tool length and tool height to be measured in mm or inches.

G-code
From Wikipedia, the free encyclopedia

G-code is a common name for the programming language that controls NC and CNC machine tools. Developed by the Electronic Industries Alliance in the early 1960s, a final revision was approved in February 1980 as RS274D.

Due to the lack of further development, the immense variety of machine tool configurations, and little demand for interoperability, few machine tool controllers (CNC) adhere to this standard. Extensions and variations have been added independently by manufacturers, and operators of a specific controller must be aware of differences of each manufacturer's product. When initially introduced, CAM systems were limited in the configurations of tools supported.

Manufacturers attempted to overcome compatibility difficulties by standardizing on a machine tool controller built by Fanuc. Unfortunately, Fanuc does not remain consistent with RS-274 or its own previous standard, and has been slow at adding new features and exploiting the increase in computing power. For example, they changed G70/G71 to G20/G21; they used parentheses for comments which caused difficulty when they introduced mathematical calculations so the use square parentheses for macro calculations; they now have nano technology recently in 32-bit mode but in the Fanuc 15MB control they introduced HPCC (high-precision contour control) which uses a 64-bit RISC (reduced instruction set computer) processor and this now has a 500 block buffer for look-ahead for correct shape contouring and surfacing of small block programs and 5-axis continuous machining.

This is also used for NURBS to be able to work closely with industrial designers and the systems that are used to design flowing surfaces. The NURBS has its origins from the ship building industry and is described by using a knot and a weight as for bending steamed wooden planks and beams.

G-code is also the name of any word in a CNC program that begins with the letter *G*, and generally is a code telling the machine tool what type of action to perform, such as:
- rapid movement
- controlled feed move in a straight line or arc
- series of controlled feed moves that would result in a hole being bored, a workpiece cut (routed) to a specific dimension, or a decorative profile shape added to the edge of a workpiece.
- change a pallet
- set tool information such as offset.

There are other codes; the type codes can be thought of like registers in a computer

- X absolute position
- Y absolute position
- Z absolute position
- A position (rotary around X)
- B position (rotary around Y)
- C position (rotary around Z)
- U Relative axis parallel to X
- V Relative axis parallel to Y
- W Relative axis parallel to Z
- M code (otherwise referred to as a "Miscellaneous" function")
- F feed rate
- S spindle speed
- N line number
- R Arc radius or optional word passed to a subprogram/canned cycle
- P Dwell time or optional word passed to a subprogram/canned cycle
- T Tool selection
- I Arc data X axis
- J Arc data Y axis.
- K Arc data Z axis, or optional word passed to a subprogram/canned cycle
- D Cutter diameter/radius offset
- H Tool length offset

Summary

CNC technology has changed the way manufacturing is done today. Quality of product and ease to create quantity has directly impacted the cost of labor in manufacturing overall.

G-Code programming is a programming language with very little consistency of standards. Because there are governing body to standardize the code, there can be and will be difference in codes between different machine tool builders and control manufacturers.

Before we continue any further, let us understand what G-code is. G-code for all intensive purposes is **Text**. There are *G-Code Editors* out there that can identify and highlight the different codes in a line, but we need to understand that it is just **Text**, not some weird language that is common in computer programming language.

This being said, understand that G-Code is something that can be layout in many different formats, most commonly .NC or .TXT.

This is important to know because you can write a program on any Text based software, like Microsoft Word or something simple as Notepad.

We first will start with the fundamentals, learn the code, and apply all of it to an application.

_____

_____

_____

_____

_____

_____

_____

_____

_____

_____

_____

_____

_____

_____

_____

_____

_____

_____

_____

_____

_____

_____

_____

_____

_____

Notes:

2 Axis Fundamentals

Fundamentals of G-Code

G-Code programming is a very simple programming language. When we were kids, we used to and may still do connect the dot puzzle games. G-code works ***exactly*** on the same principle. It takes two simple concepts to understand G-code programming, ***connect-the-dots*** and the ***number line***.

Connect-the-dots

We can draw something very simply by connecting the dots.

We do not think about it, but we are creating something tangible in the 2-axis world.

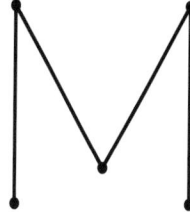

The Number Line

The number line is simply the measurement of units. Let's look at this number line:

-2   -1   0   1   2

In a straight line numbers either get bigger or smaller from Zero. Machining, along with G-Code programming, uses both sides of Zero.

Signs   +/ -

The Plus (+) sign and the Minus (-) sign are very important in machining. In machining we can also call them Positive or Negative respectively. We use these signs in two situations; location and direction.

Location

They signify what side of Zero a number is on, we can say this is a location indicator; Left for Minus and Right for Positive respectively from Zero.

Direction

These signs also are used as a tool to tell us which direction to move; Left for Minus and Right for Positive.

Addition

Let's talk about simple addition for a second. When you add or subtract numbers you get an answer. The building block of programming is simple addition. If you can not think conceptually about which side of Zero you are on, or which direction you need to go because of a negative number, just add or subtract.

Ok, let's look at some simple examples of positive and negative numbers with simple addition and subtraction.

1+1=2	-1 + -1 = -2	-1 + 4 = 3
1+2=3	-1 + -2 = -3	-4 + -1 = -5
2+2=4	-2 + -2 = -4	-6 + 2 = -4

For simplicity, always add numbers. Sometimes we get very confused subtracting negative numbers.

First.

CNC Milling Machining Centers use three axis and sometimes more. Obviously this is because the world is 3-dimensional.

Don't be scared, we will start with two. We will start by thinking in terms of that old graphing we did in algebra classes. Just think of that same number line as before with another line running perpendicular.

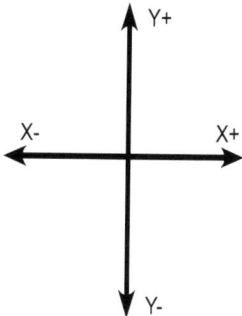

```
                    ▲ Y+
                    │
                    │
        X-          │          X+
       ◄────────────┼────────────►
                    │
                    │
                    ▼ Y-
```

These lines are all you need to get started programming. But now we have to define them. The one that goes horizontally is "**X**" and the one vertically is "**Y**".

If you can understand this simple concept, and understand that Zero has two sides, then you are on your way. We use this in programming just simply for directional positioning in a graphed area.

Quadrants

Quadrants are something to make note of simply on the basis of location. Because a machine tool uses lead screws as a means to move the table along a straight line, identifying the quadrants are important because we can identify which lead is being used to move the work piece.

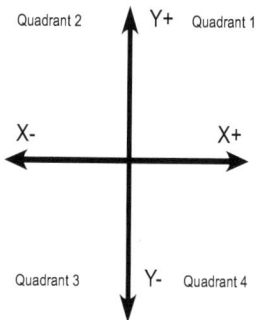

```
   Quadrant 2      ▲ Y+   Quadrant 1
                   │
                   │
        X-         │         X+
       ◄───────────┼───────────►
                   │
                   │
   Quadrant 3      ▼ Y-   Quadrant 4
```

Quadrants also help in identifying the signs of the respected axis in use.

Quadrant 1 = X+ Y+   Quadrant 3 = X- Y-
Quadrant 2 = X- Y+   Quadrant 4 = X+ Y-

Let us start by drawing that **connect-the-dots** of the Letter "**M**". If you right the letter on paper, you are actually writing it in some sort of units across a 2 dimensional surface.

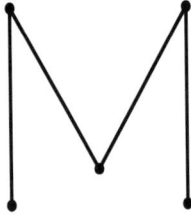

How would we describe this letter in Graphical terms applying it to our two axes?

- Move straight in the Y axis in a *positive* direction so many units.
- Then move in a *positive* X and a *negative* Y direction so many units.
- Then move in a *positive* X and a *positive* Y direction so many units.
- Then move in a *negative* Y direction so many units.

Second.

Let us take this letter "M" example and combine it with units. We will identify this scale of inches.

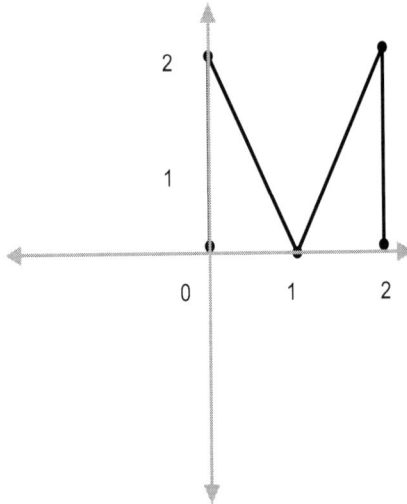

We will start at Zero.

- Move to Y2.
- Move to X1.Y0
- Move to X2.Y2.
- Move to Y0

This is the basics of programming. The combination of the right G-code in these simple lines would create the Letter "M" on a CNC Machining Center.

Absolute versus Incremental

Absolute programming is programming mode that is a reflection of each number read is from part or machine Zero.

Incremental programming is a programming mode that is a reflection from the current position.

In our Letter "M" example, the first example defined the letter from moving from a start position then on to the next position by so many units. This would be an example of *incremental* positioning. We said to move the next position from that current position.

In the second Letter "M" example adding units, we actually moved to locations with from a defined Zero position. This would be an example of *absolute* programming.

Summary

What we get from 2 Axis Fundamentals is that G-code is nothing more than numbers. What we do with G-code programming is define codes to let the machine tool know what the programmer wants to do with those numbers.

With the use of different codes we can do just about anything imaginable. These are such things like make a straight line or interpolate a circle or anything in between.

The following sections will discuss the different commonly used G-codes and M-codes along with the different complimentary aspects to assist those codes.

Notes:

Cartesian Coordinate Systems

Cartesian Coordinate Systems

The Cartesian Coordinate System

The three dimensional Cartesian coordinate system provides the three physical dimensions of space — Length, Width, and Height.

The three Cartesian axes defining the system are perpendicular to each other. The relevant coordinates are of the form (X,Y,Z). The axes are depicted in a "world-coordinates" orientation with the Z-axis pointing up.

The XY-, YZ-, and XZ-planes divide the three-dimensional space into eight subdivisions known as **Octants**, similar to the *quadrants* of 2D space. While conventions have been established for the labelling of the four quadrants of the x-y plane, only the first octant of three dimensional space is labelled. It contains all of the points whose x, y, and z coordinates are positive.

All CAD/CAM and CNC systems use some sort of Three-Dimensional Coordinate System.

This system starts by identifying a work envelope with an established origin. In CAD/CAM this is called the *World Coordinate* or *World View*. In CNC machine tools this is known as the *Machine Work Envelope*.

This three-dimensional coordinate system gives the CNC machine tool the means to interpret G-Code positioning within this Machine Work Envelope.

Using the Machine Work Envelope, the CNC can be offset to the corner of a piece of material to use a local *Work Coordinate*.

Through the use of the proper codes the CNC will use this local Work Coordinate position to interpret program numbers as it runs.

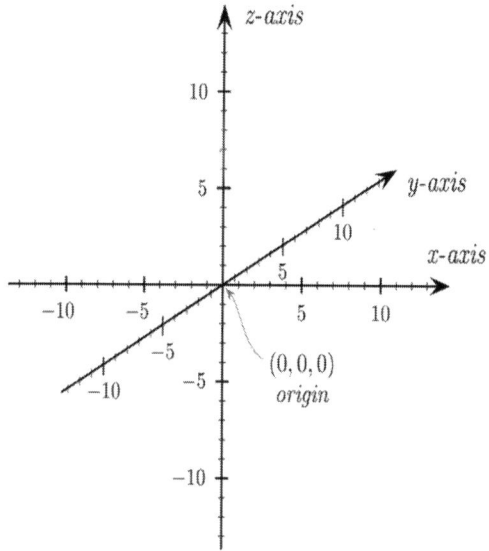

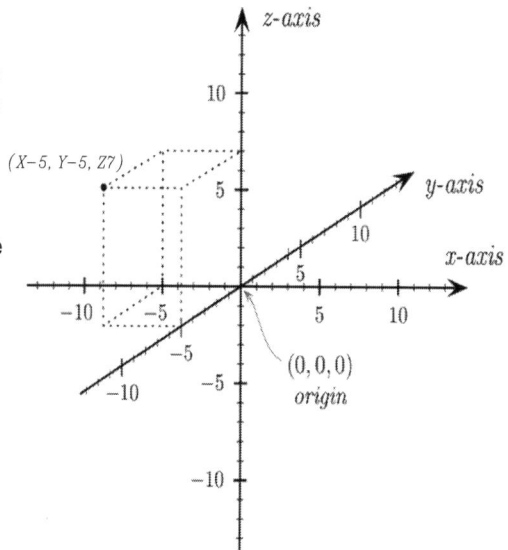

Summary

The understanding of Cartesian Coordinate Systems is very useful to CNC machining. Through the use of local Work Coordinate positions, multiple work pieces may be produced with the same program.

Notes:

Introduction

to

G-Code

Standard G-Codes

Milling

Standard G-Codes - Mill

The G-Codes are what tell the machine to do with positional reference. This is just a simple reference to what standard G-Codes do.

G0 or G00 – Rapid Movement
The fastest the Machine can go to the next defined position. If moving in multiple axis, each axis will move as fast as they can independently of one another until it reaches it's defined end points.

G1 or G01 – Linear Movement
A straight line move with a speed defined by an F. If moving in multiple axes, the machine will move proportionally in each axis until it reaches its defined end position.

G2 or G02 – Interpolation Clockwise
A circular movement in 2 axis. Will create an arc to a specified radius defined by R or I/J.

G3 or G03 - Interpolation Counter Clockwise
A circular movement in 2 axis. Will create an arc to a specified radius defined by R or I/J.

G4 or G04 – Dwell
Machine will dwell once reached position to a user defined time, P.

G9 or G09 – Exact Stop/Exact Position
Machine will not traverse to next line of code until it positions exactly to position.

G10	- Data Setting
G17	- XY plane selection
G18	- ZX plane selection
G19	- YZ plane selection
G20	- Machine in inch
G21	- Machine in MM

G28 - Return to Reference Position
Normally machine home.

G30 - Return to 2nd reference position
Normally pallet changing/tool change home if different than machine home.

G40	- Cutter Compensation Cancel
G41	- Cutter Compensation Left
	Used with user defined value, D
G42	- Cutter Compensation Right
	Used with user defined value, D
G43	- Tool Length Compensation +
	Used with user defined value, H. Common
G44	- Tool Length Compensation -
	Used with user defined value, H. Not common
G49	- Tool Length Compensation Cancel

G50   - Scaling Cancel

G51   - Scaling

G54-G59   - Work Coordinate Systems
                User defined in the Workoffset page, XYZ

G68   - Coordinate Rotation
                User defined rotation, R

G69   - Coordinate Rotation Cancel

G90   - Absolute Command
Used for absolute programming either from machine zero or work coordinate zero.

G91   - Incremental Command
                Used to incrementally move from current position.

G92   - Programming of Absolute Zero(Do Not Use)
This Code is an old way of programming. You are redefining the machine coordinate system, when using this code. Normally you move to Part Zero, and set Zero by running code G92X0Y0. This sets a new Absolute Zero for machine, overrides the Work Coordinate System. In order to reset Absolute Zero in the machine, Zero Return the machine manually to Machine Zero and run the G92X0Y0. Some machines don't like this code, *I would strongly advise against it.*

G94   - Feed Per Minute
                Sets the way the machine reads an F, inches per minute, normally.

G95   - Feed Per Revolution
                Sets the way the machine reads an F, inches per rev, normally.

G98   - Return to initial point in canned cycle
G99   - Return to R point in canned cycle

Standard Canned Cycles

G80   - Cancel Canned Cycle

R is the **Z** start height of the part for the canned cycle
Q is the size of peck in a canned cycle
P is the dwell in a canned cycle

G73   - Peck Drilling Cycle
                    Format   G98G73R.1Z-1.Q.05F10.

              Rapids to R plane
              Feeds toward Z point by Q at F
              Rapids toward R by machine parameter defined amount
              Rapids towards last Q point
              Feeds to next Q point, repeat until Z
              Rapids from Z to R

G76   Boring Cycle
                    Format   G98G86R.1Z-1.F10.

              Rapids to R plane
              Feeds to Z point by F
              Stops and orientates spindle at Z
              Rapids to R
              Turns spindle on

G81   - Drilling Cycle
                    Format   G98G81R.1Z-1.F10.

Rapids to R plane
              Feeds to Z point by F
              Rapids up to R plane

G82   - Drilling Cycle
                    Format   G98G82R.1Z-1.F10.P200

              Rapids to R plane
              Feeds Z point by F
              Dwells at Z point by P
              Rapids to R plane

G83   - Pecking Cycle
           Format   G98G83R.1Z-1.Q.1F10.

         Rapids to R plane
         Feeds to Z point by F in increments of Q
*Rapids to R and previous Q point within a machine parameter variable and begins to feed again until next Q is reached.
         Rapids to R plane

G84   Tapping Cycle
           Format   G98G84R.1Z-1.F10.

         Rapids to R plane
         Timing between Z and Spindle
*There are many different tapping formats. Refer to your machine tool manual for specifics. Normally, with G84, it is just implementing timing between the Z axis and Spindle. The feed and spindle speeds need to be calculated correctly.

G85   Boring Cycle
           Format   G98G85R.1Z-1.F10.

         Rapids to R plane
         Feeds to Z point by F
         Feeds to R plane

G86   Boring Cycle
           Format   G98G86R.1Z-1.F10.

         Rapids to R plane
         Feeds to Z point by F
         Stops spindle at Z
         Rapids to R
         Turns spindle on

G87   Back Boring Cycle
           Format   G98G87R.1Z-1.F10.

         Rapids to R plane
         Feeds to Z point by F
         Reverses Spindle at Z
         Feeds to R
         Spindle Forward at R

G-Code Quick Reference -Mill

G0 - Rapid Movement
G1 - Linear Movement
G2 - Interpolation Clockwise
G3 - Interpolation Counter Clockwise

G4 - Dwell
G9 - Exact Stop/Exact Position
G10 - Data Setting

G17 - XY plane selection
G18 - ZX plane selection
G19 - YZ plane selection

G20 - Machine in inch
G21 - Machine in MM

G28 - Return to Reference Position
G30 - Return to 2nd reference position

G40 - Cutter Compensation Cancel
G41 - Cutter Compensation Left
G42 - Cutter Compensation Right

G43 - Tool Length Compensation +
G44 - Tool Length Compensation -
G49 - Tool Length Cancel

G50 - Scaling Cancel
G51 - Scaling

G54-G59 - Work Coordinate Systems

G68 - Coordinate Rotation
G69 - Coordinate Rotation Cancel

G90 - Absolute Command
G91 - Incremental Command
G92 - Programming of Absolute Zero

G94 - Feed Per Minute
G95 - Feed Per Revolution

G98 - Return to initial point in canned cycle
G99 - Return to R point in canned cycle

G80 - Cancel Canned Cycle
G73 - Peck Drilling Cycle
G74 - Left Hand Tapping Cycle
G76 - Boring Cycle
G81 - Drilling Cycle
G82 - Drilling Cycle
G83 - Pecking Cycle
G84 - Right Hand Tapping Cycle
G85 - Boring Cycle
G86 - Boring Cycle
G87 - Back Boring Cycle

Notes:

Standard G-Codes

Lathe

Standard G-Codes - Lathe

The G-Codes are what tell the machine to do with positional reference. This is just a simple reference to what standard G-Codes do.

Please refer to <u>*Appendix: Lathe Contour Canned Cycles*</u> *in* **"CNC Programming: Basics & Tutorial Textbook"** *for examples of lathe contour canned cycles.*

G0 or G00 – Rapid Movement

> The fastest the Machine can go to the next defined position. If moving in multiple axis, each axis will move as fast as they can independently of one another until it reaches it's defined end points.

G1 or G01 – Linear Movement

> A straight line move with a speed defined by an F. If moving in multiple axes, the machine will move proportionally in each axis until it reaches its defined end position.

G2 or G02 – Interpolation Clockwise

> A circular movement in 2 axis. Will create an arc to a specified radius defined by R or I/K.

G3 or G03 - Interpolation Counter Clockwise

> A circular movement in 2 axis. Will create an arc to a specified radius defined by R or I/K.

G4 or G04 – Dwell

> Machine will dwell once reached position to a user defined time, P.

G9 or G09 – Exact Stop/Exact Position

> Machine will not traverse to next line of code until it positions exactly to position.

G10   - Data Setting
G17   - XY plane selection
G18   - ZX plane selection
G19   - YZ plane selection

G20   - Machine in inch
G21   - Machine in MM

G28   - Return to Reference Position
> Normally machine home.

G30   - Return to 2nd reference position
> Normally pallet changing/tool change home if different than machine home.

G40   - Tool Nose Radius Compensation Cancel
G41   - Tool Nose Radius Compensation Left
G42   - Tool Nose Radius Compensation Right

G50   - Spindle Speed Maximum RPM (S)

G52   - Local coordinate system setting

G53   - Machine coordinate system setting

G54-G59   - Work Coordinate Systems
           User defined in the Workoffset page, XYZ

G90   - Absolute Command
           Used for absolute programming either from machine zero or work coordinate zero.

G91   - Incremental Command
           Used to incrementally move from current position.

G92   - Thread Cutting Cycle

G96   - Constant Surface Speed
           Adjusts the spindle speed according to diameter of cut.

G97   - Constant Non-variant Spindle Speed
           Maintains the same spindle speed throughout cut.

G98   - Feed Per Minute

G99   - Feed Per Revolution

Standard Canned Cycles - Drilling

G80   - Cancel Canned Cycle

R is the **Z** start height of the part for the canned cycle
Q is the size of peck in a canned cycle
P is the dwell in a canned cycle

G81   - Drilling Cycle
                    Format   G81R.1Z-1.F.005

             Rapids to R plane
             Feeds to Z point by F
             Rapids up to R plane

G82   - Drilling Cycle
                    Format   G82R.1Z-1.F.005P200

             Rapids to R plane
             Feeds Z point by F
             Dwells at Z point by P
             Rapids to R plane

G83   - Pecking Cycle
                    Format   G83R.1Z-1.Q.1F.005

             Rapids to R plane
             Feeds to Z point by F in increments of Q
                    *Rapids to R and previous Q point within a machine parameter variable and
                    begins to feed again until next Q is reached.
             Rapids to R plane

G84   Tapping Cycle
                    Format   G84R.1Z-1.F.025

             Rapids to R plane
             Timing between Z and Spindle
                    *There are many different tapping formats. Refer to your machine tool manual for
                    specifics. Normally, with G84, it is just implementing timing between the Z axis
                    and Spindle. The feed and spindle speeds need to be calculated correctly.

Standard Canned Cycles (con't)

G85   Boring Cycle
        Format   G85R.1Z-1.F.005

        Rapids to R plane
        Feeds to Z point by F
        Feeds to R plane

G86   Boring Cycle
        Format   G86R.1Z-1.F.005

        Rapids to R plane
        Feeds to Z point by F
        Stops spindle at Z
        Rapids to R
        Turns spindle on

G-Code Quick Reference -Lathe

G0 - Rapid Movement
G1 - Linear Movement
G2 - Interpolation Clockwise
G3 - Interpolation Counter Clockwise

G4 - Dwell
G9 - Exact Stop/Exact Position
G10 - Data Setting

G17 - XY plane selection
G18 - ZX plane selection
G19 - YZ plane selection

G20 - Machine in inch
G21 - Machine in MM

G28 - Return to Reference Position
G30 - Return to 2nd reference position

G40 - Cutter Compensation Cancel
G41 - Cutter Compensation Left
G42 - Cutter Compensation Right

G43 - Tool Length Compensation +
G44 - Tool Length Compensation -
G49 - Tool Length Cancel

G50 - Scaling Cancel
G51 - Scaling

G54-G59 - Work Coordinate Systems

G68 - Coordinate Rotation
G69 - Coordinate Rotation Cancel

G90 - Absolute Command
G91 - Incremental Command
G92 - Programming of Absolute Zero

G94 - Feed Per Minute
G95 - Feed Per Revolution

G98 - Return to initial point in canned cycle
G99 - Return to R point in canned cycle

G80 - Cancel Canned Cycle
G73 - Peck Drilling Cycle
G74 - Left Hand Tapping Cycle
G76 - Boring Cycle
G81 - Drilling Cycle
G82 - Drilling Cycle
G83 - Pecking Cycle
G84 - Right Hand Tapping Cycle
G85 - Boring Cycle
G86 - Boring Cycle
G87 - Back Boring Cycle

Introduction to G-Code
Notes:

Notes:

Modal

The Groups of G-Code

Modal (Fanuc)

Codes in G-Code programming are Modal. This means that two codes from the same group cannot be executed at the same time.

There are numerous groups and may vary with specialized machine tools. These groups are:

Group 1 – Motion/Movement

This group consists of codes that create movement.
G0, G1, G2, G3, G80, and all the Standard Canned Cycles

Group 2 – Plane Selection

This group consists of codes that designate which plane is being used.
G17, G18, and G19

Group 3 – Distance/Travel Mode

This group consists of codes that designate how to interpret location.
G90 and G91

Group 4 – M code group

Group 5 – Feed Mode

This group consists of codes that designate how to feed.
G94 and G95

Group 6 – Units

This group designates the unit of measurement.
G20 and G21

Group 7 – Cutter Compensation

This group designates the use of cutter compensation.
G40, G41, and G42

Group 8 – Tool Length Compensation

This group designates the use of the tool length compensation.
G43 and G49

Group 9 – Canned Cycles

Group 10 – Return in Canned Cycle

This group designates the use of return in canned cycles.
G98 and G99

Group 14 – Coordinate System

This group designates the selected coordinate system.
G54-G59 and all extended coordinate systems.

The overall idea of the Modes in CNC is that you may not execute two of the same actions at the same time. This might seem confusing, but once you start programming, you do not even think of these groups because everything just works out.

This brief section is for exposure to the approach of how a CNC control uses the information.

Standard M-Codes

Milling

M-Codes

Standard M-Codes- Mill

M-Codes are another code that adds in the practice of G-code programming also known as *Miscellaneous Functions*. M-codes are read by the **machine tool control** that utilizes functions of the machine that are not apart of tool path generation as G-codes.

The following are *some* **common** M-codes. Beware that M codes can be defined differently by the machine tool builder and also by the machine tool control manufacturer.

M0 or M00	–	Machine Stop
M1 or M01	–	Optional Stop
M2 or M02	–	End of Program
M3 or M03	–	Spindle Start, Clockwise
M4 or M04	–	Spindle Start, Counter Clockwise
M5 or M05	–	Spindle Stop
M6 or M06	–	Tool Change
M8 or M08	–	Coolant On
M9 or M09	–	Coolant Off
M19	–	Orientate Spindle
M29	–	Rigid Tapping
M30	–	End of Program, Reset Program
M98	–	Subprogram jumpto, format M98P1
M99	–	Subprogram end, return to main program

Notes:

_____

_____

_____

_____

_____

_____

_____

_____

_____

_____

_____

_____

_____

_____

_____

_____

_____

_____

_____

_____

_____

_____

Standard M-Codes

Lathe

Standard M-Codes - Lathe

M-Codes are another code that adds in the practice of G-code programming also known as *Miscellaneous Functions*. M-codes are read by the **machine tool control** that utilizes functions of the machine that are not apart of tool path generation as G-codes.

The following are *some* **common** M-codes. Beware that M codes can be defined differently by the machine tool builder and also by the machine tool control manufacturer.

M0 or M00   –   Machine Stop

M1 or M01   –   Optional Stop

M2 or M02   –   End of Program

M3 or M03   –   Spindle Start, Counter Clockwise

M4 or M04   –   Spindle Start, Clockwise

M5 or M05   –   Spindle Stop

M8 or M08   –   Coolant On

M9 or M09   –   Coolant Off

M10   –   Chuck Clamp

M11   –   Chuck Unclamp

M17   –   Rotate Turret Forward

M18   –   Rotate Turret Reverse

M19   –   Orientate Spindle

M23   –   Angle Out of Thread On

M23   –   Angle Out of Thread Off

M30   –   End of Program, Reset Program

M36   –   Parts Catcher On

M37   –   Part Catcher Off

M97   –   Local Subprogram Call

M98   –   Subprogram jumpto, format M98P1

M99   –   Subprogram end, return to main program

M-Codes
Notes:

Notes:

The Control Panel

The Control Panel is the user interface for the Machine Tool. The panel has many different functions in order for the user to utilize the Machine Tool.

In the following section we will look over standard functions of modern Control Panel.

Generic Control Panel

Control Panels have the same basic user interface functions. Each machine tool builder and control panel manufacturer have different layouts or ways to achieve a function, but they all do the same thing.

The basic control panel has a Display, Key Inputs, and Standard User Interface Function Controls.

Let us look at these areas.

The Display

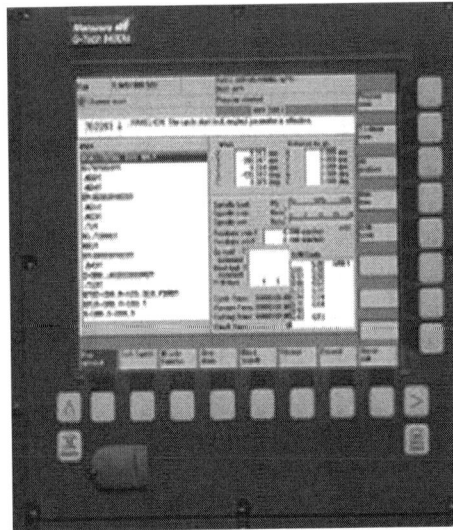

The display is used to view the different machine tool functions and inputs. There are many different screens that are viewable on the display which have specific uses for the machine tool.

Offsets

The offset screen is used to input offset numbers. This could be Work offset number or Tool Offset numbers which the machine will use in the machining process.

Program

The program screen is used to either view the G-Code program to Edit or in automatic run mode, watch the program progress.

Position

The position screen shows machine position in reference to machine home, work coordinate system zero, operator zero set, or distance to go position.

This display example along with most modern day display panels have soft-key inputs built in. These soft keys help navigate the numerous screen in the control. The numerous screens can be but not limited to graphical preview, macro, parameter, background edit, part counter, load meter, etc.

Key Inputs

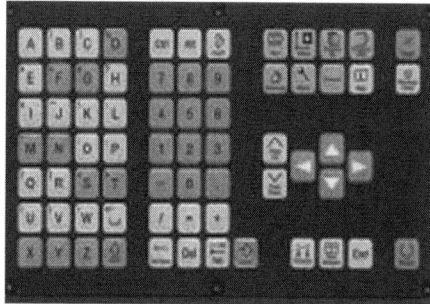

The Key Inputs are basically the equivalent of the keyboard for a personal computer. This layout lets the user input data into the machine tool control panel in order for the machine to correctly attain its function.

The inputs that can be used by this interface are type in offsets for tools or work coordinate systems, edit or create programs, and change parameter settings.

User Interface Function Controls

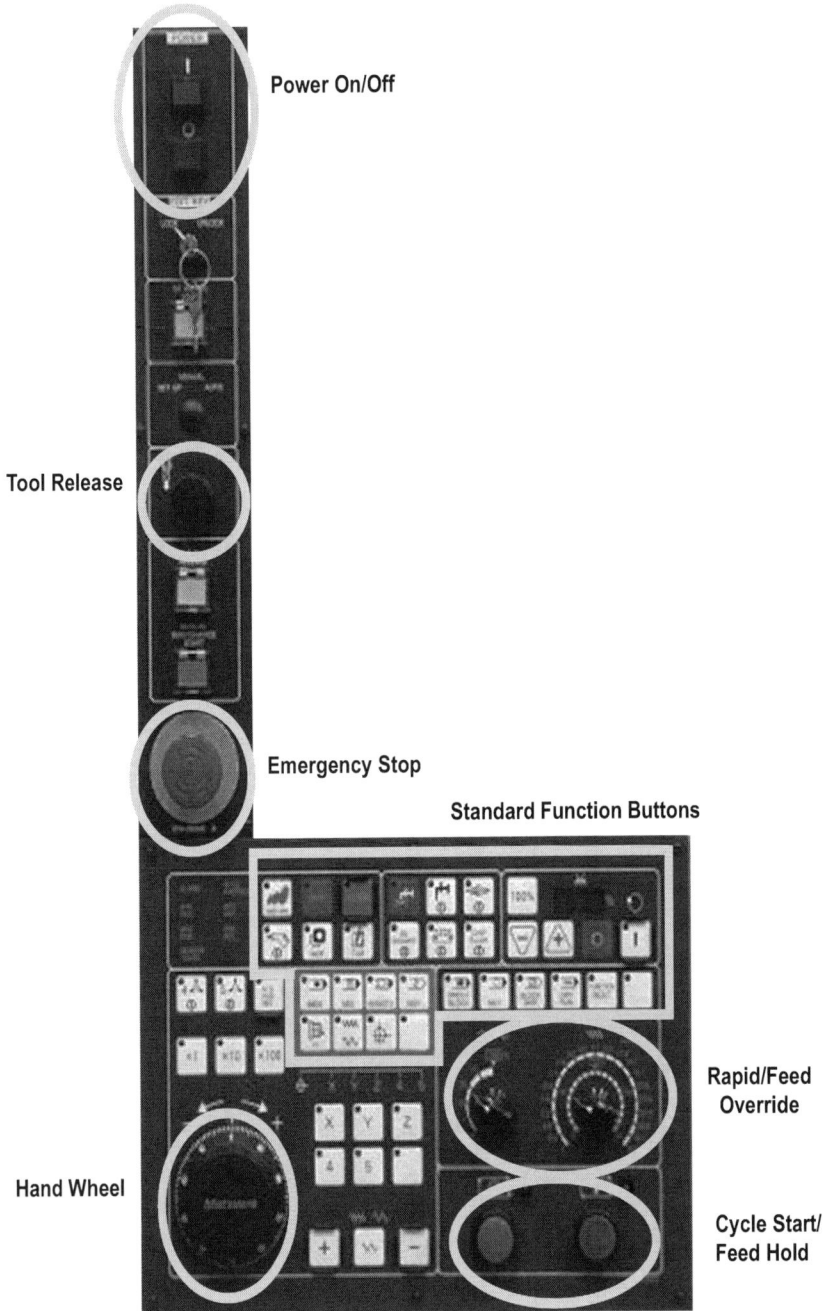

Power On/Off

Tool Release

Emergency Stop

Standard Function Buttons

Rapid/Feed
Override

Hand Wheel

Cycle Start/
Feed Hold

The User Interface Function Controls(UIFC) are standard controls and control the basic functions of the machine tool.

Each control has Power On/Off, Emergency Stop button, Tool Release button, Hand Wheel, Cycle Start/Feed Hold Button, Feedrate/Rapid Override, and Standard Function Buttons.

Most of these features are self-explanatory, but the Standard Function Buttons are something that should be addressed.

The Standard Function Buttons may not always be buttons, but could be soft switches or toggle style switches. On each control they do the same thing.

What are some of these buttons?

Single Block

When enabled, this puts the machine in a line by line, or block by block mode. This allows the machine tool to only act on one line of code at a time and will wait until the Cycle Start button is pressed to continue on.

Optional Stop

When enabled, this tells the machine tool to stop when the control reads the "M-Code" M1 or M01. Once reading this code, the machine will stop and wait for the Cycle Start button to be pressed before continuing on.

Block Skip

When enabled, the machine skips or ignores any line with "/" before it.

Memory/Auto

When enabled, the machine is set in Run mode which will run the current program in memory.

Edit

When enabled, the machine is in Edit mode, which the user can edit the current program.

MDI

When enabled, the user can manually enter code for the desired function.

The Control Panel
Notes:

_____

_____

_____

_____

_____

_____

_____

_____

_____

_____

_____

_____

_____

_____

_____

_____

_____

_____

_____

_____

_____

_____

Notes:

The Control Panel

Programming Basics

Starting with the Basics

There are fundamental basics with G-Code programming. Previously we looked over lists of G-Code and M-Codes along with how to define simple "X" and "Y" coordinates numbers.

In order to use these basics of G-Code programming, we need to understand what the basics are in the format of G-Code.

The Basic Rules

1. Each line in G-Code programming is called a **Block**.
   - A block is a single line of text with G & M Code and ends by what is called by the "End-of-Block" or "EOB" which is represented in the machine control as the semi-colon, ";".

   Note: The term Block is commonly referred to Line in shop floor terminology.
   The EOB in an Editor is nothing more than a Character Return and a semi-colon will automatically be inserted when being read by the machine tool.

2. Each program needs to be identified by a Program Number.
   - A Program Number is an identifier for the machine tool for filing in the Memory.

3. A block cannot have two G-Codes from the same Modal Group.

4. A block cannot have two M-Codes.

5. Modular. Unless defined by the current Block codes, current positional values will be interpreted by the last read Modular code.

   Examples:
   G90/G91   G68/G69   G98/G98   G1/G2/G3

6. Feedrate. The machine will recognize the last specified Feedrate until a new rate is defined.

Standards

There are some standard features that respond the same in a Milling program and a Lathe program. These things are line/block numbers, readables/comments, program numbers, and block skip.

Line Numbers

Line numbering is a common practice in G-Code programming to identify lines and also to search through the program quickly.

Line numbers are designated by the letter "N" followed by a number. The line numbers are basically ignored by the machine control unless a "GOTO" command is specified.

Example:

N1 T1M6
N2 G0G90G54X0Y0M3S6000
.

.
N789 M30

Readables

Readables are comments placed in the program by the programmer for any reason. These reasons could be to identify the toolpath or simply placed at the beginning to identify the program by part number or date. These are the text in side parentheses, "()".

Readables are ignored by the control and do not effect the function by any means.

%
O1111
(P/N,25756-001)
(TEST PART)
(1/1/08,MP)

Program Number

A program number is needed on every machining center. This is what the machine control uses for filing and identifying purposes. This is done by using the letter "O" followed by a number.

Note: Most machines are allowed to use the numbers 1-7999. Some machines have locked programs from 8000-8999 and almost all control systems lock 9000-9999.

Some newer machines will allow 5-digit program numbers.

Milling versus Lathe

Milling

Standard Milling Machining Centers work with 3-axis coordinate systems; X, Y, Z. A point to mention here is that technology has expanded the milling area to more than the standard 3-axis system into 4 and 5 axis systems, but for this basic understanding we will focus on the 3-axis system.

Milling systems work with rotatory tooling, which is nothing more than round tooling. Most machine shops program from the side of the tool. This means that the program takes into account the radius of the tool from the center of the spindle. This is the most important aspect of programming milling machines.

First let us look at some basic programming concepts.

Cutting Directions

Conventional Cutting versus Climb Cutting

Conventional cutting is when the cutter rotates in the direction opposing the feed at the point of contact and the rotation of the end mill opposes the direction of the work piece feed. When conventional milling the chip goes from thin to thick. Cutting forces tend to lift the work piece.

Climb cutting is when the cutter rotates in the same direction as the feed at the point of contact. When climb milling the chip goes from thick to thin and the pressure of the cutter will force the work down rather than lift it up.

Because rotary tooling has teeth that are directional in nature, the idea behind this cutting direction is fairly simple in graphical explanation.

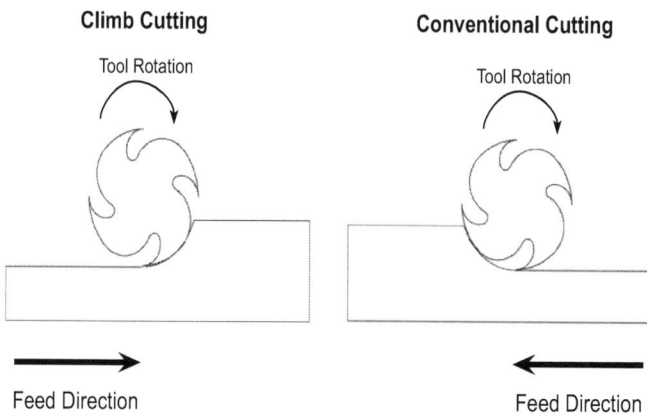

Climb Cutting

Tool Rotation

Conventional Cutting

Tool Rotation

Feed Direction

Feed Direction

Cutter Compensation

Cutter Compensation is a machine control function that allows the operator to adjust a programmed contour of G-Code.

This function is achieved by the use of G41 and G42 and cancelled by G40.

The application of cutter compensation is to control contoured toolpathes. An example of a practical application is when a 1/2" diameter tool is programmed to generate a profile of a part, but that 1/2" endmill measures actually .498" diameter. Instead of re-programming the profile of the part to this actual diameter of the tool, the user can use cutter compensation to adjust the tool path. The machine tool control will automatically adjust machine movement by the number defined by the user.

In order to use cutter compensation in the program through the use of G41 or G42 is to understand what cutter compensation adjustment is based on.

In this graphical explanation we have a programmed tool diameter of .500" and an actual tool diameter of .498".

Cutter compensation is based on distance from the center of the spindle, or for better understanding the radius of rotary tooling.

This example cutter compensation amount would be .001". There are two ways to look at this example:

1. We can take the full diameters of the tools and subtract them and take 1/2 the result.
   .500 - .498 = .002
   .002 / 2   = .001

2. We can take the radii from the tools and subtract them.
   .249 - .248 = .001

Note: For easy reference between G41 and G42 use:
   G41 for Climb Cutting
   G42 for Conventional Cutting

Programmed Tool

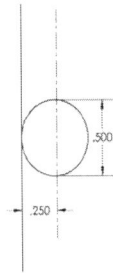

Actual Tool

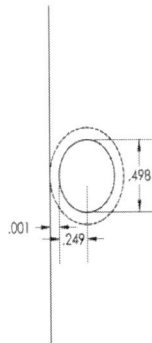

Feedrate

The feedrate is the amount of advance by the machine tool in a Feed module. This can be by either inches/revolution or inches/minute.

Inches/Revolution

This is the distance travelled in inches by one complete revolution of the spindle.

Inches/Minute

This is the distance travelled in inches in the time of one minute.

*Milling machines by machine shop default are commonly run on the Inches/Minute system feedrate.

Lathe

Standard Lathe Machining Centers work with 2-axis coordinate systems. A point of mention here with technology has expanded the lathe area to more than just the standard 2-axis system and with swiss style lathe machines they can have up to and possibly more than 13-axis systems.

Lathe systems in the standard sense rotate the part or material with stationary tooling. Standard lathe programming is programmed from the cutting point of the tool in respect to the 2-axis system, X and Z respectively.

Let us look at basic lathe concepts.

Diameter versus Radius

Most machine shops are setup to run programs on a diameter basis versus radius. This means that the X values in the program are reflective to the full diameter of the feature to be achieved.

Lathe X values are from centerline of the spindle, but in most shops the lathe is set to double in order to achieve full diameter. This is important to understand because X0 by default is the center of the part, not the side opposite of cutting edge.

Z value

The Z value of the program is a straight number of the feature that is to be achieved.

Notes:

_____

_____

_____

_____

_____

_____

_____

_____

_____

_____

_____

_____

_____

_____

_____

_____

_____

_____

_____

_____

_____

_____

The Toolpath

The Toolpath

The toolpath is the most difficult part of programming. This is the basis for actual machining.

Milling machining center programs are generated from the center of the spindle which the program reflects the radius of the tool being used, which we define of *Edge of Tool Programming*.

Edge of Tool Programming is where the side of the tool is offset in the program in relation to the center of spindle.

Lathe machining center programs are generated from the tip of the cutting tool which is offset in the "X" and "Z" axis in the control panel offset page. So each number in the program is defined by this tip of the tool and the machine control uses the appropriate offsets for the defined tool.

Linear Toolpath

In the following Graphical Example1, we see that we need to offset our program in order to cut the outer contour of the part.

In Graphical Example1 we see that we have a 1" diameter tool and need to generate a toolpath around the contour.

In order to have the program reflect a number from the center of the spindle, we need to adjust our program to the edge of the tool.

We will take 1/2 our diameter from the part. Being that the Zero of the part is the Bottom Left corner we will start there.

The first position is X-.5Y-.5.
This is positioning the spindle to the edge of the tool, 1/2 the diameter.

The following numbers are the rest of the positions for Edge of Tool Programming:

Graphical Example1

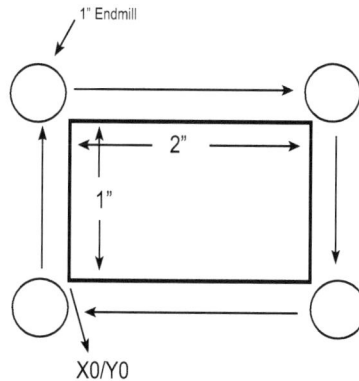

1" Endmill

2"

1"

X0/Y0

X-.5Y1.5
X2.5
Y-.5
X-.5

Interpolation is the means at which an arc, radius, or diameter is generated. Generation of a radius, arc, or diameter has many contributing factors in order to attain a result.

The I, J, K, and R are the respective letter designations for the machine tool to generate an arc, radius, or diameter. See following list:

X = I
Y = J   R = All
Z = K

The letters "I, J, and K" are *positional* distances in the respective axis from the start point to the swing point.

The letter "R" is a special letter in generating arcs, radii, and diameters. This is the *actual* diameter and needs no direction, but is limited to 180 degree movements, this will become clear as we discuss further.

First we will identify the theory of strict X and Y plane 90 degree applications.

Looking back at our G-Code list, we must identify our XY Plane with by default in Milling machining centers is G17.

In order to figure out when to use I or J and which sign +/- for it, you must first understand where you are starting from in relation to your swing point. Any time you interpolate, you are swinging around a point. Any arc, radius, or diameter has a center point, same as interpolation, you are making a arc around something.

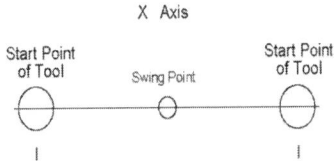

I is used when you are starting in the "X" axis from your Swing Point.

J is used when you are starting in the "Y" axis from your Swing Point.

Think about these two concepts first. Then we will decide what sign to use.

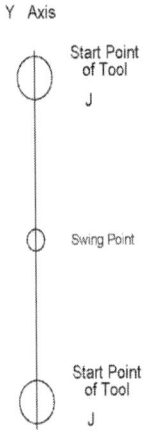

X Axis

Start Point
of Tool   Swing Point   Start Point
of Tool

I   I

Y Axis

Start Point
of Tool
J

Swing Point

Start Point
of Tool
J

Now the Sign of the I or J is defined by which side the Start Point is on from the Swing Point. This has nothing to do where you are at relative to part Zero, but only relative to the Swing Point.

See the following pictures:

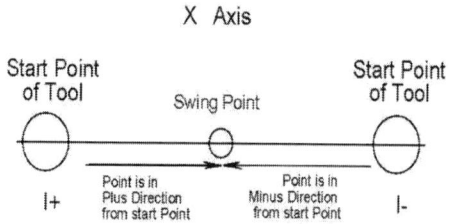

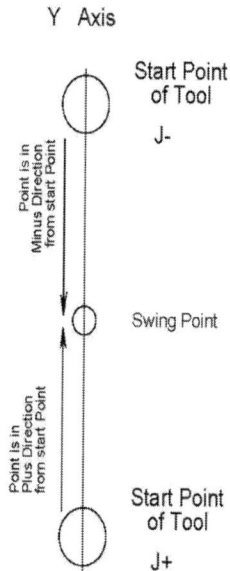

X Axis

Start Point
of Tool

Swing Point

Start Point
of Tool

Point is in
Plus Direction
from start Point

Point is in
Minus Direction
from start Point

I+

I-

Y Axis

Start Point
of Tool

J-

Point is in
Minus Direction
from start Point

Swing Point

Point is in
Plus Direction
from start Point

Start Point
of Tool

J+

The Toolpath
Second we will take the XY strict 90 degree theory to the step level when a radius is not a perfect 90 degrees.

When we generate a radius in milling G-code programming, we have two ways to achieve this; "R" or "I/J".

In Graphical Example2 we are looking at a start point from a swing point along a projected path.

Graphical Example2

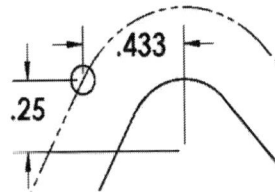

In this example we can easily see that from the start point to the swing point the "X" direction is positive and a value of .433. So this would mean our arc interpolation value would be I.433.

We can also see that from the start point to the swing po-ing in the "Y" direction is negative and a value of .25. So this would mean that our arc interpolation value would be J-.25.

So to conclude, our code to include in this particular block would be:

I.433 J-.25

Graphical Example3

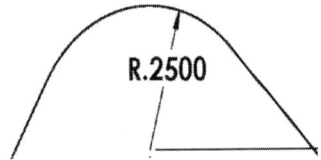

In order to use an "R" would have to know the actual ra-dius to that the machine tool should generate.

Graphical Example3 shows the actual print radius to gen-erate whereas Graphical Example4 shows the projected toolpath radius.

So to conclude, our code to include in this particular block to for the use of an "R" would be:

R.5

Graphical Example4

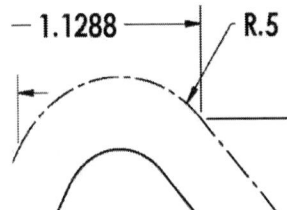

Note: These Graphical Examples are from the Angular Interpolation Part2 Tutorial.

After understanding how interpolation works in the XY plane designation, we can apply the exact same theory to the XZ plane (G18) and the YZ plane (G19).

All of the examples would be the same except the use of "K" where applicable in the "Z" plane.

Z   Axis

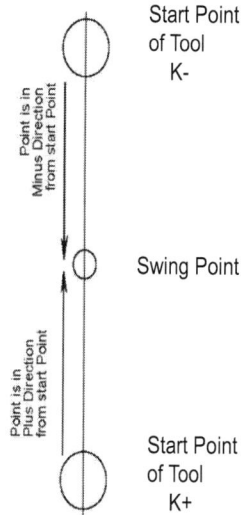

Start Point
of Tool
K-

Point is in
Minus Direction
from start Point

Swing Point

Point is in
Plus Direction
from start Point

Start Point
of Tool
K+

The Toolpath
Notes:

The Toolpath

Milling Machining

Milling Machining

Through reading over the basics of G-Codes and M-Codes tied with the section labelled "2-Axis Fundamentals" we can begin to program.

Milling machining centers need standard information to safely begin reading code and the basic program format is as follows:

1. Program Number
2. Tool Change
3. Work Coordinate System Designation
4. Tool Length Offset Designation
5. Tool Path
6. Zero Return
7. End Program

Let us go through the following two Tutorials to understand how to put it all together.

Milling Machining

Part1 Tutorial

This is a sample part tutorial to begin basic milling programming. Included is a sample print, Part1, and a G-Code program to make the part.

The following is a detailed explanation of a standard Fanuc programmed part.

This program is a Milling program, programmed to the side of the tool.

The Part Zero for programming purposes of this part are:

X0 = Left Edge of Part
Y0 = Bottom Edge of Part
Z0= Top of Part

* Refer to print on following page.

***All Feeds and Spindle speeds and reference information are from the book
"CNC Programming - Reference Book"

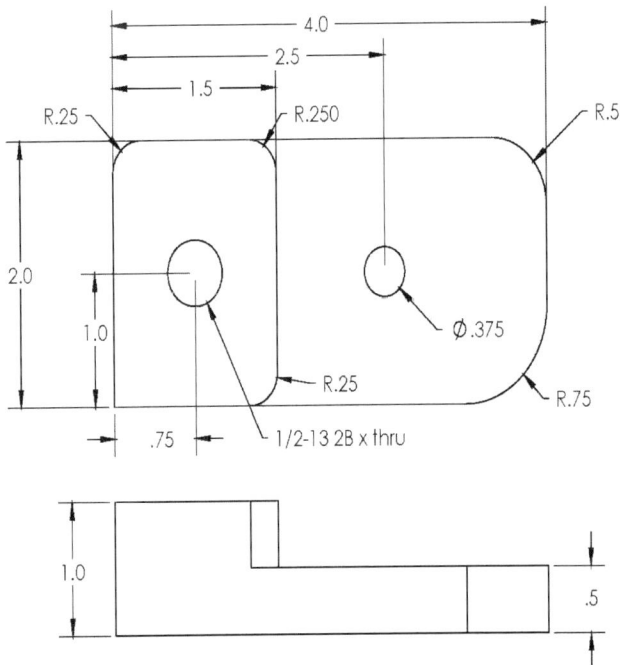

Material: Aluminum 6061

G-Code Program

```
%
O0001(PROGRAM#)
(PROGRAM NAME - PART1)
(SAMPLE PART)


N1( 1" FLAT ENDMILL TOOL )
T1M6
M1
N100G0G90G54X-1.Y0.S3056M3
G43H1Z.1M8T2
(PROFILE)
G1Z-1.F24.4
G41D51X-.5
Y1.75
G2X.25Y2.5I.75
G1X3.5
G2X4.5Y1.5J-1.
G1Y.75
G2X3.25Y-.5I-1.25
G1X0.
G2X-.5Y0.J.5
G1G40X-1.
G0Z.1

(FINISH WALL STEP3)
X1.25Y4.5
G1Z-.5
G41D51Y4.
G2X3.5Y1.75J-2.25
G1Y.25
G2X1.25Y-2.I-2.25
G1G40Y-2.5
G0Z.1
(FINISH WALL STEP 2)
Y3.75
G1Z-.5
G41D51Y3.25
G2X2.75Y1.75J-1.5
G1Y.25
G2X1.25Y-1.25I-1.5
G1G40Y-1.75
G0Z.1

(FINISH WALL)
Y3.
G1Z-.5
G41D51Y2.5
G2X2.Y1.75J-.75
G1Y.25
G2X1.25Y-.5I-.75
G1G40Y-1.
```

```
G0Z.1M9
G91G28Z0M19
M1

N2(5/8 SPOT DRILL TOOL )
(1/2-13)
T2M6
M1
N200G0G90G54X.75Y1.S2500M3
G43H2Z.1M8T3
G98G81Z-.25R.1F10.

(.375 DIAMETER)
X2.5Z-.6875R-.4
G80Z.1M9
G91G28Z0M19
M1


N3( 27/64 DRILL TOOL)
(1/2-13 DRILL)
T3M6
M1
N300G0G90G54X.75Y1.S2264M3
G43H3Z.1M8T4
G98G83Z-1.2267R.1Q.2109F9.
G80Z.1M9
G91G28Z0M19
M1


N4(1/2-13 CUT TAPRH TOOL )
T4M6
M1
N400G0G90G54X.75Y1.S130M3
G43H4Z.1M8T5
G84Z-1.35R.1F10.
G80Z.1M9
G91G28Z0M19
M1
```

```
N5( #U DRILL TOOL, .368)
(.375 DRILL)
T5M6
M1
N500G0G90G54X2.5Y1.S2595M3
G43H5Z.1M8T6
G98G83Z-1.2106R-
.4Q.184F10.4
G80Z.1M9
G91G28Z0M19
M1

N6(.375 REAMER TOOL, .375)
(.375 REAM)
T6M6
M1
N600G0G90G54X2.5Y1.S1000M3
G43H6Z.1M8T1
G98G85Z-1.2R-.4F10.
G80Z.1M9
G91G28Z0M19
G28Y0
M30
%
```

Part1 Tutorial
Notes:

Step 1: Understanding the program – Defining the beginning of the toolpath

```
N1( 1" FLAT ENDMILL TOOL )
T1M6
M1
N100G0G90G54X-1.Y0.S3056M3
G43H1Z.1M8T2
```

In this first 5 lines of this sample G-Code program, we will start by understanding what the code means.

Line 1 `N1( 1" FLAT ENDMILL TOOL )`

The "N" signifies a line number.

> Some programmers or shops will sequentially number each line of their program, this is a valuable tool so you can compare and reference different lines throughout the program.

> Some programmers or shops will designate an "N" just at the start of each tool and then that number plus "100" for the path start. This makes it easy to just quickly search through the program if you need to just run 1 tool.

> In this program example, we use the Tool Number equals the "N" number.

The Readables.

> The open and closed parentheses are referred to "Readables" or "Comment" lines. The information in this parentheses are ignored by the machine but it may contain valuable information for the program.

> In this example we use "Readables" to explain what the Tool is and reference information for the tool path.

Line 2 `T1M6`

> This is generally the Tool Change line. Some machine have different tool change formats. This example is a standard tool change format.

> We designate the "T", which is the Tool Number or Tool pot we want to change.

> The "M6" is the standard Fanuc "M-Code" for tool change.

Line 3 M1

This is an optional line by the programmer or shop to stop the machine.

"M1" or "M01" is a standard Fanuc M-Code. This is "Optional Stop". Which means, when the "M1" or "Optional Stop" button on the control is pressed, the machine will stop on this line until cycle start is pressed.

***Note: Most shops or programmers will not put this code in the program. But the reason why you may, is if you would like to look at a tool before it runs, to check if it needs to be changed. It is a simple way to let the machine change tools for you in the program and stop, without being in MDI mode.

Line 4 N100G0G90G54X-1.Y0.S3056M3

"N" is our tool path start with "100" added to Tool Number.

"G0" is to set the Modal mode of "Rapid"

"G90" is setting the Modal mode to "Absolute"

"G54" is defining a Work Offset System.

"X" and "Y" are positioning locations for the start of the toolpath.

"S3056" is to define the Spindle Speed.
> **REFERENCE:**
> This Spindle Speed Number refers back to the Surface Footage Chart in "CNC Programming - Reference Book".
>
> Material: Aluminum
> 1 Inch Diameter Tool
> Carbide (because we know it is a carbide tool we want to use)
> 800(sfm) X 3.82 = 3056
> 3056 / 1(diameter) = **3056**(spindle speed)

"M3" is to turn on Spindle Clockwise.

Line 5 `G43H1Z.1M8T2`

"G43" is Tool length Compensation

"H1" is defining the Tool Length compensation value of Tool 1.

"Z" is telling the machine what distance from Part Zero to move to.

"M8" is a standard Fanuc M-Code turning Coolant On.

"T" this tool value is used frequently to "Pre-Call" the next tool, or get it ready. This is normally only used on Tool Arm Carousel machines.

Part1 Tutorial

Step 2: The Toolpath

In this section we will talk about the actual tool path. Refer to the tool path reference print. Each position is easily understood by looking at the print and the program, with the help of understanding the code. (Refer to the Standard G-Code material).

The Solid lines are the Part from the Part Print.

The Semi-Broken lines are the Tool Path around the part.

The Dashed lines, signify the cutter diameter, 1 inch.

Tool Path Print 1

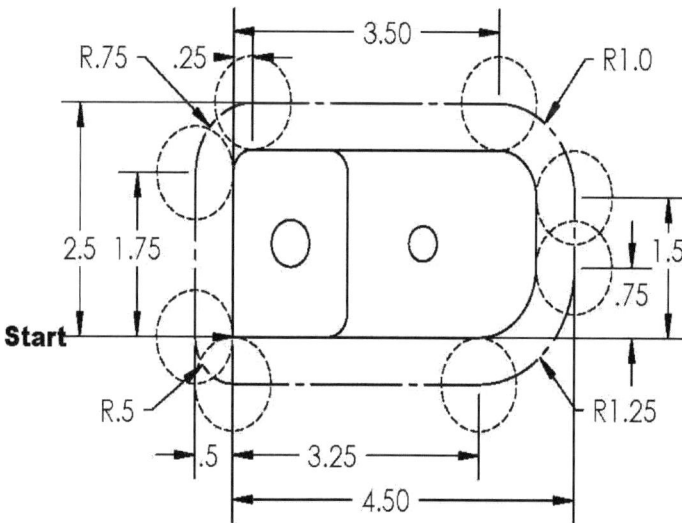

124

The Theory

*To run a path around a part, we need to adjust the path from the print dimensions "**Half**" the cutter diameter.*

This can be a little confusing at times, but once you get it, you get it. This is why the Tool Path Print has been added. Visual reference makes all the difference.

```
N1( 1" FLAT ENDMILL TOOL )
T1M6
M1
N100G0G90G54X-1.Y0.S3056M3
G43H1Z.1M8T2

(PROFILE)
G1Z-1.F24.4
G41D51X-.5
Y1.75
G2X.25Y2.5I.75
G1X3.5
G2X4.5Y1.5J-1.
G1Y.75
G2X3.25Y-.5I-1.25
G1X0.
G2X-.5Y0.J.5
G1G40X-1.
G0Z.1
```

We already explained the first 5 lines. But lets go back to the Positional "X" and "Y" in our Line 4.

> "**X-1.Y0.**" This is the position that we want to start the tool at.
>> If our left edge of the part is **"Zero"** (X-axis) and our bottom edge of the part is **"Zero"** (Y-axis), this is where we start with our numbers.
>>
>> "X-1.". This may not be clear at first, but because we want to use cutter compensation so we can adjust the cutter as we make parts, we would like to start the tool OFF the part. So we added .500 to the start position to attain this.
>>
>> "Y0". This is part Zero. Our start.

> "**(PROFILE)**". This is a readable defined to use by the programmer telling us what this tool path is doing. It is generating the outer profile of the part.

G1 Z-1.F24.4

    "G1". Modal G-Code telling the machine to feed.

    "Z-1." Is telling the machine what to feed to.

        Part Zero – Part Thickness, 1.

        0 – 1. = -1.

    "F24.4" is telling the machine at what speed to feed at.

REFERENCE:

This Feed Rate Number refers back to the Surface Footage Chart.

S3056 spindle speed

4 Flute Endmill (because it is what we want to use)

.002 FPT

3056 X 4 X .002 = 24.4

G41D51X-.5

    "G41" is turning ON Cutter Compensation Left.

        *This code is similar to G42, but since we want to Climb cut, we use G41, if you want to conventional cut, use G42.

    "D51" is the Tool Cutter Compensation Value we want to use for this tool.

        *This number can be defined to any number in the offset page. For ease, we add 50 to the Tool Number.

    "X-.5" is the location related to the Part Zero that we want the tool to position.

    The -.5 value is the number of the part reference, 0, minus half the diameter of the cutter. (0-.5 = -.5)

        *Note: The + and – are important, and confusing when you start to program. Always remember to do things in sequence, and you will never mess up.

        In this example, if you take .5 away from 0 it is just simple math, it's **-.5.**

        *Note: Because we defined the Feed code in the previous line, each move will be in the "G1" modal until the machine reads a "G0" or rapid code. It will also keep feeding at the 24.4 rate until it reads a different "F" value.

Y1.75

    This is a positional line, which is telling the machine to Feed to this "Y" position. It is feed because we stay in the Feed Modal until a different Modal is defined. Refer to Tool Path Print for understanding this location.

    *If you look at the print the part width is 2 inches, with a Raius of .250. This number is 2. - .25 = 1.75.

G2X.25Y2.5I.75

This is a Interpolation line with code.
This line says swing a radius to the "X" and "Y" stop positions by "I".

"G2" is Interpolation Clockwise

"X.25" is the stop position of Radius related to Part Zero X.
Edge of part +.25 for R.250.

"Y2.5" is stop position of Radius related to Part Zero Y.
Bottom edge to Part Width, 2. inches, plus Half cutter, .5.

"I.75" is the Radius to swing. This is the part Radius of .250 plus the Half the cutter diameter, .5.
.250 + .5 = .750

G1X3.5

This is a Linear Location Line.

"G1" defining linear modal

"X3.5" location related to print Zero.
4.00 part length minus R.5
4. - .5 = 3.5

G2X4.5Y1.5J-1.

This is a Interpolation line with code.
This line says swing a radius to the "X" and "Y" stop positions by "J".

"G2" is Interpolation Clockwise

"X4.5" is the stop position of Radius related to Part Zero X.
Length of part, 4. plus Half of Cutter, .5
4. + .5 = 4.5

"Y1.5" is stop position of Radius related to Part Zero Y.
Part Width, 2. minus R.50, 2. inches,
2. - .5 = 1.5

"J-1." is the Radius to swing. This is the part Radius of .50 plus the Half the cutter diameter, .5.
.5 + .5 = .750

G1Y.75

This is a Linear Location Line.

"G1" defining linear modal

"Y.75" location related to print Zero.
Part Zero plus R.75
0 + .75 = .75

G2X3.25Y-.5I-1.25

This is a Interpolation line with code.
This line says swing a radius to the "X" and "Y" stop positions by "I".

"G2" is Interpolation Clockwise

"X3.25" is the stop position of Radius related to Part Zero X.
Length of part, 4. minus R.75
4. - .75 = 3.25

"Y-.5" is stop position of Radius related to Part Zero Y.
Part Zero minus Half Cutter Diameter, .5
0 - .5 = -.5

"I-1.25" is the Radius to swing. This is the part Radius of .750 plus the Half the cutter diameter, .5.
.75 + .5 = 1.250

G1X0.

This is a Linear Location Line.

"G1" defining linear modal

"X0." location related to print Zero.

G2X-.5Y0.J.5

This is a Interpolation line with code.
This line says swing a radius to the "X" and "Y" stop positions by "J".

"G2" is Interpolation Clockwise

"X-.5" is the stop position of Radius related to Part Zero X.
Part Zero minus Half Cutter Diameter.
0 - .5 = -.5

"Y0" is stop position of Radius related to Part Zero Y.
Part Zero

"J.5" is the Radius to swing. This is the part Radius of 0 plus the Half the cutter diameter, .5.
0 + .5 = .5

<u>Rolling around sharp corners is a good habit, this helps against burrs.</u>

G1G40X-1.

This is a Linear Location Line.

"G1" defining linear modal

"G40" Cutter Compensation Cancel

"X-1." location related to print Zero.
Move tool off part.
0 – 1. = -1.

G0Z.1

This is a Rapid Location Line.

"G0" is defining Rapid Modal

"Z.1" is telling the machine to move to a position of .1 above the part.

Step 3: The Toolpath – Step

In this section, I am going to let you reason the Code with some reference material.

If programming by hand without the use of a CAD software package, sometimes you have to start where you have print numbers to work from and then copy that path and add to the number in order to get more paths to clean up a surface.

This next path to cut the top step, by far is not the most efficient path possible, but it is a quick programming style to get a part cut.

The Lead In to the part is .500.
> *The <u>Lead In</u> is what is referred to when you start off the part and feed into it, normally the Cutter Compensation Line distance.*

Stepover Distance is .750

The first line programmed was actually the last Group in this section, the *Finish Wall* path, and then copied and manually changed numbers by a step over distance to create a path that will fully establish the Step Surface.

Hint:

Step 1.   Reason the Finish Wall path first
Step 2.   Copy the Finish Wall path and add .750 step over to reason Finish Wall Step 2
Step 3.   Copy the Finish Wall Step 2 and add .750 step over to that one to reason
          Finish Wall Step 3.
Step 4.   Reorder the toolpath groups so machine makes part working from edge of part
          in towards wall.

> ***This is not the most efficient way to achieve this, but makes it easier to compound hard numbers quickly.*

The Solid lines are the Part from the Part Print.

The Semi-Broken lines are the Tool Path around the part.

The Dashed lines signify the cutter diameter, 1 inch.

1 Inch Tool Path Step Print

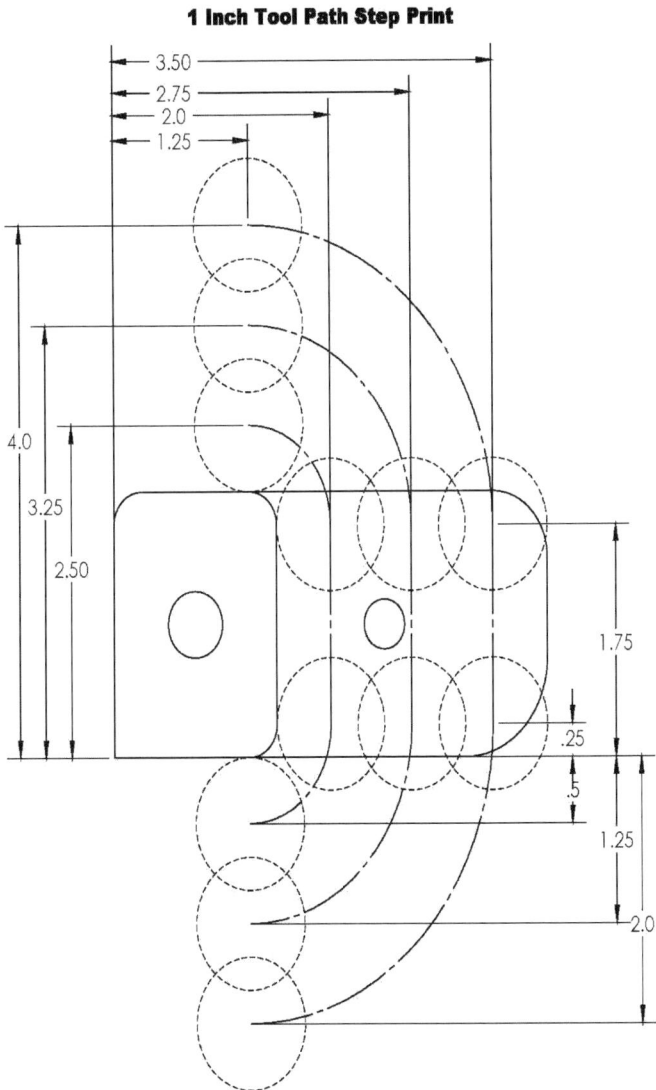

Part1 Tutorial

```
(FINISH WALL STEP3)
X1.25Y4.5
G1Z-.5
G41D51Y4.
G2X3.5Y1.75J-2.25
G1Y.25
G2X1.25Y-2.I-2.25
G1G40Y-2.5
G0Z.1

(FINISH WALL STEP 2)
Y3.75
G1Z-.5
G41D51Y3.25
G2X2.75Y1.75J-1.5
G1Y.25
G2X1.25Y-1.25I-1.5
G1G40Y-1.75
G0Z.1

(FINISH WALL)
Y3.
G1Z-.5
G41D51Y2.5
G2X2.Y1.75J-.75
G1Y.25
G2X1.25Y-.5I-.75
G1G40Y-1.
G0Z.1M9
G91G28Z0M19
M1
```

End of Tool Path

G0Z.1M9
"G0" Rapid Modal Mode
"Z.1" Location Position to .1 above Part Zero
"M9" Standard M-Code to turn coolant off.

G91G28Z0M19
"G91G28" Standard Machine Reference Position
"Z0" Axis to return to
"M19" Orient Spindle

*All together this lines tells the machine to return home in Z axis and orient spindle.

M1
"M1" Standard M-Code, Optional Stop.

132

Step 4: The Canned Cycles

In this section we will explain the use of Canned Cycles.

Canned Cycles are mostly for drilling or boring, but can be used in Plunging applications.

We are not going to cover the details of Tool #2 that have already been explained under Tool #1 in the previous area, but moreso, just focus on the use of Canned Cycles.

G-Code

```
N2(5/8 SPOT DRILL TOOL )
(1/2-13)
T2M6
M1
N200G0G90G54X.75Y1.S2500M3
G43H2Z2.1M8T3
G98G81Z-.25R.1F10.

(.375 DIAMETER)
X2.5Z-.6875R-.4
G80Z.1M9
G91G28Z0M19
M1
```

      G98G81Z-.25R.1F10.
        "G98" Standard G-Code which is refer to initial start position.
            In this example, the Initial Start position is "Z.1" which is the last designated "Z" in our "G43" line.

        "G81" this is designated the Canned Cycle to do. Refer to the Standard G-Code with formats for actual details of what this code does.

        "Z-.25" telling what depth to go to before finishing cycle.

            REFERENCE:
            This Z Number refers back to the Countersink Reference Sheet.
            .500 diameter with a 90 degree Spot drill
            .500/2 = .250

        "R.1" telling what position in ***"Z" axis*** to start canned cycle from.

        "F10." designating the feedrate at which to do Canned Cycle.

X2.5Z-.6875R-.4

"X2.5" positional location for next canned cycle.

> ***Since we want to use the same Canned Cycle we can just use a position and different parameters for new location and feature.***

"Z-.6875" telling what depth to go to before finishing cycle.

REFERENCE:
This Z Number refers back to the Countersink Reference Sheet.
.375 diameter with a 90 degree Spot drill
.375/2 = .1875
But the surface at which we are creating this feature is .500 from the top of that part, so we must add both together.
.1875 + .500 = .6875
We know the total distance is .6875, but we know it is lower then the top of that part, so total distance from top of part is **Z-.6875**

"R-.4" telling what position in **"Z" axis** to start canned cycle from.

> Z-.4, because the step in Z-.500 from top of part, and we would like to start the cycle above that surface .100
> **-.500 + .100 = -.400**

G80Z.1M9

"G80" Cancel Canned Cycle
"Z.1" positional location. .100 above part
"M9" M-Code to turn coolant off.

Step 5: The Canned Cycles - Tapping

Tapping in canned cycles is no different than any other cycle, other than defining the appropriate Spindle Speed with the right Feed Rate.

This theory varies from machine to machine. I will give you 3 examples of tapping cycles on machines.

Tapping Basics

Pitch

The Pitch of a tap is defined by the distance traveled in one revolution.
***Layman's – how much will the tap move if I turn it 360 degrees.
To find the pitch take 1, being inch and divide it by Threads Per Inch.

***All Standard Taps are in Threads per Inch, Metric are in Pitch. The Pitch on a Metric Tap is in Millimeters. So if using on a Standard system, you must covert to inches.

Example: 1/2-13 Tap

13 Thread Per Inch

1 / 13 = .0769 pitch

Threads Per Inch

The Threads Per Inch is exactly what it states, over the length of one inch, how many full threads are there.

In the Standard system, this is already called out.

In the Metric system all taps are in Pitch but Millimeters. You must covert, then figure out Thread per inch.

1. Fanuc #1

```
N4( 1/2-13 CUT TAPRH TOOL )
T4M6
M1
N400G0G90G54X.75Y1.S130M3
G43H4Z.1M8T5
G84Z-1.35R.1F10.
G80Z.1M9
G91G28Z0M19
M1
```

In this example, the program is set to correlate the Spindle with the Feedrate based by threads per inch.

If Feed is based on Thread per Inch, all you need do to find out your Spindle Speed is take the Feedrate and multiply by Threads Per Inch.

Example:
F10. X 13TPI = 130 Spindle Speed

If you know your Spindle Speed because of Tap recommended Surface Footage, to find your feedrate, just take the Spindle Speed and divide it by your Threads per inch.

Example:
130S / 13 TPI = 10. (Feed)

2. Fanuc #2

```
N4( 1/2-13 CUT TAPRH TOOL )
T4M6
M1
N400G0G90G54X.75Y1.
G43H4Z.1M8T5
M29S130
G84Z-1.35R.1F10.
G80Z.1M9
G91G28Z0M19
M1
```

This example is almost the same to #1, but with an M29S130.
This M29 syncs the spindle and feed together. Sometimes you need a pitch for the feedrate in order for this format to work. See next Example.

3. Yasnac #3

```
N4( 1/2-13 CUT TAPRH TOOL )
T4M6
M1
N400G0G90G54X.75Y1.M3S320
G43H4Z.1M8T5
G93
G84Z-1.35R.1F.0769
G80Z.1M9
G94
G91G28Z0M19
M1
```

This example is very popular on Yasnac controls.

The Spindle is the same as Fanuc examples, but it uses the Pitch as the Feedrate.

The is easily understood if you look at the "G93" and "G94" lines.

"G93" is telling the machine to switch to Feed per Revolution
So in tapping in this format, it is saying, for every time the spindle rotates 360 degrees, travel a distance of "F", which in tapping is the Pitch.

"G94" is telling the machine to switch to Feed per Inch.
This normally the most common default in milling applications.

Notes:

Part2 Tutorial

In this tutorial, we will look at process to generate a radius on an angular contour. Complex contours are easily created with the aide of a CAM system, but it is still nice to understand where the numbers come from.

When we generate a radius in milling G-code programming, we have two ways to achieve this; "R" or "I/J".

In Part1 Tutorial we discussed simply the "I/J" approach and mentioned that "R" may be substituted. In this Part2 Tutorial, in the interest of being thorough, we will show code for both.

The advantage of using an "R" is purely out of simplicity, but an "R" has limitations, whereas the use of "I/J" is unlimited.

An "R" can only be used up to 180 degrees of a circle and if you need to generate a radius that is larger than 180 degrees you would need to add additional lines, whereas "I/J" can attain 360 degrees.

The following is a detailed explanation of a standard Fanuc programmed part.

This program is a Milling program, programmed to the side of the tool.

The part Zero for programming purposes of this part are:

    X0 = Left Edge of Part
    Y0 = Bottom Edge of Part
    Z0= Top of Part

- Refer to print on following page.

Refer to the Appendix: Trigonometry *in* **"CNC Programming: Basics & Tutorial Textbook"** *for the mathematical explanation of the start and stop locations for this example.*

R.2500

60.00°

45.00°

.8428

.7753

1.9717

.5000

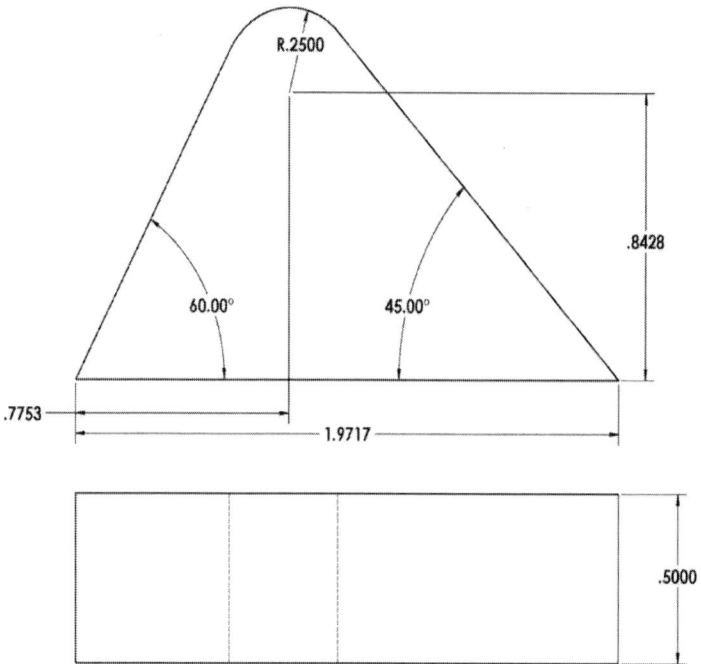

Material: Aluminum 6061

G-Code

I/J G-Code

```
%
O0001
(PROGRAM NAME -ANGLE RADIUS)
(1/2 FLAT ENDMILL)
T1M6
G0G90G54X-.6495Y.375S6112M3
G43H1Z.1M8
G1Z-.5F48.9
G41D1X-.2165Y.125
X.3423Y1.0928
G2X1.1288Y1.1964I.433J-.25
G1X2.1485Y.1768
G2X1.9717Y-.25I-.1768J.1768
G1X0.
G2X-.2165Y.125I0.J.25
G1G40X-.6495Y.375
G0Z.1M9
M5
G91G28Z0.
M30
%
```

R   G-Code

```
%
O0001
(PROGRAM NAME -ANGLE RADIUS)
(1/2 FLAT ENDMILL)
T1M6
G0G90G54X-.6495Y.375S6112M3
G43H1Z.1M8
G1Z-.5F48.9
G41D1X-.2165Y.125
X.3423Y1.0928
G2X1.1288Y1.1964R.5
G1X2.1485Y.1768
G2X1.9717Y-.25R.25
G1X0.
G2X-.2165Y.125R.25
G1G40X-.6495Y.375
G0Z.1M9
M5
G91G28Z0.
M30
%
```

For the purpose of this Tutorial, we will not discuss the layout of the program because we discussed this in the Part1 Tutorial. For this Tutorial, we are going to discuss the actual G-code positioning only and compare the differences between "R" and "I/J" in hope that we can reason the program.

First let us study the following toolpath prints for "R" and "I/J".

Tool Path Print I/J

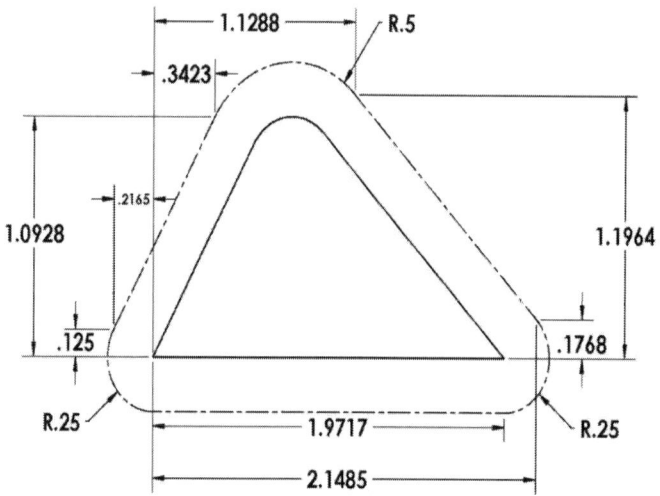

Tool Path Print R

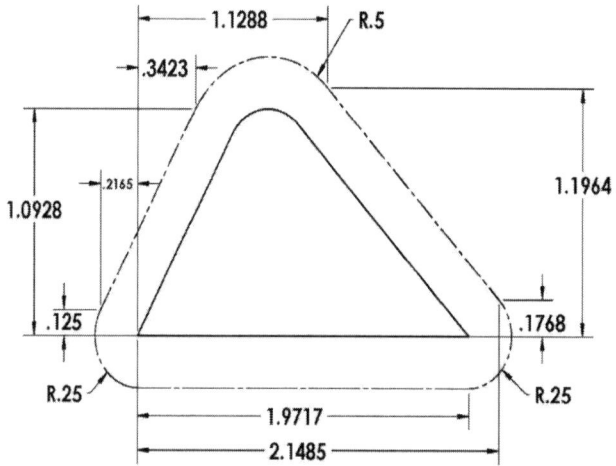

As we compare the Tool Path Prints and the G-code programs, we notice that each line with respects to the "X" and "Y" axis are identical.

We discussed in Part1 Tutorial that when we generate a full 90 degree radius, we need the end point for the swing. This is true in any situation dealing with a radius.

Let us compare the first swing of the first radius of both programs and discuss the differences.

```
G2X1.1288Y1.1964I.433J-.25          G2X1.1288Y1.1964R.5
```

First off we notice that the end points with respect to the "X" and "Y" are the same, but we notice that the "I/J" and "R" do not correlate to each other at all.

If we look at the "R" we can reason that it is just a radius from the part of .250 plus the radius of the tool .250 added together which makes .500. This is fundamentally why working with "R" is easier than "I/J", because it is simple math defined by the print and the tool.

The program is defining the start point by where the tool is currently with previous line and saying swing this R or radius to the end point.

The use of "I/J" on the other hand is more complex. We need to tell the machine where the swing point is in respect to the start point in the "X" and "Y" axis. This is where the extra trigonometry comes into.

Where does the "X" and "Y" come into play? It is there, we just need to think back to the I and J supplement. The "X" axis is "I" and the "Y" axis is "J". So in this program we can reason that the swing point is .433 in the positive direction from the tool in the "X" and .250 in the negative direction from the tool in the "Y" axis. See the following print for the graphical explanation.

Tool Path Print for Swing Points

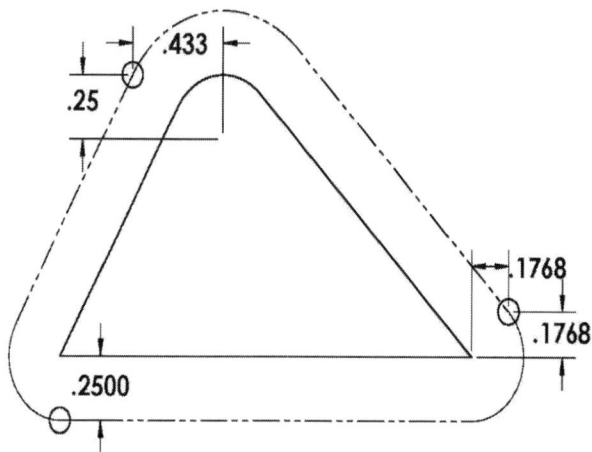

By comparing this print to the toolpath we see that the "I" and "J" numbers and signs are relative to the point at which the tool is swinging around.

So the best way to think about a G-code radius line is in this format:

"X" and "Y" definitions is the location at which the tool will be at the end of the move.

"I" and "J" definitions is the location in the "X" and "Y" coordinates at which the tool must move around.

The machine does the same move between the "R" and "I/J" code, it is just the difference in the information it is given to generate it.

The use of "R" is telling the machine to swing a radius defined by "R" to a given end point.

The use of "I/J" is telling the machine to swing around a point to an end point.

If your math is correct the feature will be generated with each practice. "R" is very popular because of the simplicity of the practice. There is no sign nor do you need to use trigonometry to figure out the swing. The "R" limitation is if the radius in larger than 180 degrees, you will need to swing 180 degrees than swing again from that point to the end of the radius, creating another line of code whereas the "I/J" could generate the same feature with one line of code.

Use the Tool Path Print for Swing Points, Tool Path Print for R and Tool Path Print for I/J to help read through the code.

Notes:

Helical Interpolation

&

Thread Milling

Helical Interpolation

Helical Interpolation is a very useful G-code programming practice. This is a circular tool path that travels in a circle in the "X" and "Y" axis while travelling up or down in the "Z" axis.

This practice is used for thread milling or for generating a feature on a part that is a diameter.

Please view the following G-code for an example of Helical Interpolation.

```
%
O0001
(PROGRAM NAME -HELICAL INTERPOLATION)
(1/2 FLAT ENDMILL)
T1M6
G0G90G54X0Y0S6112M3
G43H1Z.1M8
G1Z0F48.9
G41D1X.25
G3I-.25Z-.25
I-.25Z-.5
I-.25Z-.75
I-.25
G1G40X0
G0Z.1M9
M5
G91G28Z0.
M30
%
```

This G-code example defines a circular interpolation of a feature diameter of 1 inch.

The G3 code defines a counterclockwise interpolation path with 360 degree swing by the radius defined by "I-".

By use of the "I" in this example, if there is no end point defined, the machine control will generate a full 360 degree arc move.

The use of the "Z" in helical interpolation is also known as the pitch. This tells the machine to move in the "Z" axis end point as it swings the arc. All three axis's travel proportional with each other.

Thread Milling

Thread milling is a valuable practice in programming. There are numerous reasons to use thread milling which we not discuss, but we will discuss how to program this practice.

The practice of thread milling is done from bottom up and by the pitch of the thread.

We discussed pitch in the Part1 Tutorial, so you may need to look back at the tapping section of the tutorial.

First, we need to know the size of the *major* diameter, thread mill tool diameter, and the depth of threads.

We will assume that the minor diameter is already established by drilling or in some situations, by helical interpolation.

In this example, we will say we would like to thread mill a 1/4-20 2B thread by .500 deep.

We identify the major diameter by looking back to the Tap Drill Chart which is .500.

We will program this by using a .125 diameter thread mill.

Now we need to figure out our swing for programming and our pitch for our thread.

Swing

The swing is the diameter of the circle to make minus the tool diameter and then divide this answer by two.

.500 - .125 = .375
.375 / 2 = **.1875** the swing

Pitch

The pitch is the amount travelled in one revolution. In standard threads this is attained by dividing 1 inch by the threads per inch.

1 / 20 = .05

Please view the following G-code for this programming example.

```
%
O00001
(PROGRAM NAME -THREAD MILLING)
(.125 DIAMETER THREAD MILL)
T1M6
G0G90G54X0Y0S6000M3
G43H1Z.1M8
G1Z-.5F25.
G41D1X.1875
G3I-.1875Z-.45
I-.1875Z-.4
I-.1875Z-.35
I-.1875Z-.3
I-.1875Z-.25
I-.1875Z-.2
I-.1875Z-.15
I-.1875Z-.1
I-.1875Z-.05
I-.1875Z0
G1G40X0
G0Z.1M9
M5
G91G28Z0.
M30
%
```

By viewing this example program we can see that we are generating the major diameter by the "I-.1875" and generating the thread pitch by the "Z.05" incremental movement.

***This is absolute programming; do not confuse the use of the term *incremental movement* as incremental programming. The term is used here to signify that we need to move the "Z" up in each line the pitch to create a consistent thread.

Please refer to Appendix: Interpolation in "CNC Programming: Basics & Tutorial Textbook" for an explanation of absolute location interpolation programming.

Notes:

Lathe Machining

Lathe Machining

Through reading over the basics of G-Codes and M-Codes tied with the section labelled "2-Axis Fundamentals" and understanding how milling machining centers work with 3-axis programming we can begin to program lathe machining centers.

Lathe machining centers need standard information to safely begin reading code and the basic program format which is similar to milling but is different in some regards:

1. Program Number
2. Tool Change/Tool Length Offset Designation
3. Work Coordinate System Designation
4. Spindle Speed, Constant/Non-variable
5. Tool Path
6. Zero Return
7. End Program

Let us go through the following two Tutorials to understand how to put it all together.

Part3 Tutorial

This is a sample part tutorial to begin basic lathe programming. Included is a sample print, Part3, and a G-Code program to make the part.

The following is a detailed explanation of a standard Fanuc programmed part.

This program is a lathe program.

The Part Zero for programming purposes of this part are:

X0 = Center of Part
Z0 = Right Face of Part

* Refer to print on following page.

***All Feeds and Spindle speeds and reference information are from the book
"CNC Programming - Reference Book"

2.000

1.000

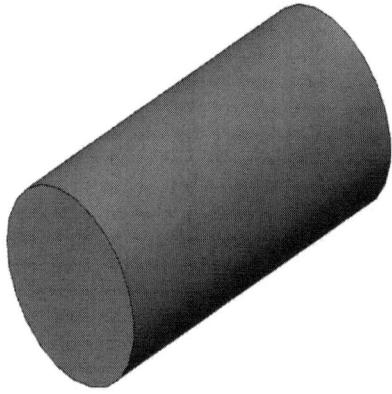

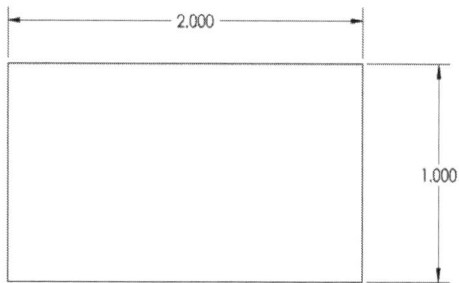

Material: Aluminum 6061

G-Code

```
%
O0001
(PROGRAM NAME -PART3)
(TURN TOOL)
G50S5000
T0101
G96M3S3056
(FACE)
G0G54G90X1.1Z0M8
G1X0F.002
G0X1.05Z.05

(1"DIA X 2."LONG)
X1.
G1Z-2.F.002
G0X6.Z5.M9
M30
%
```

In this small example of G-Code we will begin in discussing the code.

Line 1   G50S5000

> This G50 code with the defined spindle speed sets the maximum spindle speed when
> executing a constant surface speed code.

Line 2   T0101

> This T0101 line is one difference between a mill and a lathe. This line tells the lathe to change
> the turret to tool location 1 and to use Tool Offset 1.

Line 3   G96M3S3056

> This line tells the machine to turn spindle on (M3) to a spindle speed of S3056 and turn on
> Constant Surface Speed (G96). Constant surface speed means that the lathe will keep
> a constant surface speed by gradually raising the spindle speed until it reaches the above
> defined S5000.

Line 4   G0X1.1Z0M8

> Rapid to position of X1.1 and Z0. This to position to face the part, the tool tip will position .1
> away from actual part because part is 1.000" diameter and turn coolant on (M8).

Line 5   G1X0F.002

> Feed (G1) to X0 position by a feedrate of .002 (F.002) per revolution.

Line 6   G0X1.05Z.05

> Rapid (G0) to safe distance away from part to a position of X1.05 Z.05.

Line 7   X1.

> Rapid to X1. Because the G0 is modal, any positional value will be positioned by the last
> modal travel code, (G0). This X is for location before finishing the Outer Diameter, OD.

Line 8   G1Z-2.F.002

> Feed (G1) to Z-2. by a feedrate of .002 (F.002) per revolution.

Line 9   G0X6.Z5.M9

> Rapid (G0) to safe distance to clear part to position of X6.Z5. and turn coolant off (M9).

Line 10   M30

> End program, Reset.

Notes:

Part4 Tutorial

This is a sample part tutorial to begin basic lathe programming. Included is a sample print, Part4, and a G-Code program to make the part.

The following is a detailed explanation of a standard Fanuc programmed part.

This program is a lathe program.

The Part Zero for programming purposes of this part are:

X0 = Center of Part
Z0 = Right Face of Part

* Refer to print on following page.

1.500

1.500

R.125

Ø.500

Ø.625 x .75dp

.675

.062
.250

SECTION A-A

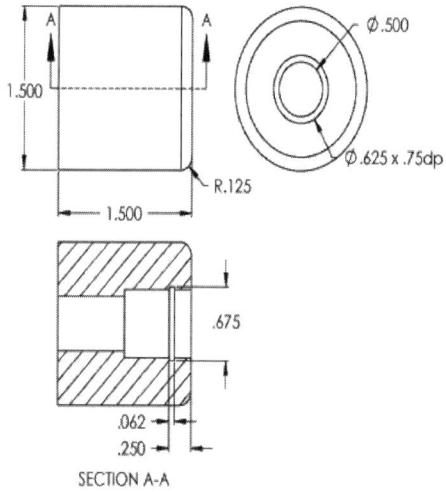

Material: Aluminum 6061

G-Code

```
%
O0001
(PROGRAM NAME -PART4)
N2(TURN TOOL,.015R)
G0G90G54
G50S3000M3
G96S2800M8
T0202
(FACE)
X1.600Z0.
G1X-.030F.003
G0X1.220Z.020
(R.125)
G1Z0F.005
G3X1.500Z-.140R.140F.001
(FINISH OD)
G1Z-1.622F.003
G0X1.600
X5.0Z5.0
M1


N3(1/2 DRILL)
G0G90G54
G50S3000M3
G97S1800M8
T0303
X0Z.060
G83R.100Z-1.650Q250F.006
G0G80Z.060
G28U0
G0Z5.0
M1


N4(3/8 BORE BAR, R.007)
G0G90G54
G50S3000M3
G97S2800M8
T0404
X.550Z.060
G1Z-.750F.005
U-.010
G0Z.060
X.600
G1Z-.750F.005
U-.010
G0Z.060
X.643
G1Z0F.005
G2X.625Z-.009R.009F.001
G1Z-.750F.002
X.480
```

```
G0Z.060
X4.0Z4.0
M1


N5(.062 WIDTH ID GROOVE TOOL)
G0G90G54
G50X3000M3
G97S1500M8
T0505
X.610Z0.
G1Z-.250F.010
X.625
G75X.675I.015F.004
G4P1.
G0G80X.610
Z.100
X4.0Z4.0
M1


N6(.122 WIDE CUTOFF TOOL)
G0G90G54
G50S3000M3
G97S1500M8
T0606
Z-1.672
X1.510
G1X1.450F.005
G0X1.510
Z-1.606
X1.500
G3X1.468W-.016R.016F.001
M36
G1X-.030F.0035
M37
G0X5.0Z5.0
M30
%
```

Discussion

The program header.

```
%
O0001
(PROGRAM NAME -PART4)
N2(TURN TOOL,.015R)
```

By now it is understood that the programmer needs to designate a program number along with any information in readables that are important to the part and program. Also the "N" in this example signifies the start of tool 2 with appropriate readables explaining the tool.

```
G0G90G54
```

This line designates rapid positioning mode, absolute travel mode, and G54 work coordinate system.

```
G50S3000M3
```

This tells the machine maximum spindle speed of defined speed and to turn spindle on in a counter clockwise direction.

```
G96S2800M8
```

Constant surface footage speed of defined spindle speed and turn on coolant.

```
T0202
```

Goto turret position and use tool offset defined. The first two digits are defining turret location, whereas the last two digits define which offset to use.

```
X1.600Z0.
```

This line says to goto X and Z location. The X1.600 is a safe starting distance from part, whereas the Z0 is the start position to face part.

```
G1X-.030F.003
```

This line feeds to X-.030, which is past X0 because of the nose radius of tool.

```
G0X1.220Z.020
```

This line rapids to start location in X and safe distance in Z.

```
G1Z0F.005
```

This line feeds to Z0 which is face of part.

```
G3X1.500Z-.140R.140F.001
```

This line generates R.125. Counter clockwise interpolation (G3), to finish OD of 1.5 (X1.5), to the end of the radius (Z-.140), which is the R.125 on part plus the R.015 of tool nose radius and swing radius of R.140, which is also the R.125 on part plus the R.015 of tool nose radius.

```
G1Z-1.622F.003
```

This line feeds to Z position which finishes the OD length of part. The 1.622 is the length plus the .122 width of the cutoff tool at the end of the program.

```
G0X1.600
```

This line rapids to safe distance off part of X.

```
X5.0Z5.0
```

Rapids to safe distance away from part to end tool path.

```
M1
```

Optional Stop.

For the rest of the description of this program, the header with the path designation will not be explained.

```
N3(1/2 DRILL)
G0G90G54
G50S3000M3
G97S1800M8
T0303
```

```
X0Z.060
```

Rapid to X and Z location. Safe distance in Z and start position for X.

```
G83R.100Z-1.650Q250F.006
```

Drilling canned cycle.

> *Please refer to **"CNC Programming: Reference Book"** for drill depth formula chart.*

```
G0G80Z.060
```

Rapid to Z and cancel canned cycle.

```
G28U0
```

Home X axis. It is popular to home out axis when lathe has either sub-spindle or turret has longer tools. Most lathe programmers will only move the turret to a safe distance to change turret tool position.

```
G0Z5.0
```

Rapid to safe Z distance.

```
M1
```

Optional Stop.

```
N4(3/8 BORE BAR, R.007)
G0G90G54
G50S3000M3
G97S2800M8
T0404
```

```
X.550Z.060
```

Rapid to X start location and safe Z location.

```
G1Z-.750F.005
```

Feed to Z location.

```
U-.010
```

An incremental move in the X axis of -.010. The "U" signifies and incremental move in X.

```
G0Z.060
```

Rapid to safe distance in Z.

```
X.600
```

Rapid position to X location.

```
G1Z-.750F.005
```

Feed to Z location.

```
U-.010
```

Incremental X move by -.010.

```
G0Z.060
```

Rapid to safe distance in Z.

```
X.643
```

Rapid to X start position. This start position is the position which is to generate a .002R plus the tool nose radius .007R which is .009. This number is doubled in the X because of diameter programming; .018.

```
G1Z0F.005
```

Feed to Z position which is face of part.

```
G2X.625Z-.009R.009F.001
```

Clockwise interpolation to X location to start finish bore, end location of Z to adjusted to R.007 of tool nose plus to generate a R.002, and to swing a R.009; tool nose plus radius to generate.

```
G1Z-.750F.002
```

Feed to Z location.

```
X.480
```

Feed to X location to finish bottom of counterbore.

```
G0Z.060
X4.0Z4.0
M1
```

Rapid to safe Z location, then safe distance to end toolpath, and optional stop.

```
N5(.062 WIDTH ID GROOVE TOOL)
G0G90G54
G50X3000M3
G97S1500M8
T0505
```

```
X.610Z0.
```

Rapid to X and Z location.

```
G1Z-.250F.010
```

Feed to Z location to start groove.

```
X.625
```

Feed to X location. Starting position in X for groove.

```
G75X.675I.015F.004
```

Groove canned cycle.

```
G4P1.
```

Dwell.

```
G0G80X.610
```

Rapid, cancel canned cycle, and position to X location.

```
Z.100
```

Rapid to Z safe location.

```
X4.0Z4.0
M1
```

Rapid to safe location and optional stop.

```
N6(.122 WIDE CUTOFF TOOL)
G0G90G54
G50S3000M3
G97S1500M8
T0606
```

```
Z-1.672
```

Rapid to Z location.

```
X1.510
```

Rapid to safe distance X location.

```
G1X1.450F.005
```

Feed to X location. This short cutoff feed is removing material in order to generate a small radius on OD to back of part prior to cutting off.

```
G0X1.510
```

Rapid to safe distance in X.

```
Z-1.606
```

Rapid to start location in Z.

```
X1.500
```

Rapid to start location in X.

```
G3X1.468W-.016R.016F.001
```

Counter clockwise interpolation. The "W" is an incremental "Z" move in lathe programming.

```
M36
```

Turn on parts catcher.

```
G1X-.030F.0035
```

Feed to X location pass X0.

```
M37
```

Turn off parts catcher.

```
G0X5.0Z5.0
M30
%
```

Rapid to safe position and end program.

Note: *This G-Code courtesy of Chad Duame, a long time co-worker and lathe programmer.*

This concludes the Part4 Tutorial. In this tutorial, there have been examples and concepts showing the programming for tool nose radius where it is not common to actually use the tool nose radius compensation G-Code. This section also shows the reader that the X and Z axis used in their own form are absolute values, whereas the programmer can substitute the "U" and "W" as incremental moves in the respective axis.

Part4 Tutorial
Notes:

Notes:

_____

_____

_____

_____

_____

_____

_____

_____

_____

_____

_____

_____

_____

_____

_____

_____

_____

_____

_____

_____

_____

Sub-Programs

Sub-Programs

Sub-Programs are programs that compliment a main program. A Sub-Program can be anything from a complete part program to individual toolpathes for a specific tool. This section will explain sub-programs from a milling machining centers, but the same principle will apply for lathes.

Duplicating Parts

The most common use of sub-programs is to utilize a toolpath in order to make numerous parts without just adding it in the main program for each new workoffset. This is to keep the overall program size small. This is very useful in older controls that have limited memory capacity.

Workoffsets

Another major use of sub-programs is to load or overwrite workoffsets. This practice allows the programmer use infinite work holding locations on any machine tool. Companies and programmers use this technique for two reasons.

The first reason is because older machine tools only support G54-G59 workoffset designations. This is only six designations, whereas a machine tool may have the travel capacity to tool/fixture many more parts at one time.

The second reason is for workoffset control. When a machine is in write-protected mode, an operator may not be allowed to change or edit the workoffsets. Another example of workoffset control is that some companies with horizontal milling machines will setup and fixture a pallet that may be removed between running a particular part. When this part is done running they may remove the complete pallet and store it on a pallet rack, and when it comes time to run that part again the pallet can be placed back in the machine and the workoffsets are already picked up and ready to go for the next run because they were preserved in the program.

Multiple Parts/Different Pallet

Due to scheduling, programmers have to create a program that will produce one part number on one pallet of a horizontal milling machine and another completely different part number on another pallet and run in tandem. This is easily achieved with a sub-program.

Format and Use

Understanding how a sub-program is used by the machine tool control is very simple, but first the programmer needs to understand the basics.

In the main program the programmer must callup the sub-program properly. The basic way to achieve a sub-program call is by the appropriate M-Code and the correct Program number.

M98P0002

> The M98 is the sub-program jumpto or callup.
> The P0002 is the correct way to designate a program with the M98. In the program file list the program is listed as O0002, the "P" is the format used for sub-programs.

M99

> In order for the machine control jump back to the main, the sub-program needs to have an M99 at the end of the program. **Note:** If there is an M2 or M30 the machine will interpret that as an end of program.

When the machine tool control reads through the program, it will read the M98 line and jump into that sub-program, when the control reads the M99 it will jump back to the *previous* program and read the next line after the M98. The previous program is important, because the programmer can have a sub-program in a sub-program. The control will always go back to the program that called up the sub-program. If the programmer has a sub-program that calls up another sub-program when a M99 is read, it does not mean it will return to the main program.

Duplicating Parts

In the following examples, the application is to create two parts at one time without having a long redundant code program. The following is code from Part1 Tutorial code, Example 1 has redundant code whereas Example 2 has sub-programs to create the same application.

Some programmers may say that for contour passes it makes a the overall program size smaller but using canned cycles it makes it more complicated and is not worth it for drilling cycles.

In this particular example, the programmer has to understand that if there are any changes to the program, the use of sub-programs to create duplicate parts is beneficial when there are an edits to be made. The programmer will only have to edit one toolpath or drill cycle. If there were six or 100 parts being made in this program, just imagine how easy it would be to edit if it was only in the sub-program versus editing each redundant toolpath in the main program.

```
%
O0001(PROGRAM#)
(PROGRAM NAME - PART1)
(SAMPLE PART)


N1( 1" FLAT ENDMILL TOOL )
T1M6
M1
N100G0G90G54X-1.Y0.S3056M3
G43H1Z.1M8T2
(PROFILE)
G1Z-1.F24.4
G41D51X-.5
Y1.75
G2X.25Y2.5I.75
G1X3.5
G2X4.5Y1.5J-1.
G1Y.75
G2X3.25Y-.5I-1.25
G1X0.
G2X-.5Y0.J.5
G1G40X-1.
G0Z.1

(FINISH WALL STEP3)
X1.25Y4.5
G1Z-.5
G41D51Y4.
G2X3.5Y1.75J-2.25
G1Y.25
G2X1.25Y-2.I-2.25
G1G40Y-2.5
G0Z.1
(FINISH WALL STEP 2)
Y3.75
G1Z-.5
G41D51Y3.25
G2X2.75Y1.75J-1.5
G1Y.25
G2X1.25Y-1.25I-1.5
G1G40Y-1.75
G0Z.1

(FINISH WALL)
Y3.
G1Z-.5
G41D51Y2.5
G2X2.Y1.75J-.75
G1Y.25
G2X1.25Y-.5I-.75
G1G40Y-1.
G0Z.1

(SECOND PART)
G55X-1.Y0.
(PROFILE)
G1Z-1.F24.4
G41D51X-.5
Y1.75
G2X.25Y2.5I.75
G1X3.5
G2X4.5Y1.5J-1.
G1Y.75
G2X3.25Y-.5I-1.25
G1X0.
G2X-.5Y0.J.5
G1G40X-1.
G0Z.1

(FINISH WALL STEP3)
X1.25Y4.5
G1Z-.5
```

```
G41D51Y4.
G2X3.5Y1.75J-2.25
G1Y.25
G2X1.25Y-2.I-2.25
G1G40Y-2.5
G0Z.1
(FINISH WALL STEP 2)
Y3.75
G1Z-.5
G41D51Y3.25
G2X2.75Y1.75J-1.5
G1Y.25
G2X1.25Y-1.25I-1.5
G1G40Y-1.75
G0Z.1

(FINISH WALL)
Y3.
G1Z-.5
G41D51Y2.5
G2X2.Y1.75J-.75
G1Y.25
G2X1.25Y-.5I-.75
G1G40Y-1.
G0Z.1
M9
G91G28Z0M19
M1

N2(5/8 SPOT DRILL TOOL )
(1/2-13)
T2M6
M1
N200G0G90G54X.75Y1.S2500M3
G43H2Z.1M8T3
G98G81Z-.25R.1F10.
(.375 DIAMETER)
X2.5Z-.6875R-.4
G80Z.1

(SECOND PART)
G55X.75Y1.
G98G81Z-.25R.1F10.
(.375 DIAMETER)
X2.5Z-.6875R-.4
G80Z.1
M9
G91G28Z0M19
M1

N3( 27/64 DRILL TOOL)
(1/2-13 DRILL)
T3M6
M1
N300G0G90G54X.75Y1.S2264M3
G43H3Z.1M8T4
G98G83Z-1.2267R.1Q.2109F9.
G80Z.1

(SECOND PART)
G55X.75Y1.
G98G83Z-1.2267R.1Q.2109F9.
G80Z.1
M9
G91G28Z0M19
M1

N4(1/2-13 CUT TAPRH TOOL )
T4M6
M1
N400G0G90G54X.75Y1.S130M3
G43H4Z.1M8T5
G84Z-1.35R.1F10.
G80Z.1
```

```
(SECOND PART)
G55X.75Y1.
G84Z-1.35R.1F10.
G80Z.1
M9
G91G28Z0M19
M1

N5( #U DRILL TOOL, .368)
(.375 DRILL)
T5M6
M1
N500G0G90G54X2.5Y1.S2595M3
G43H5Z.1M8T6
G98G83Z-1.2106R-.4Q.184F10.4
G80Z.1

(SECOND PART)
G55X2.5Y1.
G98G83Z-1.2106R-.4Q.184F10.4
G80Z.1
M9
G91G28Z0M19
M1

N6(.375 REAMER TOOL, .375)
(.375 REAM)
T6M6
M1
N600G0G90G54X2.5Y1.S1000M3
G43H6Z.1M8T1
G98G85Z-1.2R-.4F10.
G80Z.1

(SECOND PART)
G55X2.5Y1.
G98G85Z-1.2R-.4F10.
G80Z.1
M9
G91G28Z0M19
G28Y0
M30
%
```

Example 2

```
%
O0001(PROGRAM#)
(PROGRAM NAME - PART1)
(SAMPLE PART)
(MAIN PROGRAM)

N1( 1" FLAT ENDMILL TOOL )
T1M6
M1
N100G0G90G54X-1.Y0.S3056M3
G43H1Z.1M8T2
M98P0011
```

(SECOND PART)
```
G55X-1.Y0.
M98P0011
G0Z.1M9
G91G28Z0M19
M1
```

```
N2(5/8 SPOT DRILL TOOL )
(1/2-13)
T2M6
M1
N200G0G90G54X.75Y1.S2500M3
G43H2Z.1M8T3
M98P0012
```

(SECOND PART)
```
G55X.75Y1.
M98P0012
G80Z.1M9
G91G28Z0M19
M1
```

```
N3( 27/64 DRILL TOOL)
(1/2-13 DRILL)
T3M6
M1
N300G0G90G54X.75Y1.S2264M3
G43H3Z.1M8T4
M98P0013
```

(SECOND PART)
```
G55X.75Y1.
M98P0013
G80Z.1M9
G91G28Z0M19
M1
```

```
N4(1/2-13 CUT TAPRH TOOL )
T4M6
M1
N400G0G90G54X.75Y1.S130M3
G43H4Z.1M8T5
M98P0014
```

(SECOND PART)
```
G55X.75Y1.
M98P0014
G0G80Z.1M9
G91G28Z0M19
M1
```

```
N5( #U DRILL TOOL, .368)
(.375 DRILL)
T5M6
M1
N500G0G90G54X2.5Y1.S2595M3
G43H5Z.1M8T6
M98P0015
```

(SECOND PART)

```
G55X2.5Y1.
M98P0015
G80Z.1M9
G91G28Z0M19
M1
```

```
N6(.375 REAMER TOOL, .375)
(.375 REAM)
T6M6
M1
N600G0G90G54X2.5Y1.S1000M3
G43H6Z.1M8T1
M98P0016
```

(SECOND PART)
```
G55X2.5Y1.
M98P0016
G80Z.1M9
G91G28Z0M19
G28Y0
M30
```

```
O0011
(SUBPROGRAM O1)
(T1-1" TOOLPATH)
X-1.Y0.
(PROFILE)
G1Z-1.F24.4
G41D51X-.5
Y1.75
G2X.25Y2.5I.75
G1X3.5
G2X4.5Y1.5J-1.
G1Y.75
G2X3.25Y-.5I-1.25
G1X0.
G2X-.5Y0.J.5
G1G40X-1.
G0Z.1
```

```
(FINISH WALL STEP3)
X1.25Y4.5
G1Z-.5
G41D51Y4.
G2X3.5Y1.75J-2.25
G1Y.25
G2X1.25Y-2.1-2.25
G1G40Y-2.5
G0Z.1
(FINISH WALL STEP 2)
Y3.75
G1Z-.5
G41D51Y3.25
G2X2.75Y1.75J-1.5
G1Y.25
G2X1.25Y-1.25I-1.5
G1G40Y-1.75
G0Z.1
```

```
(FINISH WALL)
Y3.
G1Z-.5
G41D51Y2.5
G2X2.Y1.75J-.75
G1Y.25
G2X1.25Y-.5I-.75
G1G40Y-1.
G0Z.1
M99
```

```
O0012
(SUBPROGRAM O1)
(T2-5/8" TOOLPATH)
X.75Y1.
G98G81Z-.25R.1F10.
```

```
(.375 DIAMETER)
X2.5Z-.6875R-.4
G80Z.1
M99
```

```
O0013
(SUBPROGRAM O1)
(T3-27/64" TOOLPATH)
X.75Y1.
G98G83Z-1.2267R.1Q.2109F9.
G80Z.1
M99
```

```
O0014
(SUBPROGRAM O1)
(T4-1/2-13" TOOLPATH)
X.75Y1.
G84Z-1.35R.1F10.
G80Z.1
M99
```

```
O0015
(SUBPROGRAM O1)
(T5-U DRILL TOOLPATH)
X2.5Y1.
G98G83Z-1.2106R-.4Q.184F10.4
G80Z.1
M99
```

```
O0016
(SUBPROGRAM O1)
(T6-375 REAMER TOOLPATH)
X2.5Y1.
G98G85Z-1.2R-.4F10.
G80Z.1
M99
%
```

Workoffsets

As discussed earlier in this section, workoffsets in the sub-program is very popular and useful. It is very simple format to utilize this feature.

Note: This is a common Fanuc control format where different control manufacturers may differ slightly.

The G10

G10G90L2P1X-13.1050Y-2.2135Z-1.2012

This format designates G10 which is Data Input, along with G90 Absolute, L2 is the Workoffsets, and P1 is designating which workoffset. P1 is G54, P2 is G55,...P6 is G59.

Also, the X,Y,Z are the values to override. A/B values may be used if there is the axis available in the Workoffset screen.

Read through the following Example 3 and note the amount of workoffset sub-programs.

```
%
O0001(PROGRAM#)
(PROGRAM NAME - PART1)
(SAMPLE PART)
(MAIN PROGRAM)

N1( 1" FLAT ENDMILL TOOL )
T1M6
M1
(WORKOFFSET1)
M98P0021
N100G0G90G54X-1.Y0.S3056M3
G43H1Z.1M8T2
M98P0011
(SECOND PART)
G55X-1.Y0.
M98P0011
G0Z.1
(THIRD PART)
G56X-1.Y0.
M98P0011
G0Z.1
(FOURTH PART)
G57X-1.Y0.
M98P0011
G0Z.1
(FIFTH PART)
G58X-1.Y0.
M98P0011
G0Z.1
(SIXTH PART)
G58X-1.Y0.
M98P0011
G0Z.1
(WORKOFFSET2)
M98P0022
(SEVENTH PART)
G54X-1.Y0.
M98P0011
(EIGHTH PART)
G55X-1.Y0.
M98P0011
G0Z.1
(NINTH PART)
G56X-1.Y0.
M98P0011
G0Z.1
(TENTH PART)
G57X-1.Y0.
M98P0011
G0Z.1
(ELEVENTH PART)
G58X-1.Y0.
M98P0011
G0Z.1
(TWELFTH PART)
G58X-1.Y0.
M98P0011
G0Z.1
M9
G91G28Z0M19
M1

N2(5/8 SPOT DRILL TOOL )
(1/2-13)
T2M6
M1
(WORKOFFSET1)
M98P0021
N200G0G90G54X.75Y1.S2500M3
G43H2Z.1M8T3
M98P0012
(SECOND PART)
```

```
G55X.75Y1.
M98P0012
(THIRD PART)
G56X.75Y1.
M98P0012
(FOURTH PART)
G57X.75Y1.
M98P0012
(FIFTH PART)
G58X.75Y1.
M98P0012
(SIXTH PART)
G59X.75Y1.
M98P0012


(WORKOFFSET2)
M98P0022
(SEVENTH PART)
G54X.75Y1.
M98P0012
(EIGHTH PART)
G55X.75Y1.
M98P0012
(NINTH PART)
G56X.75Y1.
M98P0012
(TENTH PART)
G57X.75Y1.
M98P0012
(ELEVENTH PART)
G58X.75Y1.
M98P0012
(TWELFTH PART)
G59X.75Y1.
M98P0012
G80Z.1M9
G91G28Z0M19
M1


N3( 27/64 DRILL TOOL)
(1/2-13 DRILL)
T3M6
M1
(WORKOFFSET1)
M98P0021
N300G0G90G54X.75Y1.S2264M3
G43H3Z.1M8T4
M98P0013
(SECOND PART)
G55X.75Y1.
M98P0013
(THIRD PART)
G56X.75Y1.
M98P0013
(FOURTH PART)
G57X.75Y1.
M98P0013
(FIFTH PART)
G58X.75Y1.
M98P0013
(SIXTH PART)
G59X.75Y1.
M98P0013

(WORKOFFSET2)
M98P0022
(SEVENTH PART)
G54X.75Y1.
M98P0013
(EIGHTH PART)
G55X.75Y1.
M98P0013
(NINTH PART)
G56X.75Y1.
M98P0013
```

```
(TENTH PART)
G57X.75Y1.
M98P0013
(ELEVENTH PART)
G58X.75Y1.
M98P0013
(TWELFTH PART)
G59X.75Y1.
M98P0013
G80Z.1M9
G91G28Z0M19
M1

N4(1/2-13 CUT TAPRH TOOL )
T4M6
M1
(WORKOFFSET1)
M98P0021
N400G0G90G54X.75Y1.S130M3
G43H4Z.1M8T5
M98P0014
(SECOND PART)
G55X.75Y1.
M98P0014
(THIRD PART)
G56X.75Y1.
M98P0014
(FOURTH PART)
G57X.75Y1.
M98P0014
(FIFTH PART)
G58X.75Y1.
M98P0014
(SIXTH PART)
G59X.75Y1.
M98P0014


(WORKOFFSET2)
M98P0022
(SEVENTH PART)
G54X.75Y1.
M98P0014
(EIGHTH PART)
G55X.75Y1.
M98P0014
(NINTH PART)
G56X.75Y1.
M98P0014
(TENTH PART)
G57X.75Y1.
M98P0014
(ELEVENTH PART)
G58X.75Y1.
M98P0014
(TWELFTH PART)
G59X.75Y1.
M98P0014
G0G80Z.1M9
G91G28Z0M19
M1

N5( #U DRILL TOOL, .368)
(.375 DRILL)
T5M6
M1
(WORKOFFSET1)
M98P0021
N500G0G90G54X2.5Y1.S2595M3
G43H5Z.1M8T6
M98P0015
(SECOND PART)
G55X2.5Y1.
M98P0015
(THIRD PART)
G56X2.5Y1.
```

M98P0015
(FOURTH PART)
G57X2.5Y1.
M98P0015
(FIFTH PART)
G58X2.5Y1.
M98P0015
(SIXTH PART)
G59X2.5Y1.
M98P0015

(WORKOFFSET2)
M98P0022
(SEVENTH PART)
G54X2.5Y1.
M98P0015
(EIGHTH PART)
G55X2.5Y1.
M98P0015
(NINTH PART)
G56X2.5Y1.
M98P0015
(TENTH PART)
G57X2.5Y1.
M98P0015
(ELEVENTH PART)
G58X2.5Y1.
M98P0015
(TWELFTH PART)
G59X2.5Y1.
M98P0015
G80Z.1M9
G91G28Z0M19
M1

N6(.375 REAMER TOOL, .375)
(.375 REAM)
T6M6
M1
(WORKOFFSET1)
M98P0021
N600G0G90G54X2.5Y1.S1000M3
G43H6Z.1M8T1
M98P0016
(SECOND PART)
G55X2.5Y1.
M98P0016
(THIRD PART)
G56X2.5Y1.
M98P0016
(FOURTH PART)
G57X2.5Y1.
M98P0016
(FIFTH PART)
G58X2.5Y1.
M98P0016
(SIXTH PART)
G59X2.5Y1.
M98P0016

(WORKOFFSET2)
M98P0022
(SEVENTH PART)
G54X2.5Y1.
M98P0016
(EIGHTH PART)
G55X2.5Y1.
M98P0016
(NINTH PART)
G56X2.5Y1.
M98P0016
(TENTH PART)
G57X2.5Y1.
M98P0016
(ELEVENTH PART)

G58X2.5Y1.
M98P0016
(TWELFTH PART)
G59X2.5Y1.
M98P0016
G80Z.1M9
G91G28Z0M19
G28Y0
M30

O0011
(SUBPROGRAM O1)
(T1-1" TOOLPATH)
X-1.Y0.
(PROFILE)
G1Z-1.F24.4
G41D51X-.5
Y1.75
G2X.25Y2.5I.75
G1X3.5
G2X4.5Y1.5J-1.
G1Y.75
G2X3.25Y-.5I-1.25
G1X0.
G2X-.5Y0.J.5
G1G40X-1.
G0Z.1

(FINISH WALL STEP3)
X1.25Y4.5
G1Z-.5
G41D51Y4.
G2X3.5Y1.75J-2.25
G1Y.25
G2X1.25Y-2.I-2.25
G1G40Y-2.5
G0Z.1
(FINISH WALL STEP 2)
Y3.75
G1Z-.5
G41D51Y3.25
G2X2.75Y1.75J-1.5
G1Y.25
G2X1.25Y-1.25I-1.5
G1G40Y-1.75
G0Z.1

(FINISH WALL)
Y3.
G1Z-.5
G41D51Y2.5
G2X2.Y1.75J-.75
G1Y.25
G2X1.25Y-.5I-.75
G1G40Y-1.
G0Z.1
M99

O0012
(SUBPROGRAM O1)
(T2-5/8" TOOLPATH)
X.75Y1.
G98G81Z-.25R.1F10.
(.375 DIAMETER)
X2.5Z-.6875R-.4
G80Z.1
M99

O0013
(SUBPROGRAM O1)
(T3-27/64" TOOLPATH)
X.75Y1.
G98G83Z-1.2267R.1Q.2109F9.
G80Z.1
M99

O0014
(SUBPROGRAM O1)
(T4-1/2-13" TOOLPATH)
X.75Y1.
G84Z-1.35R.1F10.
G80Z.1
M99

O0015
(SUBPROGRAM O1)
(T5-U DRILL TOOLPATH)
X2.5Y1.
G98G83Z-1.2106R-.4Q.184F10.4
G80Z.1
M99

O0016
(SUBPROGRAM O1)
(T6-375 REAMER TOOLPATH)
X2.5Y1.
G98G85Z-1.2R-.4F10.
G80Z.1
M99

O0021
(WORKOFFSET1)
G10G90L2P1X-1.1000Y-1.0125Z-1.1021
G10G90L2P2X-5.12500Y-1.0125Z-1.1021
G10G90L2P3X-10.3520Y-1.0125Z-1.1021
G10G90L2P4X-15.1579Y-1.0125Z-1.1021
G10G90L2P5X-20.8778Y-1.0125Z-1.1021
G10G90L2P6X-25.3479Y-1.0125Z-1.1021
M99

O0022
(WORKOFFSET2)
G10G90L2P1X-1.1520Y-10.8795Z-1.1021
G10G90L2P2X-5.1253Y-11.7785Z-1.5211
G10G90L2P3X-10.8720Y-11.0335Z-1.1021
G10G90L2P4X-15.4379Y-12.6645Z-1.1021
G10G90L2P5X-20.3258Y-13.3215Z-1.1021
G10G90L2P6X-25.3339Y-14.7795Z-1.1021
M99
%

Sub-Programs

Multiple Parts/Different Pallet

Technology is increasingly changing, and with the use of horizontal machining centers that have pallet pools or racking systems, there are needs to create different parts on different pallets.

In Example 5 we need to create two pieces from Part1 Tutorial and one piece from Part2 Tutorial.

Pallet change codes very between manufacturers, for this example, we will assume that M71 is designated to change to pallet #1 and M72 is designated to change to pallet #2.

Sub-Programs

```
%
O2323
(MAIN PROGRAM)
(PART1 & PART2)
M71
M98P0001
M72
M98P1001
M30


O0001(PROGRAM#)
(SUBPROGRAM NAME - PART1)
(SAMPLE PART)
(SUB PROGRAM)


N1( 1" FLAT ENDMILL TOOL )
T1M6
M1
N100G0G90G54X-1.Y0.S3056M3
G43H1Z.1M8T2
M98P0011


(SECOND PART)
G55X-1.Y0.
M98P0011
G0Z.1M9
G91G28Z0M19
M1


N2(5/8 SPOT DRILL TOOL )
(1/2-13)
T2M6
M1
N200G0G90G54X.75Y1.S2500M3
G43H2Z.1M8T3
M98P0012


(SECOND PART)
G55X.75Y1.
M98P0012
G80Z.1M9
G91G28Z0M19
M1


N3( 27/64 DRILL TOOL)
(1/2-13 DRILL)
T3M6
M1
N300G0G90G54X.75Y1.S2264M3
G43H3Z.1M8T4
M98P0013


(SECOND PART)
G55X.75Y1.
M98P0013
G80Z.1M9
G91G28Z0M19
M1


N4(1/2-13 CUT TAPRH TOOL )
T4M6
M1
N400G0G90G54X.75Y1.S130M3
G43H4Z.1M8T5
M98P0014


(SECOND PART)
G55X.75Y1.
M98P0014
G0G80Z.1M9
G91G28Z0M19
M1


N5( #U DRILL TOOL, .368)
(.375 DRILL)
```

```
T5M6
M1
N500G0G90G54X2.5Y1.S2595M3
G43H5Z.1M8T6
M98P0015


(SECOND PART)
G55X2.5Y1.
M98P0015
G80Z.1M9
G91G28Z0M19
M1


N6(.375 REAMER TOOL, .375)
(.375 REAM)
T6M6
M1
N600G0G90G54X2.5Y1.S1000M3
G43H6Z.1M8T1
M98P0016


(SECOND PART)
G55X2.5Y1.
M98P0016
G80Z.1M9
G91G28Z0M19
M99


O0011
(SUBPROGRAM O1)
(T1-1" TOOLPATH)
X-1.Y0.
(PROFILE)
G1Z-1.F24.4
G41D51X-.5
Y1.75
G2X.25Y2.5I.75
G1X3.5
G2X4.5Y1.5J-1.
G1Y.75
G2X3.25Y-.5I-1.25
G1X0.
G2X-.5Y0.J.5
G1G40X-1.
G0Z.1


(FINISH WALL STEP3)
X1.25Y4.5
G1Z-.5
G41D51Y4.
G2X3.5Y1.75J-2.25
G1Y.25
G2X1.25Y-2.I-2.25
G1G40Y-2.5
G0Z.1
(FINISH WALL STEP 2)
Y3.75
G1Z-.5
G41D51Y3.25
G2X2.75Y1.75J-1.5
G1Y.25
G2X1.25Y-1.25I-1.5
G1G40Y-1.75
G0Z.1


(FINISH WALL)
Y3.
G1Z-.5
G41D51Y2.5
G2X2.Y1.75J-.75
G1Y.25
G2X1.25Y-.5I-.75
G1G40Y-1.
G0Z.1
M99
```

```
O0012
(SUBPROGRAM O1)
(T2-5/8" TOOLPATH)
X.75Y1.
G98G81Z-.25R.1F10.
(.375 DIAMETER)
X2.5Z-.6875R-.4
G80Z.1
M99


O0013
(SUBPROGRAM O1)
(T3-27/64" TOOLPATH)
X.75Y1.
G98G83Z-1.2267R.1Q.2109F9.
G80Z.1
M99


O0014
(SUBPROGRAM O1)
(T4-1/2-13" TOOLPATH)
X.75Y1.
G84Z-1.35R.1F10.
G80Z.1
M99


O0015
(SUBPROGRAM O1)
(T5-U DRILL TOOLPATH)
X2.5Y1.
G98G83Z-1.2106R-.4Q.184F10.4
G80Z.1
M99


O0016
(SUBPROGRAM O1)
(T6-375 REAMER TOOLPATH)
X2.5Y1.
G98G85Z-1.2R-.4F10.
G80Z.1
M99


O1001
(SUBPROGRAM NAME -ANGLE RADIUS)
(SAMPLE PART2)
(1/2 FLAT ENDMILL)
T7M6
M1
G0G90G56X-.6495Y.375S6112M3
G43H7Z.1M8
G1Z-.5F48.9
G41D7X-.2165Y.125
X.3423Y1.0928
G2X1.1288Y1.1964I.433J-.25
G1X2.1485Y.1768
G2X1.9717Y-.25I-.1768J-.1768
G1X0.
G2X-.2165Y.125I0.J.25
G1G40X-.6495Y.375
G0Z.1M9
M5
G91G28Z0.
M99
%
```

Summary

Through the use of Sub-Programs, creating continual running and fluid programs can be very simplistic with infinite programming possibilities. Through the use of other G-Code practices, the programmer may be able to Scale or Rotate or Mirror a single toolpath and cancel that code and run the path in a regular state on the next work location or fixture.

_____

_____

_____

_____

_____

_____

_____

_____

_____

_____

_____

_____

_____

_____

_____

_____

_____

_____

_____

_____

_____

_____

_____

Notes:

_____

_____

_____

_____

_____

_____

_____

_____

_____

_____

_____

_____

_____

_____

_____

_____

_____

_____

_____

_____

_____

Sub-Programs

Macros

Macros

As discussed in the Introduction to CNC section macros are defined by very different definitions. For the purposes of this section, the discussion of macros will be what is known as variable macro programming and will be very brief.

Variable macro programming is a very complicated subject and there are complete texts that focus strictly on programming for macros. We will discuss basic understanding of what macros can do and the potential.

What is a variable macro?

In programming G-Code variable macros are nothing more than a variable that can be substituted for a value of a directional or positional code. These codes can be substituted for G & M codes but mostly are for purposes other than those. These macros can also be used in many different mathematical expressions to use the control to find an answer for a user defined problem.

Variable macros are identified by "#" followed by a number. The following examples are a standard Fanuc based variable macro interpretation, for different controls or macro formats please refer to that control's programming manual.

What can you do with macros?

The programmer can do just about anything that can be imaginable. The programmer can make a short macro program to change tools in sequence in order to take many tools out of a machine without having to manually type in each tools where the operator does not have access to the tool magazine. The programmer can make a more in depth program that can control similar features on a family of parts without having to make a completely separate program. The programmer can also create a complicated program that has mathematical expressions to find the location of a part which is rotating around an axis, such as horizontal or indexers.

What does a macro program look like?

In this short example, the programmer creates a simple program to change the tool in a milling machine in order to quickly put tools in or take tools out. This program will change the tool and automatically add "1" to the tool value each time to program is started.

```
%
O1
(TOOL CHANGE)
/#101=1
T#101 M6
#102 = [#101+1]
#101 = #102
M30
%
```

/#101=1

> This line designates macro 101 to the value of 1. The block skip is set because after the initial designation, the operator must enable the block skip switch/button, so the machine will not overwrite the value in macro 101. This is important because as we read through the program we will notice the program will change this macro 101 position. If the user does not enable block skip the value would be reset.

T#101 M6

> This line changes the tool with the value in macro 101.

#102 = [#101+1]

> This line adds a value of "1" to macro 101. The brackets, "[ ]" are used for a mathematical expression.

#101 = #102

> This lines overwrites macro 101 with macro 102

M30

> This line resets or ends the program.

In this example we notice that each time the cycle start button is pressed the machine will change the tool to the next value.

The first time the button is pressed the machine reads the program to change T1. The second time the button is pressed with block skip feature enabled, the machine reads the program to change T2 and so on and so forth.

Most programmers will leave out the first line which would have to be manually inputted in the Macro screen of the control panel by the operator. This is helpful if the operator would want to start at a different tool number.

What is a more practical example?

The overall most common use for variable macro programming is when there are a family of parts with identical features except for a variance in one single feature.

In this example there is a simple drilling feature that has a different location depending on the Part Number.

Part Number 2008-1   X1.25   Y.500
Part Number 2008-2   X2.375   Y1.500
Part Number 2008-3   X3.245   Y1.650

```
%
O1
(DRILL HOLE)
(2008-FAMILY)
(#101 = X VALUE)
(#102 = Y VALUE)

(DRILL)
T1M6
G0G90X#101Y#102M3S2536
G43H1Z.1M8
G83R.1Z-.3758Q.1057F11.5
G80Z.1M9
G91G28Z0M19
G28Y0
M30
%
```

In this example, depending on the part number the operator has to make, the value only needs to be manually changed in the Macro screen to the appropriate value.

This is a very simple example for family of parts but should allow the reader the exposure to understand the potential of macros.

Macros
Notes:

_____

_____

_____

_____

_____

_____

_____

_____

_____

_____

_____

_____

_____

_____

_____

_____

_____

_____

_____

_____

_____

_____

_____

_____

Notes:

Macros

Appendix: Trigonometry of Part2 Tutorial

The section will explain the mathematics of Part2 Angular Tutorial toolpath positions.

Figures 1 & 4: The hypotenuse is the distance of the radius of the tool and radius to generate.
Figures 2 & 3: The hypotenuse is the distance of the radius of the tool.

Note: Please refer to the Trigonometry chart in **"CNC Programming: Reference Book"**.

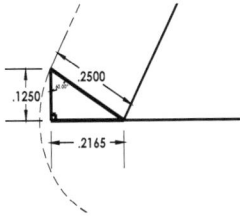

Figure 1

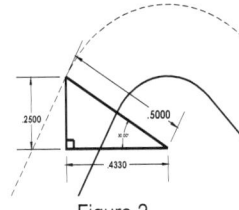

Figure 2

Known Sides/Angles c and B
Need *a* and *b*

a = c x cos B   b = c x sin B

a = .250(cos 60)   *b = .250(sin 60)*
a = .250(.5)   *b = .250(.8660)*
a= .125   *b = .2165*

Known Sides/Angles c and A
Need *a* and *b*

a = c x sin A   b = c x cos A

a = .500(sin 30)   *b = .500(cos 30)*
a = .500(.5)   *b = .500(.8660)*
a= .250   *b = .4330*

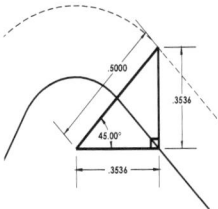

Figure 3

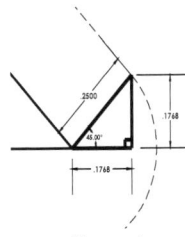

Figure 4

Known Sides/Angles c and B
Need *a* and *b*

a = c x cos B   b = c x sin B

a = .500(cos 45)   *b = .500(sin 45)*
a = .500(.7071)   *b = .500(.7071)*
a= .3536   *b = .3536*

Known Sides/Angles c and B
Need *a* and *b*

a = c x cos A   b = c x sin A

a = .250(cos 45)   *b = .250(sin 45)*
a = .250(.7071)   *b = .250(.7071)*
a= .1768   *b = .1768*

Appendix: Interpolation

In the sections covering Interpolation, Helical Interpolation and Thread Milling we discussed the basics of interpolating diameters where the hole location is at Zero. Most situations for interpolation are not at Zero.

When the diameter is not at Zero, it is fairly simple to program, but the programmer needs to understand the positional values accordingly.

In the example from Helical Interpolation we note the hole is at Zero. Notice the same example where the hole location is at X2.5 Y-3.125.

Example 1 Location Zero

```
%
O0001
(PROGRAM NAME -HELICAL INTERPOLATION)
(1/2 FLAT ENDMILL)
T1M6
G0G90G54X0Y0S6112M3
G43H1Z.1M8
G1Z0F48.9
G41D1X.25
G3I-.25Z-.25
I-.25Z-.5
I-.25Z-.75
I-.25
G1G40X0
G0Z.1M9
M5
G91G28Z0.
M30
%
```

Example 2 Location X2.5 Y-3.125

```
%
O0001
(PROGRAM NAME -HELICAL INTERPOLATION)
(1/2 FLAT ENDMILL)
T1M6
G0G90G54X2.5Y-3.125S6112M3
G43H1Z.1M8
G1Z0F48.9
G41D1X2.75
G3I-.25Z-.25
I-.25Z-.5
I-.25Z-.75
I-.25
G1G40X2.5
G0Z.1M9
M5
G91G28Z0.
M30
%
```

The programmer will need to adjust the absolute value of the diameter location. In the examples from above, changing the start and stop positional "X" values are all that need to be changed. The "I" stays the same because this value is swing from diameter center.

Note: If the start and stop are in the "Y" the programmer adjusts the location values exactly the same as if it where the "X" axis.

There is a large debate over the use of what is known as Lathe Contour Canned Cycles. These are canned cycles that are similar to drill/bore canned cycles. The programmer sets parameters in a line of code and the machine control uses those parameters to create an internal parameter based movement to fulfill the canned cycle argument.

The problems with Contour Canned Cycles are that the user or operator does not have control over the operation with regards to make adjustments for taper and with different controls/control versions contour canned cycle formats can and do vary.

The following are Control specific examples of Lathe Contour Canned Cycles. *Note: These are just a few examples of Lathe Contour Canned Cycles, see the control manual for specific formats and defines canned cycles for the specific machine.*

Takisawa TC-3 Fanuc Series 15-T

G71   Rough Turn/Bore

G71 U_ W_ P_ Q_ D_ F_

U = Amount of Stock X Axis for Finish Turn
W = Amount of Stock Z Axis for Finish Turn
P = First Line "N" Number
Q = Last Line "N" Number
D = Depth of Cut on one side (no decimal)
F = Feed Rate

This canned cycle uses G-Code in the program as its path to follow. By reading through the variables defined in the cycle, the machine tool automatically adjusts for multiple passes according to the stock and depth of cuts.

Takisawa TC-3 Fanuc Series 16/18 & OT

G71   Rough Turn/Bore

G71 U_ R_
G71 U_ W_ P_ Q_ F_

First Line: U = Depth of Cut on a side
R = Retracting Amount
Second Line: U = Amount of Stock X Axis
W = Amount of Stock Z Axis
P = First Line "N" Number
Q = Last Line "N" Number
F = Feed Rate

This canned cycle uses G-Code in the program as its path to follow. By reading through the variables defined in the cycle, the machine tool automatically adjusts for multiple passes according to the stock and depth of cuts.

Appendix: Lathe Contour Canned Cycle

Takisawa TC-3 Fanuc Series 15-T

G74   Peck drilling in Z-axis

G74 Z_ K_ F_

Z = Depth to Drill
K = Depth of Each Peck
F = Feedreate

Note: The amount of peck retract is set by an "Internal Parameter"

Takisawa TC-3 Fanuc Series 16/18

G74   Peck drilling in Z-axis

G74 R_
G74 Z_ Q_ F_

First Line: R = Retract Amount
Seond Line: Z = Depth to Drill
              Q = Depth of each Peck (no decimal)
              F = Feedrate

Takisawa TC-3 Fanuc Series 16/18

G75   Outer/Inner Peck Grooving in X-axis

G75 R_
G75 X_ P_ F_

First Line: R = Retract Amount
Seond Line: X = Diameter to Turn
              P = Depth of each Peck (no decimal)
              F = Feedrate

This canned cycle uses the defined parameters to create a groove. The previous line should have the X and Z start location prior to starting the canned cycle.

Takisawa TC-3 Fanuc Series 15-T

G75   Outer/Inner Grooving in X-axis

G75 X_ I_ F_

X = Diameter to Turn
I = Depth of each Peck (no decimal)
F = Feedrate

This canned cycle uses the defined parameters to create a groove. The previous line should have the X and Z start location prior to starting the canned cycle.

Note: The amount of peck retract is set by an "Internal Parameter"

Index

Index

Wikipedia:Text of the GNU Free Documentation License
From Wikipedia, the free encyclopedia

Version 1.2, November 2002
Copyright (C) 2000,2001,2002 Free Software Foundation, Inc.
51 Franklin St, Fifth Floor, Boston, MA 02110-1301 USA
Everyone is permitted to copy and distribute verbatim copies of this license document, but changing it is not allowed.

0. PREAMBLE
The purpose of this License is to make a manual, textbook, or other functional and useful document "free" in the sense of freedom: to assure everyone the effective freedom to copy and redistribute it, with or without modifying it, either commercially or noncommercially. Secondarily, this License preserves for the author and publisher a way to get credit for their work, while not being considered responsible for modifications made by others.

This License is a kind of "copyleft", which means that derivative works of the document must themselves be free in the same sense. It complements the GNU General Public License, which is a copyleft license designed for free software.

We have designed this License in order to use it for manuals for free software, because free software needs free documentation: a free program should come with manuals providing the same freedoms that the software does. But this License is not limited to software manuals; it can be used for any textual work, regardless of subject matter or whether it is published as a printed book. We recommend this License principally for works whose purpose is instruction or reference.

1. APPLICABILITY AND DEFINITIONS
This License applies to any manual or other work, in any medium, that contains a notice placed by the copyright holder saying it can be distributed under the terms of this License. Such a notice grants a world-wide, royalty-free license, unlimited in duration, to use that work under the conditions stated herein. The "Document", below, refers to any such manual or work. Any member of the public is a licensee, and is addressed as "you". You accept the license if you copy, modify or distribute the work in a way requiring permission under copyright law.

A "Modified Version" of the Document means any work containing the Document or a portion of it, either copied verbatim, or with modifications and/or translated into another language.

A "Secondary Section" is a named appendix or a front-matter section of the Document that deals exclusively with the relationship of the publishers or authors of the Document to the Document's overall subject (or to related matters) and contains nothing that could fall directly within that overall subject. (Thus, if the Document is in part a textbook of mathematics, a Secondary Section may not explain any mathematics.) The relationship could be a matter of historical connection with the subject or with related matters, or of legal, commercial, philosophical, ethical or political position regarding them.

The "Invariant Sections" are certain Secondary Sections whose titles are designated, as being those of Invariant Sections, in the notice that says that the Document is released under this License. If a section does not fit the above definition of Secondary then it is not allowed to be designated as Invariant. The Document may contain zero Invariant Sections. If the Document does not identify any Invariant Sections then there are none.

The "Cover Texts" are certain short passages of text that are listed, as Front-Cover Texts or Back-Cover Texts, in the notice that says that the Document is released under this License. A Front-Cover Text may be at most 5 words, and a Back-Cover Text may be at most 25 words.

A "Transparent" copy of the Document means a machine-readable copy, represented in a format whose specification is available to the general public, that is suitable for revising the document straightforwardly with generic text editors or (for images composed of pixels) generic paint programs or (for drawings) some widely available drawing editor, and that is suitable for input to text formatters or for automatic translation to a variety of formats suitable for input to text formatters. A copy made in an otherwise Transparent file format whose markup, or absence of markup, has been arranged to thwart or discourage subsequent modification by readers is not Transparent. An image format is not Transparent if used for any substantial amount of text. A copy that is not "Transparent" is called "Opaque".

Examples of suitable formats for Transparent copies include plain ASCII without markup, Texinfo input format, LaTeX input format, SGML or XML using a publicly available DTD, and standard-conforming simple HTML, PostScript or PDF designed for human modification. Examples of transparent image formats include PNG, XCF and JPG. Opaque formats include proprietary formats that can be read and edited only by proprietary word processors, SGML or XML for which the DTD and/or processing tools are not generally available, and the machine-generated HTML, PostScript or PDF produced by some word processors for output purposes only.

The "Title Page" means, for a printed book, the title page itself, plus such following pages as are needed to hold, legibly, the material this License requires to appear in the title page. For works in formats which do not have any title page as such, "Title Page" means the text near the most prominent appearance of the work's title, preceding the beginning of the body of the text.

A section "Entitled XYZ" means a named subunit of the Document whose title either is precisely XYZ or contains XYZ in parentheses following text that translates XYZ in another language. (Here XYZ stands for a specific section name mentioned below, such as "Acknowledgements", "Dedications", "Endorsements", or "History".) To "Preserve the Title" of such a section when you modify the Document means that it remains a section "Entitled XYZ" according to this definition.

The Document may include Warranty Disclaimers next to the notice which states that this License applies to the Document. These Warranty Disclaimers are considered to be included by reference in this License, but only as regards disclaiming warranties: any other implication that these Warranty Disclaimers may have is void and has no effect on the meaning of this License.

2. VERBATIM COPYING
You may copy and distribute the Document in any medium, either commercially or noncommercially, provided that this License, the copyright notices, and the license notice saying this License applies to the Document are reproduced in all copies, and that you add no other conditions whatsoever to those of this License. You may not use technical measures to obstruct or control the reading or further copying of the copies you make or distribute. However, you may accept compensation in exchange for copies. If you distribute a large enough number of copies you must also follow the conditions in section 3.

You may also lend copies, under the same conditions stated above, and you may publicly display copies.

3. COPYING IN QUANTITY
If you publish printed copies (or copies in media that commonly have printed covers) of the Document, numbering more than 100, and the Document's license notice requires Cover Texts, you must enclose the copies in covers that carry, clearly and legibly, all these Cover Texts: Front-Cover Texts on the

front cover, and Back-Cover Texts on the back cover. Both covers must also clearly and legibly identify you as the publisher of these copies. The front cover must present the full title with all words of the title equally prominent and visible. You may add other material on the covers in addition. Copying with changes limited to the covers, as long as they preserve the title of the Document and satisfy these conditions, can be treated as verbatim copying in other respects.

If the required texts for either cover are too voluminous to fit legibly, you should put the first ones listed (as many as fit reasonably) on the actual cover, and continue the rest onto adjacent pages.

If you publish or distribute Opaque copies of the Document numbering more than 100, you must either include a machine-readable Transparent copy along with each Opaque copy, or state in or with each Opaque copy a computer-network location from which the general network-using public has access to download using public-standard network protocols a complete Transparent copy of the Document, free of added material. If you use the latter option, you must take reasonably prudent steps, when you begin distribution of Opaque copies in quantity, to ensure that this Transparent copy will remain thus accessible at the stated location until at least one year after the last time you distribute an Opaque copy (directly or through your agents or retailers) of that edition to the public.

It is requested, but not required, that you contact the authors of the Document well before redistributing any large number of copies, to give them a chance to provide you with an updated version of the Document.

4. MODIFICATIONS

You may copy and distribute a Modified Version of the Document under the conditions of sections 2 and 3 above, provided that you release the Modified Version under precisely this License, with the Modified Version filling the role of the Document, thus licensing distribution and modification of the Modified Version to whoever possesses a copy of it. In addition, you must do these things in the Modified Version:

A. Use in the Title Page (and on the covers, if any) a title distinct from that of the Document, and from those of previous versions (which should, if there were any, be listed in the History section of the Document). You may use the same title as a previous version if the original publisher of that version gives permission.

B. List on the Title Page, as authors, one or more persons or entities responsible for authorship of the modifications in the Modified Version, together with at least five of the principal authors of the Document (all of its principal authors, if it has fewer than five), unless they release you from this requirement.

C. State on the Title page the name of the publisher of the Modified Version, as the publisher.

D. Preserve all the copyright notices of the Document.

E. Add an appropriate copyright notice for your modifications adjacent to the other copyright notices.

F. Include, immediately after the copyright notices, a license notice giving the public permission to use the Modified Version under the terms of this License, in the form shown in the Addendum below.

G. Preserve in that license notice the full lists of Invariant Sections and required Cover Texts given in the Document's license notice.

H. Include an unaltered copy of this License.

I. Preserve the section Entitled "History", Preserve its Title, and add to it an item stating at least the title, year, new authors, and publisher of the Modified Version as given on the Title Page. If there is no section Entitled "History" in the Document, create one stating the title, year, authors, and publisher of the Document as given on its Title Page, then add an item describing the Modified Version as stated in the previous sentence.

J. Preserve the network location, if any, given in the Document for public access to a Transparent copy of the Document, and likewise the network locations given in the Document for previous versions it was based on. These may be placed in the "History" section. You may omit a network location for a work that was published at least four years before the Document itself, or if the original publisher of the version it refers to gives permission.

K. For any section Entitled "Acknowledgements" or "Dedications", Preserve the Title of the section, and preserve in the section all the substance and tone of each of the contributor acknowledgements and/or dedications given therein.

L. Preserve all the Invariant Sections of the Document, unaltered in their text and in their titles. Section numbers or the equivalent are not considered part of the section titles.

M. Delete any section Entitled "Endorsements". Such a section may not be included in the Modified Version.

N. Do not retitle any existing section to be Entitled "Endorsements" or to conflict in title with any Invariant Section.

O. Preserve any Warranty Disclaimers.

If the Modified Version includes new front-matter sections or appendices that qualify as Secondary Sections and contain no material copied from the Document, you may at your option designate some or all of these sections as invariant. To do this, add their titles to the list of Invariant Sections in the Modified Version's license notice. These titles must be distinct from any other section titles.

You may add a section Entitled "Endorsements", provided it contains nothing but endorsements of your Modified Version by various parties--for example, statements of peer review or that the text has been approved by an organization as the authoritative definition of a standard.

You may add a passage of up to five words as a Front-Cover Text, and a passage of up to 25 words as a Back-Cover Text, to the end of the list of Cover Texts in the Modified Version. Only one passage of Front-Cover Text and one of Back-Cover Text may be added by (or through arrangements made by) any one entity. If the Document already includes a cover text for the same cover, previously added by you or by arrangement made by the same entity you are acting on behalf of, you may not add another; but you may replace the old one, on explicit permission from the previous publisher that added the old one.

The author(s) and publisher(s) of the Document do not by this License give permission to use their names for publicity for or to assert or imply endorsement of any Modified Version.

5. COMBINING DOCUMENTS

You may combine the Document with other documents released under this License, under the terms defined in section 4 above for modified versions, provided that you include in the combination all of the Invariant Sections of all of the original documents, unmodified, and list them all as Invariant Sections of your combined work in its license notice, and that you preserve all their Warranty Disclaimers.

The combined work need only contain one copy of this License, and multiple identical Invariant Sections may be replaced with a single copy. If there are multiple Invariant Sections with the same name but different contents, make the title of each such section unique by adding at the end of it, in parentheses, the name of the original author or publisher of that section if known, or else a unique number. Make the same adjustment to the section titles in the list of Invariant Sections in the license notice of the combined work.

In the combination, you must combine any sections Entitled "History" in the various original documents, forming one section Entitled "History"; likewise combine any sections Entitled "Acknowledgements", and any sections Entitled "Dedications". You must delete all sections Entitled "Endorsements."

6. COLLECTIONS OF DOCUMENTS

You may make a collection consisting of the Document and other documents released under this License, and replace the individual copies of this License in the various documents with a single copy that is included in the collection, provided that you follow the rules of this License for verbatim copying of each of the documents in all other respects.

You may extract a single document from such a collection, and distribute it individually under this License, provided you insert a copy of this License into the extracted document, and follow this License in all other respects regarding verbatim copying of that document.

7. AGGREGATION WITH INDEPENDENT WORKS

A compilation of the Document or its derivatives with other separate and independent documents or works, in or on a volume of a storage or distribution medium, is called an "aggregate" if the copyright resulting from the compilation is not used to limit the legal rights of the compilation's users beyond what the individual works permit. When the Document is included in an aggregate, this License does not apply to the other works in the aggregate which are not themselves derivative works of the Document.

If the Cover Text requirement of section 3 is applicable to these copies of the Document, then if the Document is less than one half of the entire aggregate, the Document's Cover Texts may be placed on covers that bracket the Document within the aggregate, or the electronic equivalent of covers if the Document is in electronic form. Otherwise they must appear on printed covers that bracket the whole aggregate.

8. TRANSLATION

Translation is considered a kind of modification, so you may distribute translations of the Document under the terms of section 4. Replacing Invariant Sections with translations requires special permission from their copyright holders, but you may include translations of some or all Invariant Sections in addition to the original versions of these Invariant Sections. You may include a translation of this License, and all the license notices in the Document, and any Warranty Disclaimers, provided that you also include the original English version of this License and the original versions of those notices and disclaimers. In case of a disagreement between the translation and the original version of this License or a notice or disclaimer, the original version will prevail.

If a section in the Document is Entitled "Acknowledgements", "Dedications", or "History", the requirement (section 4) to Preserve its Title (section 1) will typically require changing the actual title.

9. TERMINATION

You may not copy, modify, sublicense, or distribute the Document except as expressly provided for under this License. Any other attempt to copy, modify, sublicense or distribute the Document is void, and will automatically terminate your rights under this License. However, parties who have received copies, or rights, from you under this License will not have their licenses terminated so long as such parties remain in full compliance.

10. FUTURE REVISIONS OF THIS LICENSE

The Free Software Foundation may publish new, revised versions of the GNU Free Documentation License from time to time. Such new versions will be similar in spirit to the present version, but may differ in detail to address new problems or concerns. See http://www.gnu.org/copyleft/.

Each version of the License is given a distinguishing version number. If the Document specifies that a particular numbered version of this License "or any later version" applies to it, you have the option of following the terms and conditions either of that specified version or of any later version that has been published (not as a draft) by the Free Software Foundation. If the Document does not specify a version number of this License, you may choose any version ever published (not as a draft) by the Free Software Foundation.

How to use this License for your documents
To use this License in a document you have written, include a copy of the License in the document and put the following copyright and license notices just after the title page:
Copyright (c) YEAR YOUR NAME.
Permission is granted to copy, distribute and/or modify this document
under the terms of the GNU Free Documentation License, Version 1.2
or any later version published by the Free Software Foundation;
with no Invariant Sections, no Front-Cover Texts, and no Back-Cover Texts.
A copy of the license is included in the section entitled "GNU
Free Documentation License".

If you have Invariant Sections, Front-Cover Texts and Back-Cover Texts, replace the "with...Texts." line with this:
with the Invariant Sections being LIST THEIR TITLES, with the
Front-Cover Texts being LIST, and with the Back-Cover Texts being LIST.
If you have Invariant Sections without Cover Texts, or some other combination of the three, merge those two alternatives to suit the situation.

If your document contains nontrivial examples of program code, we recommend releasing these examples in parallel under your choice of free software license, such as the GNU General Public License, to permit their use in free software.

Notes:

Notes:

Notes:

Notes:

Notes:

Notes:

Notes:

Notes:

Notes:

Notes:

Notes:

Notes:

Notes:

Notes:

Notes:

Notes:

28405305R00129

Printed in Great Britain
by Amazon

Anderson Correia

Evaluation of Level of Service at Airport Passenger Terminals

Individual Components and Overall Perspectives

Lambert Academic Publishing

Impressum/Imprint (nur für Deutschland/ only for Germany)

Bibliografische Information der Deutschen Nationalbibliothek: Die Deutsche Nationalbibliothek verzeichnet diese Publikation in der Deutschen Nationalbibliografie; detaillierte bibliografische Daten sind im Internet über http://dnb.d-nb.de abrufbar.

Alle in diesem Buch genannten Marken und Produktnamen unterliegen warenzeichen-, marken- oder patentrechtlichem Schutz bzw. sind Warenzeichen oder eingetragene Warenzeichen der jeweiligen Inhaber. Die Wiedergabe von Marken, Produktnamen, Gebrauchsnamen, Handelsnamen, Warenbezeichnungen u.s.w. in diesem Werk berechtigt auch ohne besondere Kennzeichnung nicht zu der Annahme, dass solche Namen im Sinne der Warenzeichen- und Markenschutzgesetzgebung als frei zu betrachten wären und daher von jedermann benutzt werden dürften.

Verlag: Lambert Academic Publishing AG & Co. KG
Theodor-Heuss-Ring 26, 50668 Köln, Deutschland
Telefon +49 681 3720-310, Telefax +49 681 3720-3109, Email: info@lap-publishing.com

Herstellung in Deutschland:
Schaltungsdienst Lange o.H.G., Berlin
Books on Demand GmbH, Norderstedt
Reha GmbH, Saarbrücken
Amazon Distribution GmbH, Leipzig
ISBN: 978-3-8383-1757-1

Imprint (only for USA, GB)

Bibliographic information published by the Deutsche Nationalbibliothek: The Deutsche Nationalbibliothek lists this publication in the Deutsche Nationalbibliografie; detailed bibliographic data are available in the Internet at http://dnb.d-nb.de.

Any brand names and product names mentioned in this book are subject to trademark, brand or patent protection and are trademarks or registered trademarks of their respective holders. The use of brand names, product names, common names, trade names, product descriptions etc. even without a particular marking in this works is in no way to be construed to mean that such names may be regarded as unrestricted in respect of trademark and brand protection legislation and could thus be used by anyone.

Publisher:
Lambert Academic Publishing AG & Co. KG
Theodor-Heuss-Ring 26, 50668 Köln, Germany
Phone +49 681 3720-310, Fax +49 681 3720-3109, Email: info@lap-publishing.com

Printed in the U.S.A.
Printed in the U.K. by (see last page)
ISBN: 978-3-8383-1757-1

Acknowledgements

I thank my supervisor, Dr. S. C. Wirasinghe for his unlimited support during my PhD studies at the University of Calgary. I really appreciate his guidance, invaluable criticism, encouragement, as well his friendship for the development of this research.

I am also indebted to Dr. A. G. de Barros and Dr. J. D. Hunt, members of the committee, who took the time off their busy schedules to read the thesis and offer many suggestions and corrections. Thanks also to Dr. N. M. Waters and Dr. V. Tossic for participating in the examination committee. Dr. Tossic came from University of Belgrade especially for this purpose.

I am grateful to the staff of the São Paulo/Guarulhos International Airport, São Paulo/Congonhas International Airport, Rio de Janeiro International Airport, and Calgary International Airport for the assistance during the collection of data for this research. I am also grateful to Mr. J. Montoya, Mr. R. Correia, and Mr. A. Nanayakara for participating as surveyors during the data collection.

Special thanks for the many friends that helped make my stay in Calgary more significant. Those include the Rosa, Eaty, Prado, Yontz, Wilson, and Gilkes families. A special gratitude goes to my parents Edeci and João Batista for all the love and support during all years of my life. My sincere appreciation goes to my wife Fernanda for all love, patience, encouragement and inspiration during all these years. I also thank to my sons Daniel and Lucas for all the happiness they brought me during all these years. Last but not least, I thank God for giving me the capability and intelligence to accomplish this thesis research.

This research was made possible by CAPES, a research support agency from the Brazilian Ministry of Education, and in part by NSERC - Canada.

Dedication

To my wife Fernanda and my children Daniel and Lucas

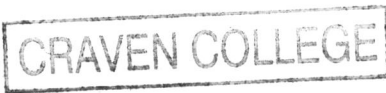

TABLE OF CONTENTS

List of Tables

List of Figures

CHAPTER ONE: INTRODUCTION

1.1. Motivation

The motivation for developing level of service (LOS) measures is twofold. First, since one of the goals of airport planning is to improve, or at least maintain, the level of service experienced by the airport user, it is necessary to be able to measure LOS in order to know whether this goal is being achieved. Second, airport passenger terminals improvements rarely are without expense. To know whether a particular expenditure is justified, it is necessary to be able to measure the change in LOS resulting from it. (Gosling, 1988).

Establishing measures to evaluate operational performance of the airport landside and quality of service is one of the major problems facing the airlines and airport operators. Humphreys and Francis (2000) affirm that LOS evaluation in American Airports have been undertaken at individual airports, with no standard method or reporting system for this on a national scale. Research is also needed in developing countries, mainly to generate references for planning airport infrastructure. In this regard, Fernandes and Pacheco (2002) stress that the lack of studies in Brazil to enable parameters reflecting Brazilian conditions to be estimated means that estimates made on the basis of conditions at other countries' airports are used without proper further evaluation. According to them, the issues of domestic traffic, in particular, deserve special attention in terms of Brazilian specifics.

Airport landside LOS and capacity have been topics of research interest over the past two decades or so. More recently, owing to the critical nature of airport LOS issues, a number of studies have been initiated on the identification of the landside problem in general, and on capacity and service measures in particular. Despite all the studies developed in the last decades, in comparison with the status of LOS analysis in highway engineering, it is in a rudimentary state of development in airport design. In 1986 the FAA responded to concerns of inadequate understanding of landside capacity constraints by commissioning the Transportation Research Board to conduct a study of ways to measure airport landside capacity. This study (TRB, 1987) recognized that the capacity of any given landside facilities cannot be evaluated without defining acceptable LOS standards, but that there is currently little agreement on how to do this. Lemer (1988) reviews the study's principal findings and recommendations, presented in the final report. The author of the paper concluded that the effort represented a valuable first step toward definitive guidelines for capacity assessment, but much remained to be done. Thus, the development of appropriate ways to measure airport landside LOS is a critical research need.

The measurement of LOS of airport passenger terminals is also an important issue considering the recent trends for airport privatization and the further regulation of privatized facilities. There are concerns that efforts to regulate the prices charged by airports can result in under-investment and decline service standards. In Australia for example, newly privatized airports would be subjected to price regulation in the form of price-caps on aeronautical charges; there is a concern about their effect on the incentive faced by the enterprise to downgrade quality (Forsyth, 1997). This makes it important to monitor not only the cost-efficiency and cost-effectiveness, but also the service-effectiveness of airports (Hooper and Hensher, 1997). Gillen and Lall (1997) agree with their view and state that while airports should be asked to adhere to private financial standards, they must also be judged in the context of their overall goals.

1.2. Objectives and Scope of Study

On the basis of all the issues that affect airport planners, designers and managers, we propose a methodology to evaluate LOS of airport passenger terminals. We could summarize the objective of this work as to provide LOS standards for:

Planning and design of new facilities

Current airport passenger terminal planning and design techniques rely mainly on subjective intuition and past experience of consulting groups, with usually no participation or inputs representing user real needs at a terminal. The LOS standards proposed in this thesis will be a valuable input to current planning practices.

Management of existing facilities

The Airports Council International – ACI (2000) proposes that measuring quality of service should be regarded as part of a whole quality system which works in a continuous cycle, and should lead to a system of continuous improvement. According to them, the "Quality Chain" which follows is composed of five elements:

- Evaluate customer needs and expectations.
- Implement adequate service.
- Achieve the service.
- Measure quality of service.
- Evaluation of causes and corrective action.

In this work, we intend to provide LOS standards that will be useful for measuring the actual level of service according to user perceptions. With this, it will be possible to provide corrective actions as necessary.

Benchmarking

No customer satisfaction research program can be considered complete if it focuses only on the company's own product and service quality. It has to include a probing survey of what the best of the competition is doing. There is a section in this thesis dealing with this subject, where one airport can be compared with other competing airports.

1.3. Definition of Some Terms Used in this Thesis

Many terms that might not be particularly familiar to the reader are featured in this thesis. It is intended to define them at this stage so that the reader may have a full comprehension of this research without the need of a special dictionary. The definitions are appropriate to this thesis; they may have other definitions when used in other contexts. Other terms which are not frequently employed will be defined as used.

Curbside: the interface between the terminal building and the ground transportation system.

Landside: as opposed to the airside of the airport, it represents the airport passenger terminal.

LOS (Level of Service): the quality of the experience that the passenger has when processed in an airport passenger terminal.

Operational Components: components of the airport passenger terminal that are mandatory for passenger processing. Example: check-in counter, passport control, departure lounge, etc.

Orientation: knowing where one is in relation to known landmarks.

Overall LOS Measure: a quantitative measure representing the overall level of service of a single component or the airport passenger terminal as a whole.

Passenger Perceptions: the opinion of a passenger concerning the LOS provided at the airport passenger terminal.

Qualitative Measure: a LOS measure, subjective by nature, which can not be numerically quantified. Example: aesthetics.

Quantitative Measure: a quantifiable measure that might represent the level of service an individual component or the terminal. Example: waiting time of 25 minutes.

Security Environment: represents the sensation of being secured at the airport passenger terminal.

Temporal/Spatial Measures: LOS measures as a function of the time incurred or space available for passengers.

Transborder: a flight between two bordering countries. Example: flights between Canada and United States.

1.4.   Thesis Layout

This thesis is organized as follows. Chapter One contains an Introduction and gives definitions of some of the terms used in the thesis. Chapter Two presents the review of literature relevant to this research. Chapter Three provides a methodology for LOS measurement, illustrated with a real application. Chapter Four provides an explanation of the survey method employed and the benefits and difficulties associated with it. Chapter Five studies the relationship between LOS ratings and characteristics of facilities; the following facilities are evaluated: curbside, check-in counter, security screening, departure lounge, and baggage claim. Chapter Six studies the relationship between overall LOS ratings and overall measures as total time, walking distance and orientation. Chapter Seven studies the relationship between overall terminal LOS and LOS of individual components; this chapter also presents a section dealing with airport benchmarking. Chapter Eight, the final chapter, presents the conclusions and recommendations.

CHAPTER TWO: LITERATURE REVIEW

2.1. Introduction

There has been considerable research and discussion in the profession concerning the adoption of LOS standards and associated criteria to evaluate the level of service afforded in the design of landside processing systems. Although it is relatively simple to develop relationships between aircraft delay on the airside and its economic consequences, such relationships are difficult to either define or develop on the airport landside. Much of the difficulty is related to the fact that the various constituent groups associated with airports view quality of service or LOS from different perspectives (Horonjeff and McKelvey, 1994).

2.2. Literature Review on Airport LOS Methods

In a Transportation Research Board workshop, Heathington and Jones (1975) examined 25 characteristics relevant to the airport terminal. Some of these are availability of seating, walking distance, accessibility, orientation, waiting time and occupancy. In the same meeting, Brink and Madison (1975) considered that for passengers at the airport terminal, LOS is a subjective impression of the quality of the transfer between the access mode and the aircraft. They consider this subjective perception of quality dependent on a series of factors, including (but not necessarily limited to):

a) Time necessary to be processed through the landside,

b) Reliability or predictability of processing time,

c) Reaction to overall landside environment,

d) Physical comfort and convenience,

e) Treatment by airline, concessionaire, security and other airport personnel,

f) Cost of air fare and airport services,

g) Type of passenger and purpose of trip,

h) Frequency of air travel, and

i) Expectation of level of service.

According to the authors, in practice, however, processing times at the different facilities are used to represent the levels of service. They suggest that a LOS rating can be assigned to the airport, which is a measure of the total time required to complete all processing, and it can be obtained by summing the processing times for the different facilities.

Novak (1978) proposes a humanistic design process as an answer to the question of how an airport designer can act to increase the weight of morality in design. By a humanistic design process, the author means a design process based on the assumption that people are supremely important and that indicators of their welfare should constitute the ultimate criteria of good and bad design. The primary goals of this process are to achieve a balanced treatment of various values by the investigation, description, and protection of such human values as freedom, dignity, privacy, and security. According to the author, the primary goals of current design practice virtually disregard certain important ethical human values while emphasizing other issues. The humanistic design process should create the information necessary to keep many fundamental values from being neglected relative to financial, technological, or political considerations.

The proposed process was illustrated through the investigation of many airports in the United States, according to three primary evaluation values: attachment, independence, and freedom from anxiety (considered to be one aspect of the more complex value of comfort). After the analyses, recommendations have been proposed for future airport design criteria. At the final of the thesis, it is suggested that future research be focused on the refinement of the humanistic design process and specifically on the refinement of observation techniques and the measurement of values. According to the author, empirically testing is also clearly needed.

Paul (1981) followed the general idea presented by Heathington and Jones (1975). He presented a methodology for predicting passenger evaluations of airport terminal facilities through the development of relationships between measures of passenger evaluation of the facility and factors that influence their evaluation. Rating technique and multiple regression analysis were applied for analyzing passenger evaluations in that research. The main objective of the study was its incorporation into the existing framework for evaluating passenger acceptance of the short-haul air transportation system. Nevertheless, the author suggests that his methodology may be useful for evaluating the airport terminal functions and components for management and planning purposes. The author applied a seven-point rating scale, varying from very comfortable to very uncomfortable. The data collected was divided in four main areas:

1) Data on the design characteristics of the terminal.
2) Data on variables that changed gradually with time (temperature and humidity).
3) Data on potential predictors which change rapidly with time or from one passenger to the next (crowding, delays, passenger's characteristics, etc).
4) Data on some of the Airline Characteristics.

Muller (1987) recognizes two important failures in Paul's approach:

- There is no way to sort all potential explanatory variables for the most important ones. This approach requires that all of the variables are considered in the proposed model, and so data must be collected for more than thirty factors.
- The approach simply uses the service quality rating obtained from a survey as the dependent variable of the model. The researcher did not realize that the quality rating obtained represented only the user perception of service quality on a qualitative discrete (ordinal) scale. Therefore, the data he gathered are not directly appropriate to the modeling proposed in his study. To perform his

proposed modeling, a transformation of qualitative discrete data into quantitative continuum data is required.

Another initiative to evaluate passenger perception of quality of service at airport terminals was developed by Mumayiz (1985). The methodology proposed would be an alternative to the former methods developed by transportation agencies, since most of them lacked measures to assess the passenger perception on the LOS provided by the airport authorities. Structurally, the methodology is arranged to deal with two procedures: LOS and capacity measures.

The factor utilized for the evaluation of LOS at the airport components was delay for passengers. The user perceptions were obtained through surveys applied directly to the passengers at some British Airports. Subsequently, a panel of experts was organized to ask the participants to state their perception of service, in this way representing the view and opinions of their own airports. The methodology applied perception-response (P-R) curves. The P-R model depicts the relationship between the percentage of passengers stating their level of satisfaction with service encountered at a particular facility and the value of a measure of service. The percentage of passengers replying to whether a certain amount of time (delay or time spent) at a particular facility was perceived as good, tolerable, or bad is related to amount of time (delayed or spent). The conceptual diagram for this model is shown in Figure 2.1. Time values (T1 and T2) are deduced, representing the frontier between good/tolerable and tolerable/bad level of service respectively. Only processing facilities were considered in that work. The methodology was presented at a Transportation Research Board by Mumayiz and Ashford (1986).

The main drawback of the mentioned methodology is that it allows the evaluation of only one attribute per time. Nevertheless, Ashford (1988) suggested that strong interaction exists between space provision and time; in this way, that interaction can not be obtained by the P-R concept as it has been presented. Mumayiz (1991) stated that a three-dimensional P-R concept could be developed accounting for the variations of delay and crowding, but, according to the author, no work has been done to support this hypothesis because of problems associated with adequately interpreting and collecting user perceptions of crowdedness and space provided. In addition to that deficiency, recent LOS studies in airport passenger terminal processing components have shown that perceived and actual time revealed large discrepancies (Park, 1994; Park, 1999; Yen et. al., 2001). Those discrepancies indicate that obtaining data by stated-preference technique must be used with caution.

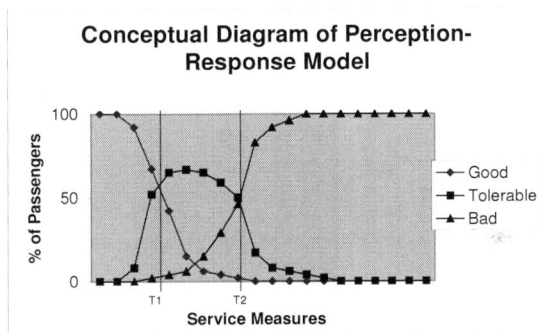

Figure 2.1: Conceptual Diagram of Perception-Response Model
(Mumayiz, 1985)

Müller (1987) proposed a framework for evaluating quality of service at airport passenger terminals according to user perceptions, using a psychological scaling technique. The objective of the research is to provide the support required to enable the transformation of the qualitative discrete passenger information into a quantitative continuum quality scale; it attempts to address the question of which are the relevant factors and their relative importance in influencing the perception of overall service quality. They assumed that there is a consistent causal relationship between the measurable passenger experience at a facility (e.g., amount of time the passenger has to wait, degree of crowding, etc.) and the perceived quality of service. The modeling of passenger perception of the airport terminal quality of service considers that when passengers evaluate the quality of service a discriminal process enables them to place their perception of quality at a point on a quality scale. The modeling approach follows two steps. First it is considered that the passenger evaluates each terminal facility individually and secondly the overall terminal quality of service is evaluated; on this second step evaluation process, it is assumed that there is a causal relationship between facility ratings and the overall terminal quality of service rating. Figure 2.2 illustrates this assumed quality perception process. An attempt was made to evaluate passenger benefits in dollars when evaluating capacity expansions, which was possible through the exploration of the passenger value of time concept. Two important considerations can be observed with respect to the mentioned research:

1. Although the author has proposed a methodology for the evaluation of overall terminal LOS, he was not able to calibrate the mathematical equations with the available data, and no further study has been able to demonstrate the applicability of the methodology to the overall terminal LOS evaluation.

2. The author provides a list of facilities importance ratings, but no effort is spent to provide the adequate quality of service measures for each of them, e.g. information, aesthetics, security, curb, shops, eating facilities, etc. The only two measures employed on the study are waiting time and crowding; obviously these measures can not account for the evaluation of many important facilities at the airport passenger terminal.

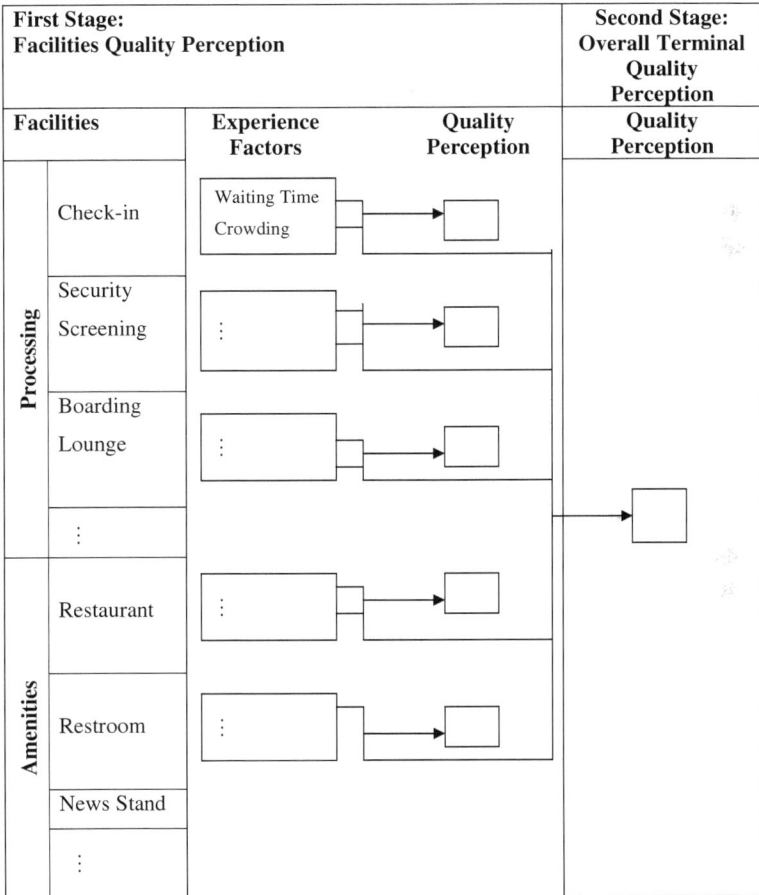

First Stage: Facilities Quality Perception				Second Stage: Overall Terminal Quality Perception
Facilities		Experience Factors	Quality Perception	Quality Perception
Processing	Check-in	Waiting Time / Crowding		
	Security Screening	⋮		
	Boarding Lounge	⋮		
	⋮			
Amenities	Restaurant	⋮		
	Restroom	⋮		
	News Stand			
	⋮			

Figure 2.2: Assumed Quality Perception Process
(Muller, 1987)

The survey application was also very simplistic. An attempt was made to observe passengers in the airport, thus collecting data in the form of experienced waiting time and crowding. As opposed to collecting actual stimulus, he collected average waiting times and crowding at every 15 minutes and then asked passengers to indicate in the survey the time they arrived at the airport. By the time indicated by the passengers he correlated this information with the average measures collected every 15 minutes. There is one important issue that might arise: it is very difficult for passengers to note (at a 15 minutes precision) the time they arrived at the airport. Even if they could indicate that precisely, there is a possibility that passengers might spend some time at the parking, curbside, circulation, washroom or any other activity before getting into the check-in area. And this lag cannot be obtained by the survey developed.

Another important issue of the research employed by Muller was that he asked passengers to provide an evaluation of quality of service for a specific component as opposed to provide evaluation for specific measures (waiting time and crowding). When correlating user responses of the components' quality of service with two measures, the data needs were very high. If the method proposed has to be applied using three or four measures at the same time, the application would be impractical.

Finally, passengers provided the responses through a mail-back questionnaire. In this case, the questionnaire was filled on the flight or later in the hotel or back home. This time lag might present a bias that could affect the validity of responses.

Taking into account these considerations, research should be done to evaluate the most adequate measures for each component of the airport passenger terminal and to estimate the overall terminal LOS according to the users perceptions.

Davis and Braaksma (1987) undertook to develop a new set of LOS criteria to platooning pedestrian traffic in airport terminal arrival corridors. According to the authors, these corridors make an ideal laboratory because of their high incidence of platoon formation. A LOS framework that includes speed, flow, and area as service measures was proposed and behavioral surveys were done at Montreal International Airport (Mirabel), Ottawa International Airport, and Lester B. Pearson International Airport Terminal 2 (Toronto). The authors conclude that the applicability of these platoon flow LOS standards to other walkway environments must be assessed in terms of the prevalence and uniformity of platooning behavior.

Khan (1986), in an attempt to study cost-effectiveness of the airport system, proposes a utility theoretic approach for LOS evaluation of terminal facilities. He presents a correlation of utility value ranges related to LOS gradations from A to E. Omer and Khan (1988), applied that concept in research where they developed a method applying the utility and cost-effectiveness theories for measuring user-perceived LOS and for establishing economical design criteria on airport landside. The methodology proposes the application of attitudinal survey techniques to ask the users to indicate the relative importance of LOS factors (e.g. waiting time, processing time, space availability) and to rate each LOS attribute/factor through a scaling method. After that, the weight rates would be transformed to a relative value scale and then combined into a utility measure. That methodology was applied at some Canadian airports for the check-in, baggage claim, boarding lounge and preliminary inspection line (PIL) area subsystems; the results of that research are presented by Omer (1990), where he provides composite utility equations for each of the subsystems mentioned. Figure 2.3 illustrates the relationship between physical measures, utility and level of service for the case of check-in and baggage claim facilities. Muller and Gosling (1991) criticize their methodology, suggesting that there are a number of serious flaws in that approach. According to them, rank numbers are ordinal not cardinal, and cannot therefore be summed together, and most service measures do not have upper bounds and cannot be converted to a scale of 0 to 1. These problems could be circumvented by rating rather than by ranking (as described by de Neufville and Stafford, 1971, pp. 203-208). Ndoh and Ashford (1993) also criticize their approach, saying that the direct use of survey rating scales in the model suggested in their paper is thought to be inappropriate.

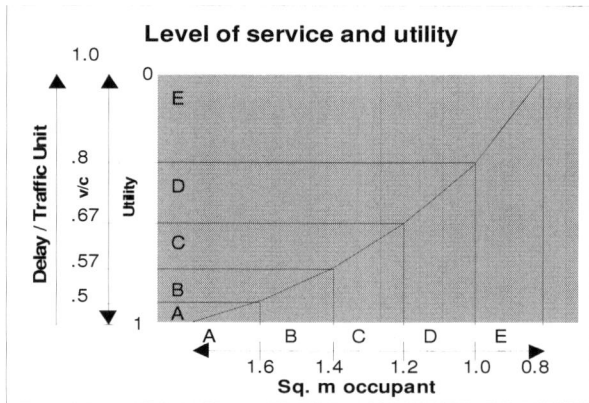

Figure 2.3: Level of service and utility: check-in and baggage claim
(Omer and Khan, 1988)

Martel and Seneviratne (1990) analyzed the factors influencing quality of service (QOS) in passenger terminal buildings. Through a personal interview survey of departing passengers, the answers were that availability of space is the most significant factor influencing quality of service from the passenger point of view. Within the circulation elements, 53 percent of the respondents believed that information is the most important factor. Similarly, for the waiting areas, the most important factor was the availability of seats and for the processing elements it was the waiting time. According to the survey, there are many factors to be considered other than space or time when it comes to evaluating QOS from the passenger point of view. The study conclude that QOS is a complex concept that is inappropriate to evaluate with one indicator and the factors influencing QOS differ depending on the element of the passenger terminal building that one is considering. Figures 2.4-2.6 illustrate the research findings.

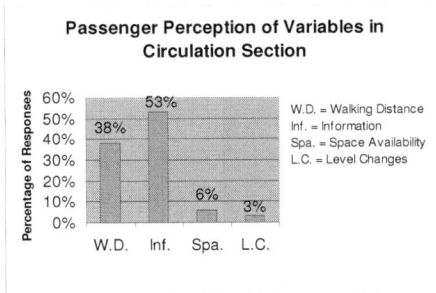

Figure 2.4: Passenger Perception of Variables in
Circulation Section (Martel and Seneviratne, 1990)

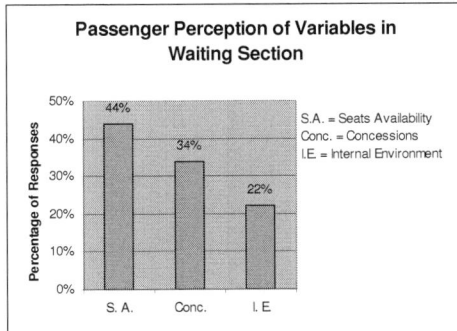

Figure 2.5: Passenger Perception of Variables in
Waiting Section (Martel and Seneviratne, 1990)

Passenger Perception of Variables in Processing Section

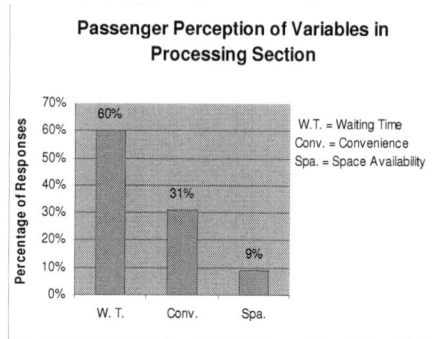

Figure 2.6: Passenger Perception of Variables in
Circulation Section (Martel and Seneviratne, 1990)

Seneviratne and Martel (1991) applied the results of the previous mentioned survey on the measurement of performance variables for passenger terminal buildings. The measures were developed through the suggestion of global indices for the most important variables that have a bearing on the evaluation of LOS for airport passenger terminals, according to the passenger views related on the survey. Most of these global indexes proposed were applied on further research by Seneviratne and Martel (1994); they used six indices to describe terminal subsystem characteristics:

a) availability of seats;

b) walking distance;

c) accessibility;

d) orientation (i.e., availability of information);

e) waiting time; and

f) occupancy (i.e. density).

Six LOS intervals were defined for each measure. The basis for the calculation of LOS was different for each of the components studied; the authors applied some research in landside planning available on the literature. The methodology proposed needs some improvements, including:

1. The measures corresponding to each LOS interval were defined arbitrarily, with hidden assumptions. An adequate research improvement would be the correlation of these indexes to some measure of quality according to the passenger perceptions.

2. The authors were not able to develop a composite index capable of considering all the subsystems as a whole unit; according to the authors, these could be achieved only through extensive attitudinal surveys.

Ndoh and Ashford (1993) employed the theories of perception scaling and categorical judgment to evaluate airport access LOS. The categories were graded "very satisfactory", "satisfactory", "indifferent", "unsatisfactory", and "very unsatisfactory". Data was collected by stated preference technique. The analysis considered 12 attributes (e.g. mode economy, mode comfort, access information, etc). At the end of the work the authors presented the scale values for each access mode (private car, taxi, metro, etc) for each attribute considered. Although the research provides insight on the scale values of numerous qualitative attributes, the results are not useful for facility planning; in the cases where there exists a need for improvement, the method provides no objective basis for deciding what a reasonable target might be. More research should be done to propose consistent LOS standards obtained through passenger perceptions, allowing the measurement of benefits derived from the necessary improvements.

Ndoh and Ashford (1994) explored fuzzy set theory, particularly linguistic fuzzy set models, as a technique for evaluating transportation LOS through the incorporation of qualitative components such as convenience and comfort. It was the opinion of the authors that the last approaches used to estimate LOS provided crisp scale values of LOS that cannot be given linguistic values that are precise in comparison with the manner in which passengers originally expressed their perception of services. The authors apply the methodology proposed to evaluate processing services at an airport (check-in, security inspection and passport control subsystems) using hypothetical values. Although the methodology seems reasonable for application to airport LOS evaluation, it was not properly validated through any real case-study. Finally, the method does not offer any goodness-of-fit test to assess the quality of the measurement.

Siddiqui (1994) applies the utility theory approach on the evaluation of LOS for curbside facilities at airport passenger terminals. An attempt was made to develop a relationship between the actual service level at the terminal curbside and the user perceived value of the service levels. The methodology proposed was supposed to cover the deficiencies of the former approaches to terminal curbside LOS evaluation, as follows, according to the author:

- They proposed procedures for curbside design for vehicles and not for people.
- Perceptions of travelers were not included in LOS criteria and standards, although they are real users.
- Only time was included in LOS definition, while another factor, distance was ignored.
- No specific level was universally accepted as basic, to facility sizing, in planning and design procedures.

A survey was designed to collect the perceptions of curb users with reference to the following two factors:

- Time that each vehicle requires to find an unloading/loading position in the curb area, measured from the moment of passing the entrance ramp.
- The distance that a user travels by foot, between the unloading/loading position and entrance door.

The author presents utility equations for the departure and arrival curbs, relating perceived quality to the two above measured factors. Furthermore, user perception of the

LOS was related to a monetary value, that users attributed to associated psychological and physical utilities. A method has been established to take into account social costs in design procedures, through a graphical method. According to the recommendations, if social costs are taken into account, the most cost effective LOS is "C"; for projects with a long life cycle or high rate of demand increase, LOS "B" might be considered.

The methodology applied is very similar to the one employed by Omer and Khan (1988), having the same flaws and deficiencies associated with the linear transformations and ranking of service measures. Unless those deficiencies are corrected, such methodology may be considered inappropriate for further applications.

Park (1994) employs fuzzy set theory for the LOS airport terminal evaluation based on user perceptions, considering three types of factors: temporal or spatial as quantitative measures; and comfort factors and reasonable service factors as qualitative measures. The methodology utilizes an expert panel to obtain the degree of importance of the several terminal components and a passenger survey at Seoul Kimpo Airport to obtain the quality ratings of facilities on five different areas of the airport terminal: service processing, holding, circulation, ground access and concessions. The surveys explored the use of linguistic expressions as bearable, long, accepted, complicated, tolerable, bad, etc. The outputs of the expert panel and the user survey were further applied on a fuzzy multi-decision model through a computer program to obtain the quantitative quality ratings of the facilities surveyed. In addition to that, the author provided a comparison between real service performance indicators (temporal measures) and perceived values obtained by the perception-response (P-R) research that was developed by Mumayiz (1985). The comparison of results of the two methods shows a totally different perception of service standards, in particular for the security screening service and for the passport control. According to the author, those differences indicate that the P-R model as originally developed has many important failures, mainly because of the lag-time between the service experience and filling out of the questionnaire by the airport user.

Although the multi-decision fuzzy model was capable of obtaining the quality of service evaluation according to the user perceptions, it was not able to associate actual physical measures to the LOS ratings. Not only so, the research does not suggest any physical measure appropriate for the measurement of most of the factors presented. Further study must be developed to correct that deficiency and adjust the methodology, so that it may become relevant for planning purposes.

Yen (1995) conducted a survey at the municipal airport of Austin, Texas. He applied binary logit models to estimate a "long" model and a "short" model to predict the probabilities that a passenger will rate a service on the basis of perceived time measures. The long and short models were then used to build a mechanism to define different service levels. The waiting times and delays were stated by the passengers (stated preference data) as were the proportion of responses (short - not short, long - not long). By using these two types of data the binary logit models were developed, whose results are presented in Table 2.1.

Table 2.1: LOS Standards

Service Operation	$T_a(0.5)$	$T_c(0.5)$	$T_a(0.6)$	$T_c(0.4)$	$T_a(0.7)$	$T_a(0.3)$	$T_a(0.8)$	$T_c(0.2)$
Check-in	9.5	64.0	6.5	58.5	3.0	50.0	*	38.5
Baggage claim	9.5	19.0	8.0	18.0	6.5	16.5	4.5	15.5
Departure delay	10.0	39.0	7.5	36.5	4.5	33.5	1.0	30.5
Arrival delay	9.5	35.5	7.5	31.5	4.5	26.5	1.0	20.5

Source: Yen (1995)   (The time unit in the Table is minutes)

The utility variable used in the logit models was supposed to be a function of the waiting time and delay values, and other explanatory variables (purpose of travel, gender, and family income). However the results of calculations show only the waiting time and delay coefficients as statistically significant.

For instance, the waiting time at check-in should be shorter than 9.5 minutes so that 50% of passengers rate it as short; it should be shorter than 6.5 minutes so that 60% of passengers rate it as short. On the other hand, the waiting time at check-in should be longer than 64 minutes so that 50% of passengers rate it as long; it should be longer than 58.5 minutes so that 40% of passengers rate it as long. Values below Ta represent LOS A; values above Tc represent LOS C; LOS B values lie between Ta and Tc. It is worth noticing that the range of values representing LOS B is very large (9.5-64.0 minutes). It should be useful to split this range into more ranges (A-E or A-F LOS ranges).

Although the author provides a model that forecasts the proportion of passengers pleased with certain waiting time and delay values, he does not recommend any standard values that might be applicable for airport planning and design.

Yen et al. (2001) presents two advantages of that model:

- it measures the level of service at airport passenger terminals on the basis of a well-defined behavioral model;
- the model has the capacity of forecasting.

Dada (1997) developed quantitative models to evaluate human orientations in airport passenger terminals. Particularly, the effects of number of signs, or decision points and number of level changes on visual access were investigated and a relationship between the slowness in reaching a target, the number of decision points, and the number of level changes was developed. LOS A to E and LOS A to C were defined: he proposed values of visibility indexes (VI) and inter-connection densities (ICD) and the combinations of the two measures that correspond to the LOS previously defined. VI is an index based primarily on available sight line, which measures the ease of way finding in a building; ICD is a numerical measure of building layout complexity: the higher the value, the more complex the building is and the more difficult it would be to navigate through it. Future research can be undertaken to associate the measures proposed with the passenger perception of LOS related to orientation in airport passenger terminals.

Caves and Pickard (2001) review the physical and psychological needs of all users of airport terminals (employees, passengers and visitors). According to the authors, all the occupants of terminals share the need for a suitable environment in terms of safety and comfort. In addition, the employees, passengers and visitors all require needs that are specific to their intended activities. The current LOS standards suggested by air transport agencies were reviewed by the paper and are characterized as not very satisfactory; the authors affirm that they are based on handbook formulas that are insensitive to the realities of each situation. They should be improved by a realistic appreciation of the dynamics and behavior of sequences of queues, the psychology of crowds in such situations, and the ways airport users truly allocate the time they spend in passenger terminals. In the paper, attention is focused on the users, with particular reference to navigating, or wayfinding, within the terminal, especially for those with disabilities. Applying the connectivity index proposed by Dada and Wirasinghe (1999), the authors developed a case-study of some airports in Europe and concluded that providing for the needs of users has been rather neglected in those airports. Finally, they provide some recommendation for improving wayfinding for those with visual impairments.

The Airports Council International (ACI) undertook to develop a quality survey with its members. The inquiry took place in 2000, with questions concerning:

- objective performance measurement and design standards, and whether results are published;
- perceived satisfaction ratings and whether results are published;
- quality system management;
- certification (especially ISO 9001/2/3): benefits and problems encountered.

The ACI differentiates two kinds of measurement:

- Objective measurement, which is provided by the measurement of defined criteria, with indicators that help in achieving objective measures. The results cannot be subject to value criticism.
- Subjective measurement, which depends on the subjective value attributed to quality of service by passengers. These values can be given by surveys, or comment cards, or complaints.

According to the survey, 61.7% of respondents make use of subjective criteria and 43.3% make use of objective criteria; 31.7% make use of both objective and subjective criteria.

Table 2.2 presents the results of the survey, listing the objective criteria used by airports to assess the quality of service to passengers:

Table 2.2: Objective Criteria Employed by ACI Airport Members

Objective criteria	Airport (s) Applying this Criterion
General	
Response to/analysis of complaints/mail/comments	13
Response to phone calls	8
Flight Information Display System (FIDS)	4
Monitoring of information to passengers	3
Availability of automated services	2
Ticketing waiting time	2
Availability of telecommunications	1
Availability of lifts/escalators/moving walkways/conveyors/stairs	12
Repair/maintenance monitoring	3
Availability of trolleys	20
Cleanliness	12
Availability of assistance for disabled	4
Seat congestion	2
Shops/restaurants and bars	
Shops/restaurants and bars-waiting time	1
Shops/restaurants and bars-prices	5
Shops/restaurants and bars-opening hours	3
Check-in	
Check-in waiting time/queue	29
Check-in transaction time	4
Security check	
Security check waiting time/queue	18
Immigration/police	
Immigration/police waiting time/queue	21

Loading/unloading process	
Performance of airside buses at gate	6
Performance of passenger boarding bridges (air bridges)	2
Air bridge usage rate	4
Flight punctuality	7
Baggage delivery	
Baggage delivery time	28
Baggage waiting time	4
Availability of baggage belts	2
Mis-handled baggage monitoring	4
Customs	
Customs waiting time/queue	8
Overall process	
Overall process time monitoring	7
Transfer process	
Connecting time	5
Special services	
Plant quarantine treatment	1
Examination and clearance for animals and products	1
Animal treatment at quarantine	1
Control of contagious diseases	1
Medical assistance to the sick	1
Clearance for imported food	1
Ground access	
Car park congestion	7
Car park exit waiting time	7
Car park-inability to operate	3
Car park systems (automated cashier, barriers)	2
Long distance bus (between airport and city)-punctuality	3
Long distance bus (between airport and city)-waiting time/availability	4
Long distance car park bus to terminal-waiting time/availability	3
Inter-terminal bus-waiting time/availability	1
Taxi-waiting time/availability	10
Inter-terminal connection performance	1

In addition to Table 2.2, the survey presents a long list of subjective criteria applied by airports. The criteria most used are: overall customer satisfaction, signage, overall cleanliness, telecommunication facilities, FIDS (flight information display systems), overall satisfaction, food overall satisfaction, shops overall satisfaction, ground access in general, car park areas overall standard and availability of baggage carts.

Although there is no worldwide procedure for assessing quality of service at airports, the trends for processing components of airport passenger terminals is focused on measuring basically the waiting/processing time associated with individual facilities.

Yen et. al. (2001) presents a quantitative model to define the level of service at airport passenger terminals. The model uses the fuzzy concept to relate subjective service ratings to time measurements of associated waiting or service processes. Respondents were asked to subjectively rate each service from five possible options: very satisfied, satisfied, neutral, unsatisfied and very unsatisfied; following the calculation of their five consecutive membership functions of service ratings, the thresholds can be estimated mathematically to set up the interval of each service level. By the analysis of empirical data, the authors conclude that in each process the mean of perceived time is always greater than the one actually measured by researchers and perceptive measurements have more deviation from their means than objective measurements.

Fernandes and Pacheco (2002) employ data envelopment analysis (DEA) to evaluate the capacity of 35 Brazilian domestic airports. DEA is a non-parametric method designed to measure the performance of a firm, organization, program, etc.; that is, whatever is produced by a decision-making unit (DMU). This procedure is a mathematical technique based on linear programming, which does not require that the functional form relating inputs to outputs be specified. Unlike regression analysis, which optimizes a single regression plane in all observations, DEA optimizes at each observation for the purpose of constructing an Efficient Frontier (Figure 2.7).

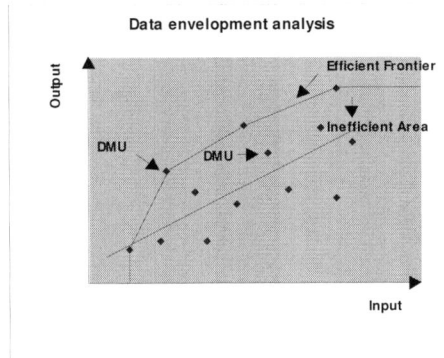

Figure 2.7: Data envelopment analysis
(Fernandes and Pacheco, 2002)

The objective of the study was to determine which airports were efficient in terms of the number of passengers processed. The model uses domestic passenger, boarded plus disembarked as the outputs. The inputs of the model are:

- Area of apron (m^2);
- Departure lounge (m^2);
- Number of check-in counters;
- Curb frontage (m^2);
- Number of vehicle parking spaces;
- Baggage claim area (m^2).

After evaluation of actual values, the authors utilized demand forecasts projected by Brazil's Civil Aviation Department to determine, for each airport, the periods when capacity expansions would become necessary to maintain services at standards currently perceived by passengers.

Although the technique seems to be powerful for system analysis, in that work all the results were analyzed considering relative efficiency. According to the authors, determining the frontier sets the benchmark for the efficiency of the sample, but no suggestion was made to obtain such a frontier that could determine the ideal operating conditions according to users' perceptions.

2.3. Conclusions

The main conclusions of the literature review can be summarized as follows:

- There is no accepted current standard or procedure for LOS evaluation at airports.

- LOS of airport terminals is a function of many quantitative and qualitative variables, but for simplifications purposes, the airport planners have tried to develop methods of LOS evaluations constituting of either time or space measures. It is interesting, though, that many researches have shown that time/space measures are not the only important ones, according to user perceptions.

- In general, most of the methods available from the literature that propose different factors other than temporal or spatial measures have one of the following deficiencies. (1) They evaluate LOS ratings according to user perceptions, but are unable to correlate those quality ratings to performance measures of the airport terminal facilities; (2) they propose some performance measures, but are unable to assess the user perceptions about these values.

- Much of the research has concluded that their approach is sufficiently data hungry and suggest that more data is needed to validate their methodologies, especially when considering the evaluation of overall terminal LOS. In this way, much of the research developed to date has not been totally validated, leaving the airport planners and managers without a tested and approved methodology for LOS evaluation.

- Many methodologies proposed have serious flaws in their approaches, ranging from oversimplifications to conceptual development failures.

31

- Little research has been developed to assess LOS of airport terminals located in developing countries; most of the research has been done in the North America/Europe-Pacific axis. In this way, the research in LOS is a critical need in most of other regions of the globe, including the south-American continent.
- There exists in the literature no method capable of assessing and measuring LOS of airport terminals as a function of the security environment. That is a critical issue and perhaps the most important one (at some specific countries) according to the user views, especially considering the September, 11th event.
- Most of the research developed considers only departing passengers. Little effort has been spent on transfers and arriving passengers.
- There exists no method capable of assessing and measuring overall terminal LOS. The methodologies proposed are able to evaluate LOS for individual components only.

In the face of all issues and difficulties presented, we can conclude that research on the evaluation of LOS of airport passenger terminals is a very critical need today and much effort must be spent to improve the methods available on the literature, which deal with LOS evaluation.

CHAPTER THREE: METHODOLOGY PROPOSED

In this chapter, the available theoretical methods that might be useful for a LOS evaluation at airport passenger terminals are presented. One of these methods will be employed for further analysis and its selection is also justified in this chapter. Finally, the details of the theoretical framework are thoroughly explained.

According to the literature review provided in the Chapter Two of this thesis, the most critical needs can be summarized as follows:

- Correlation between LOS user ratings and characteristics of facilities.

- Overall Terminal LOS for various passenger types.

- LOS evaluation according to user perceptions.

In this case, the method selected should be capable of providing an effective, reasonable, and practical way of addressing these issues.

3.1. Objective

The objective of this work is to provide meaningful measures of LOS in airport passenger terminals, taking into account the representative variables that have a bearing on the user perception of LOS.

With this objective in mind and the critical needs previously mentioned in the literature review, we could simplify our intended methodology into three steps:

1) Determine the principal variables influencing the user perception of LOS in airport passenger terminals.

2) Provide measures of LOS for individual components.

3) Provide an overall measure of LOS for various passenger types: departing, arriving, and transferring.

3.2.   LOS Attributes

Determining the LOS attributes is a difficult task, since it involves passenger attitudes, preferences and motivations. Rather than applying a survey to inquire what they should be, this investigation might be developed by the use of qualitative marketing research.

Qualitative research is a widely used term for research that does not subject research findings to quantification or quantitative analysis. Qualitative research examines the attitudes, feelings and motivations of product users (Proctor, 2000).

Qualitative research is characterized by small samples and this has always been the focus of criticism. Executives are reluctant to base important strategy decisions on small-sample research because it relies so much on the subjectivity and interpretation of the researcher. Executives show a preference for a large sample with computer analysis and a summary Table of results. Despite the apparent preference of executives, qualitative research has grown in popularity, for three reasons. First, it is usually much cheaper than quantitative research. Second, it produces a good mechanism for coming to an understanding of customer attitudes and motivations. Third, it can improve the efficiency of quantitative research.

One of the most used qualitative techniques in marketing research is the focus group. It comprises eight to twelve persons who are led by a moderator in an in-depth discussion on a particular topic or concept. The aim of focus-group research is to learn and understand what people have to say about a topic and understand their arguments. We might divide the focus groups into three categories (Proctor, 2000):

- Exploratory focus groups: are often used at the exploratory phase of marketing research to help to define the problem precisely.
- Experiencing focus groups: allows the researcher to experience a real customer.
- Clinical focus groups: are used because a person's true motivations and feelings are subconscious in nature.

In addition to the focus groups techniques, there are other qualitative marketing research techniques that might me employed in this stage of the methodology, like depth interview and projective techniques. The application of qualitative marketing research demands a high skilled professional not only for knowing the subject being discussed but also to effectively lead the group.

Fortunately, many researchers such as Brink and Madison (1975), Heathington and Jones (1975), Condom (1987), Mumayiz (1987), Muller (1987), Martel and Seneviratne (1990), Park (1994), and many others have successfully attempted to determine the main variables having a bearing on the user perceptions of level of service at airport passenger terminals. Some of these researchers made use of qualitative research like focus groups; others have employed quantitative research, like surveys of passengers; finally others have determined it based on their own experience. These works have shown that LOS evaluation is a variable dependent on innumerable factors ranging from the ones easily quantifiable to the comfort measures such as beauty and aesthetics. The difficulty in measuring the attributes that passengers evaluate as having a high degree of importance has led the researchers and planners to focus on temporal/spatial measures, which lend themselves to measurement. Although these two measures may be sufficient when evaluating processing components, they may not make a representative sample when evaluating other components and the overall LOS. Although most of the researchers have reduced the number of LOS evaluation factors to the least possible, on the other side, some have tried to evaluate overall LOS considering a vast range of attributes. For instance, we can refer to Paul (1981), who undertook to evaluate airport terminal LOS considering more than thirty factors; obviously his approach is impractical making itself impossible to be applied in practice.

In this research, we will explore other attributes in addition to temporal/spatial factors when evaluating LOS for airport passenger terminals. Nevertheless, we will narrow the choice of attributes to pick the most important ones according to the user perceptions. An exaggerated number of factors not only makes the measurement impractical, but provides high correlation between attributes, leading to modeling errors. We want to prevent these two possible issues, because we intend that our research be applied by the airport planners and managers in practice, providing reliable results that can assist in the decision making process during the planning and operational stage of airport facilities.

3.3. Measures for Individual Components

We have shown in the 'Literature Review' section of this work that most of the methods available on the literature have failed to correlate characteristics of airport terminal facilities with the user perceptions of LOS. To proceed with this correlation we should be able to get LOS ratings for individual components according to user perceptions and characteristics of these facilities.

LOS ratings might be obtained by the use of a measuring scale. Measurement is the process by which scores or numbers are assigned to the attributes of people or objects. The scales used in the different types of measurement are termed nominal, ordinal, interval and ratio respectively (Proctor, 2000).

- *Nominal scales* allow us to place an object in one and only one of a set of mutually exclusive classes with no implied ordering.

- *Ordinal-scaled* data involves ranking. This means we can say that an object has more or less or the same amount of an attribute as some other object.

- *Interval-scaled* data reflects how much more one object has of an attribute than another object. It is possible to tell how far apart two or more objects are with respect to the attribute.

- *Ratio-scaled* data possess the same kind of properties as interval-scaled data but also possess an absolute or natural origin.

Table 3.1 exemplifies the four types of scales (Proctor, 2000):

Table 3.1: Illustration of the Four Types of Scales

Nominal data	John, Sally, Fred, Peter, Winnie
Ordinal data	John is taller than Sally; Sally is taller than Fred
Interval data	John is twice the amount taller than Sally as Sally is taller than Fred
Ratio data	John is 1m 92cm tall; Sally is 1m 84cm tall; Fred is 1m 80 cm tall.

Interval and ratio data are sometimes grouped together and referred to as either cardinal data or continuous data (Miles and Shelvin, 2001).

It is clear that for the purpose of obtaining a quantitative correlation between LOS ratings and characteristics of facilities, we should make use of cardinal data.

There are two broad classes of measurement scales: comparative and non-comparative scales. With *comparative scaling* the respondent is asked to compare one set of objects against another. Results have to be interpreted in relative terms and have ordinal or rank-order properties. The scores obtained indicate that one brand is preferred to another, but not by how much. In *non-comparing scaling* respondents are required to evaluate each object independently of other objects being investigated.

The types of scale used in marketing research can be represented in Table 3.2 (Proctor, 2000):

Table 3.2: Comparative and Non-comparative Types of Scale

Types of scale	
Comparative	Non-comparative
Paired comparison	Line marking/continuous rating
Rank order	Itemized rating
Constant sum	
Line marking/continuous rating	
Q-sort	

To choose between the different types of scales, we will provide an application example. Suppose we want to evaluate LOS of a check-in counter facility at an airport terminal. A research project could be undertaken to survey passengers at an airport terminal. Since we are looking for a correlation between LOS ratings and characteristics of facilities (in this example, waiting time), we must find out the user LOS ratings, since an external observer can measure the waiting time incurred for this passenger.

Suppose that a single passenger has experienced a waiting time of 10 minutes. In practice the passenger can not compare this waiting time of 10 minutes with any other stimulus, since in most of the cases he/she has waited in line for check-in just once during this trip. The use of comparative scales is impractical for our research purposes. We should be able to provide a non-comparative scale to a surveyed passenger, like a line marking/continuous rating scale or an itemized rating scale. The description of these two scales is represented below:

Line marking/continuous rating scales

A line marking or continuous rating scale can be used in a non-comparative format. In this case the respondent is required to assign a rating by placing a mark at the appropriate position on a line, usually about 10 cm long, which best describes the subject under study. No standard for comparison is given. The resulting scores are usually analyzed as interval data.

Itemized rating scale

Here the respondent is provided with a scale that has numbers and/or a brief description associated with each category. They are asked to select one of the categories, ordered in terms of scale position that best describes the object under study. The scale can take on various formats reflecting the number of categories used, the nature and degree of verbal description, the number of favorable and unfavorable categories, and the presence of the neutral position. This kind of scale can have any number of response categories. However, the controlling factor concerns the respondent's ability to discriminate among categories. Various types of verbal descriptions and numeric formats can be employed and the former does help to ensure that respondents are operating from the same base. However, the presence of verbal descriptions will influence the responses obtained. Pictures and other types of graphics may also be used.

Both the line marking and the itemized rating scales could be used in this research. We will make use of the itemized rating scale because it has been widely used in LOS and quality research for airport passenger terminals.

The method used to collect the characteristics of facilities (e.g. waiting time, availability of space) will be discussed in Chapter 4.

3.4. Overall Evaluation

The last stage of evaluation is at the overall terminal level. At this stage, passengers consider their individual experiences at the facilities and transform them into an overall perception of the terminal LOS for their activity, e.g. departure.

3.4.1. Optional and Required Components

An airport passenger terminal contains various components, each of them supplying a specific passenger need. We could classify them into two categories: required and optional components. For instance, the security screening area is a required component on the departing path, while a hotel, though it might be important for some passengers, is an optional component, since its absence in an airport passenger terminal does not directly impact its operation. Although this classification may look simple, important components sometimes are classified into the optional category, while they are essential for air travelers, deserving a LOS evaluation as any other operational component. Despite this fact, most LOS studies have not included these components when developing LOS measurements. Considering this fact, we will provide our own list of required components, as they would be necessary for departing, arriving and connecting passengers.

3.4.2. Approaches to Overall LOS Calculation

It is useful here to discuss the different assumptions, based on which the methodology for overall LOS can be based. For our research development we will consider the following three hypotheses: weighted average, maximum value and minimum value.

Based on the weighted average assumption it is supposed that passengers combine their experiences through different components into a weighted average of individual LOS. An important step in this method is determining the weights associated with each component, that is, their relative importance as assigned by passengers. These assigned weights are of high importance for managers and designers, because they can focus their attention on the most important components. Considering this hypothesis, a bad passenger experience in a given component can be counterbalanced by a good experience in another component.

Another approach that can be employed for overall LOS evaluation is based on the maximum LOS value. In this case, it is supposed that passengers assign an overall terminal LOS, according to the maximum LOS value of all components that they pass through. Considering this, a departing passenger experiencing LOS A during check-in procedures, but LOS C for all remaining components, will still assign LOS A for the overall terminal level of service. The opposite of this approach is considering that passengers evaluate their overall terminal LOS according to the worst experience they

41

face. In this case, independently of the LOS experienced by the passenger during all other components, the overall LOS will be based on the worst experience. For instance, if on arriving, a passenger experiences LOS A for all components, except for baggage claim, where he assigns a LOS E, his overall terminal experience will be still assigned LOS E, according to this approach. Although these two hypotheses are very simplistic in nature, they represent an alternative concept to the weighted average approach, which requires data (component weights) that are difficult to gather.

An improvement to the maximum and minimum LOS approaches would be employing statistical measures of LOS, like mode, median or mean. Suppose for various airport passenger terminal components, we can get a vector representing LOS evaluations for all the individual components:

$$V: (A, B, D, A, A, B, B, A) \qquad (3.1)$$

For instance this vector could represent LOS evaluations for a departing path, e.g., terminal curb (LOS A), check-in counter (LOS B), departing lounge (LOS D), etc. The most frequent value represented in the above vector is LOS A (four times), which is the modal value. The median is between A and B, and the mean may be determined only if numerical values are assigned to the letters. Coincidentally, LOS A is also the maximum LOS value but that might not be the case for other situations. The minimum value (LOS D) is very far from the mode and occurs for just one component. The unfairness of applying the minimum LOS value approach on this evaluation is clear, especially if the component represented by LOS D is not "so important" according to the user perceptions. The mode, median and mean value approach can also be criticized based on a relative weight perspective; it might be the case that the most frequent LOS value actually represents components, which do not have important weights according to passengers' perceptions. We must stress that although the weighted average approach is more complex, requiring data that are relatively difficult to obtain, it is able to represent a balanced and adequate overall LOS evaluation. We intend to use this approach: we must find out a suitable methodology to determine the relative weights of different parameters from the user point of view.

3.5.   Alternative Overall Evaluation

With the objective of providing a straightforward evaluation of the overall LOS for various passenger types at airport passenger terminals, this research also intends to present an alternative approach based on a single scale. For instance, the overall terminal LOS could be based on total time incurred in the departing process. We call it an alternative approach, since it exempts the analyst from gathering data for individual components, such as the components' LOS values and the relative weights.

The investigation of the alternative overall LOS according to the user perception will be done using surveys, by obtaining two types of data: (1) LOS ratings; and (2) terminal characteristics.

Three variables will be applied for overall LOS evaluation:

- Total waiting + processing time;
- Walking Distance;
- Travel Time Differential (a measure of the ease of orientation).

The explanation of how these variables will be measured is a subject of chapter 6.

43

3.6. Illustration Chart

A simplified chart illustrating the methodology is presented in Figure 3.1.

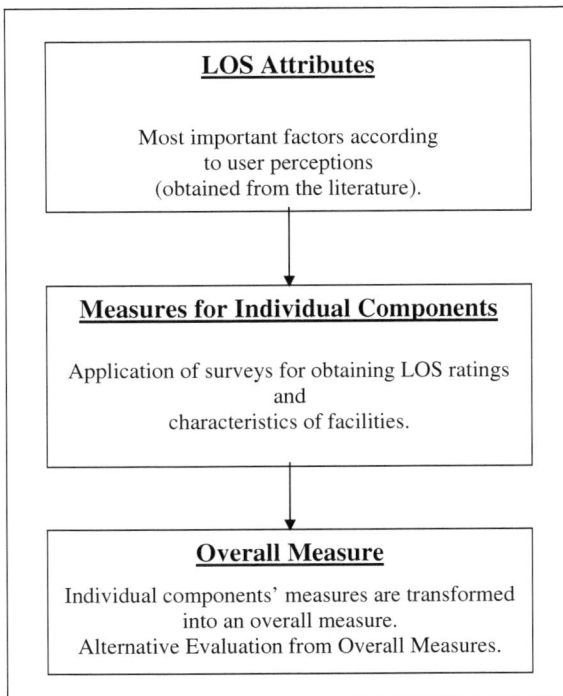

Figure 3.1: Conceptual procedure diagram

3.7. Available Methods

Analyzing the methods available on the literature, we have identified several techniques useful for LOS evaluation of airport passenger terminals. Table 3.3 presents a review of the different methods developed:

Table 3.3: Summary of Techniques Employed at LOS Evaluation

Technique Employed	Authors
Fuzzy set theory	Park (1994); Ndoh and Ashford (1994); Teng (2000); Yen et. al (2001); Yeh and Kuo (2002).
Utility theoretic approach	Omer and Khan (1998); Khan (1990); Siddiqui (1994).
Psychometrical scaling theory	Muller (1987); Muller and Gosling (1991); Ndoh and Ashford (1993).
Perception-response concept	Mumayiz (1985); Mumayiz and Ashford (1986); Ashford (1986); Mumayz (1991); Park (1999).
Logit Models	Yen (1995)

Considering the objectives proposed by this research, we discard the application of the perception-response concept and logit models, in that as originally presented, they are not able to provide a multi-attribute analysis. Additionally, they were developed to evaluate level of service as a function of only three categories (e.g., A, B, and C). This shortcoming makes the application somewhat limited. In the following, we present a summary of the techniques considered for further application in this research.

3.7.1. Fuzzy Set Theory

Fuzzy set theory provides a means for representing uncertainties. It is a marvelous tool for modeling the kind of uncertainty associated with vagueness, with imprecision, and/or with a lack of information regarding a particular element of the problem at hand. Fuzzy logic seems to be most successful in two kinds of situations: (1) very complex models where understanding is strictly limited or, in fact, quite judgmental, and (2) processes where human reasoning, human perception, or human decision making are inextricably involved (Ross, 1995). Fuzzy set theory was first proposed by Zadeh (1965). By his definition, a fuzzy set is characterized by a membership function that maps each point in its domain to a real number, labeled as membership grade, in the interval [0,1]. Similar to the ordinary crisp sets, the operation rules such as intersection and union as well as the arithmetics of the fuzzy sets have been well developed by Zadeh (1965). Recognizing that the perception of delay such as "satisfied" or "unsatisfied" is a subjective attribute rather than an objective one, the fuzzy concept is used by Yen et. al. (2001) to interpret passengers' subjective ratings of waiting period or services incurred at airports. In the specific topic of the mentioned research, fuzzy sets define the passengers' subjective notion of his or her rating associated with each waiting or service, and membership functions map waiting/service time to the respective membership grades of the notion sets.

3.7.2. Utility Theoretic Approach

The methods for determining utility have a common characteristic: they establish equivalence between a stimulus and a response. The stimulus is provided in the measuring process to provoke a person's response, indicating the intensity of preference, the utility. The process is analogous to radar identification of objects: a signal goes out and the response is interpreted (Neufville, 1990). For application to airport passenger terminals, the stimuli are considered to be the actual measures experienced by passengers. The response to the stimulus is the quality of service rating obtained by passenger interviews, which can be represented by a utility function. The utility function exists on a particular cardinal scale, on which values can be calculated meaningfully. It is then possible, within the limits defined by the axioms of utility, to measure the utility function

The utility function for each individual performance measure can be represented by a variety of functional forms, where two specific kinds are usual. The exponential function (Equation 3.2) has been favored in the past (de Neufville, 1990).

$$U(X) = a + be^{-cX} \qquad (3.2)$$

where

X = a given performance measure (waiting time, processing time, etc)

$U(X)$ = utility value of performance measure X

a, b, c = constants

This function has some nice properties mainly to do with the obsolescent concept of "risk aversion". Another option is the power function (Equation 3.3):

$$U(X) = a + bX^{c} \qquad (3.3)$$

In practice it appears to be as effective as the exponential. Either is fitted to the data in the same way: by adjusting the functional parameters so that the function generates the values of $U(X)$ assumed at the endpoints of the range and gives the best fit of intermediate points.

No specific function can be defined as an ideal to be employed. The most appropriate function must be selected according to its fit to existing data. That will be the approach to be applied in this research.

3.7.3. Psychometrical Scaling Theory

The psychometrical scaling technique allows the scaling of user perceptions of LOS attributes from categorical data. Categorical data are collected by most airports from passenger surveys in which passengers are asked to rate service attributes of preference, importance, or satisfaction. In applying the psychometric technique it is assumed that (Ndoh and Ashford, 1993):

- A scale continuum, partitioned into k category boundaries is defined. Any particular LOS attribute j, has a unique perception scale value (U) that can be placed between two category boundaries. This scale value is unique irrespective of the person providing the scale measure.

- A category k in which the mean scale value (U) is placed has lower and an upper boundary on the scale continuum. The lower boundary of the first category is minus infinity, and the last upper boundary of the last category is plus infinity.

- Any passenger providing a perception scale for an attribute j will ascribe a scale value V, which is related to the mean scale value U of j, the category boundaries t and $t + 1$, and a variance value specific to the passenger. The location of the category boundaries are defined as composed of fixed components on the continuum and a random component that allows for variations in the interpretation of the category boundary k by different passengers. Figure 3.2 shows the spatial descriptions of the scale values and categories boundaries.

- Over the whole population or a homogeneous sample, the sample mean scale value for any LOS attribute can be determined. The deduced scale is a discriminant process based on a specified probability distribution function. The normal distribution is assumed as this distribution for both the scale value and the category boundaries.

48

The application of the psychometrical scaling theory provides a quantitative measure representing quality of service at airport passenger terminals; this numerical measure can be applied by regression analysis to be correlated to actual performance measures obtained through attitudinal surveys (Muller, 1987):

$$FQ_{jq} = f_{jq}(FC_{q1},..., FC_{qi},...)$$ (3.4)

where:

FQ_{jq} = mean quantitative quality rating of facility q's service by group passengers in group j,

f_{jq} = functional form for facility q and passengers in group j,

FC_{qi} = quantitative characteristic i of facility q (e.g., waiting time and crowding).

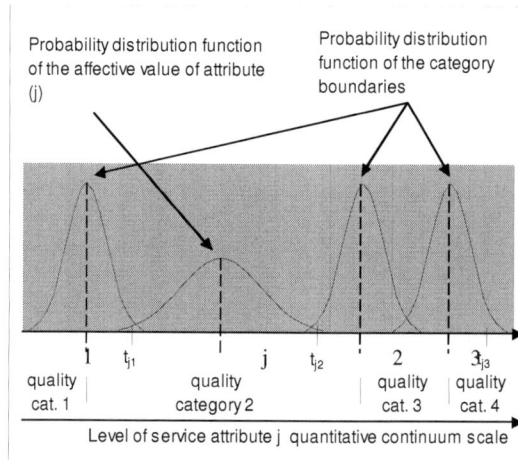

Figure 3.2: Spatial description of scale continuum
(Ndoh and Ashford, 1993)

3.7.4. Marketing Research on Quantitative Data Analysis

In addition to the methods employed by previous researchers on the airport terminal LOS evaluation, we would like to discuss the marketing research methods for quantitative data analysis. These methods could be useful for LOS evaluation.

Malhotra (1999) provided a classification of multivariate techniques employed by marketing researchers (Figure 3.3):

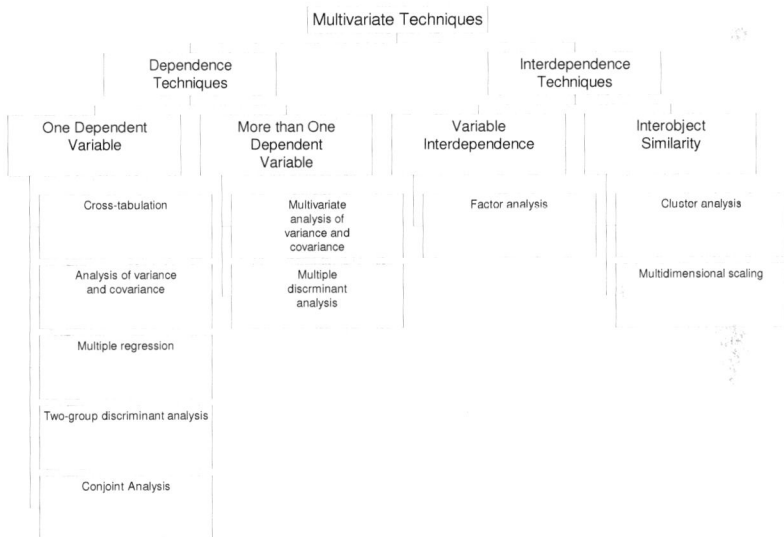

```
                          Multivariate Techniques

          Dependence                        Interdependence
          Techniques                         Techniques

  One Dependent    More than One      Variable          Interobject
    Variable        Dependent      Interdependence       Similarity
                    Variable

  Cross-tabulation   Multivariate    Factor analysis    Cluster analysis
                     analysis of
                     variance and
                     covariance

  Analysis of variance   Multiple                       Multidimensional scaling
  and covariance         discrminant
                         analysis

  Multiple regression

  Two-group discriminant analysis

  Conjoint Analysis
```

Figure 3.3: Marketing Research Techniques (Malhotra, 1999)

Cross-Tabulations help answer questions about how variables link or associate with other variables. For example,

- How many brand-loyal users are men?

50

- Is product use (measured in terms of heavy users, medium users, light users, and nonusers) related to interest in outdoor activities (high, medium, and low)?
- Is product ownership related to income (high, medium, and low)?

Analysis of Variance and Analysis of Covariance are used for examining the differences in the mean values of the dependent variable associated with the effect of the controlled independent variables, after taking into account the influence of the uncontrolled independent variables. Essentially, analysis of variance (ANOVA) is used as a test of means for two or more populations.

Marketing researchers are often interested in examining the differences in the mean values of the dependent variable for several categories of a single independent variable or factor. For example,

- Do the various segments differ in terms of their volume of product consumption?
- Do the brand evaluations of groups exposed to different commercials vary?
- Do retailers, wholesalers, and agents differ in their attitudes toward the firm's distribution policies?
- How do consumers' intentions to buy the brand vary with different price levels?

The answer to these and similar questions can be determined by conducting one-way ANOVA. N-way ANOVA is often interested in the effect of more than one factor simultaneously. A major advantage of this technique is that it enables the researcher to examine interactions among the factors. Interactions occur when the effects of one factor on the dependent variable depend on the level (category) of the other factors.

Regression Analysis is a powerful and flexible procedure for analyzing associative relationships between a metric dependent variable and one or more independent variables. It can be used to:

1. Determine whether the independent variables explain a significant variation in the dependent variable (whether a relationship exists);
2. Determine how much of the variation in the dependent variable can be explained by the independent variables (strength of the relationship);
3. Determine the structural form of the relationship (the mathematical equation relating the independent and dependent variables); and
4. Predict the values of the dependent variable.

Regression analysis deals with the nature and degree of association between variables and does not imply or assume any causality.

Discriminant Analysis is a technique for analyzing data when the criterion or dependent variable is categorical and the predictor or independent variables are interval in nature. For example, the dependent variable may be the choice of a brand of personal computer (brand A, B, or C), and the independent variables may be ratings of attributes of computers on a seven-point Likert scale. The objectives of discriminant analysis are as follows:

1. Development of discriminant functions or linear combinations of the predictor or independent variables that will best discriminate between the categories of the criterion or dependent variable (groups);
2. Examination of whether significant differences exist among the groups, in terms of the predictor variables;
3. Determination of which predictor variables contribute to most of the intergroup differences;

4. Classification of cases to one of the groups on the basis of the values of the predictor variables; and

5. Evaluation on the accuracy of classification.

Examples of discriminant analysis abound in marketing research. This technique can be used to answer questions such as:

- In terms of demographic characteristics, how do customers who exhibit store loyalty differ from those who do not?
- Do heavy, medium, and light users of soft drinks differ in terms of their consumption of frozen foods?
- What psychographic characteristics help differentiate between price-sensitive and non-price-sensitive buyers of groceries?
- Do the various market segments differ in their media consumption habits?

Factor Analysis is a general name denoting a class of procedures primarily used for data reduction and summarization. In marketing research, there may be a large number of variables, most of which are correlated and must be reduced to a manageable level. Relationships among sets of many interrelated variables are examined and represented in terms of a few underlying factors.

Factor analysis is used in the following circumstances:

1. To identify underlying dimensions, or factors, that explain the correlations among a set of variables;

2. To identify a new, smaller set of uncorrelated variables to replace the original set of correlated variables in subsequent multivariate analysis (regression or discriminant analysis); or

3. To identify a smaller set of salient variables from a larger set for use in subsequent multivariate analysis.

53

Factor analysis has many applications in marketing research. For example,

- In product research, factor analysis can be employed to determine the brand attributes that influence consumer choice. Toothpaste brands might be evaluated in terms of protection against cavities, whiteness of teeth, taste, fresh breath, and price.
- In pricing studies, factor analysis can be used to identify the characteristics of price-sensitive consumers. For example, these consumers might be methodical, economy-minded, and home-centered.

Cluster Analysis is a class of techniques used to classify objects or cases into relatively homogeneous groups called *clusters*. Objects in each cluster tend to be similar to one another and dissimilar to objects in the other clusters.

Cluster analysis has been used in marketing for a variety of purposes, including the following:

- Segmenting the market.
- Understanding buyer behaviors.
- Identifying new product opportunities.
- Selecting test markets.
- Reducing data.

Multidimensional scaling (MDS) is a class of procedures for representing perceptions and preferences of respondents spatially by means of a visual display. It has been used in marketing to identify.

1. The number and nature of dimensions consumers use to perceive different brands in the marketplace.
2. The positioning of current brands on these dimensions, and
3. The positioning of consumers' ideal brand on these dimensions.

Conjoint Analysis attempts to determine the relative importance consumers attach to salient attributes and the utilities they attach to the levels of attributes. This information is derived from consumers' evaluations of brands or brand profiles composed of these attributes and their levels. Conjoint analysis has been used in marketing for a variety of purposes, including.

1. Determining the relative importance of attributes in the consumer choice process. A standard output from conjoint analysis consists of derived relative importance weights for all the attributes used to construct the stimuli used in the evaluation task. The relative importance weights indicate which attributes are important in influencing consumer choice.

2. Estimating market share of brands that differ in attribute levels. The utilities derived from conjoint analysis can be used as input into a choice simulator to determine the share of choices, and thus the market share, of different brands.

3. Determining the composition of the most preferred brand. The brand features can be varied in terms of attribute levels and the corresponding utilities determined. The brand features that yield the highest utility indicate the composition of the most preferred brand.

3.8.   Summary

We have presented a summary of three theories that can be used for the evaluation of LOS at airport passenger terminals. It is worth mentioning, though, that these methodologies have limitations associated with their applications and the modeler must be aware of these when implementing these techniques. Table 3.4 illustrates the advantages associated with the application of each approach.

55

Table 3.4: Advantages Associated with LOS Evaluation Techniques

Fuzzy Sets	• Allows utilization of linguistic expressions as good, tolerable, bad, etc on the LOS investigation. • It is a suitable theory for application on problems with uncertainty associated with vagueness, imprecision, and/or a lack of information. • Represents an alternative to the traditional approaches.
Utility	• Provides a goodness of fit test for the utility functions. • It is a traditional theory used for measurements on the varied fields of engineering.
Psychometric	• Provides a goodness of fit test for the utility functions. • It is a traditional theory used for measurements on the varied fields of engineering. • Allows transformation of qualitative data into quantitative data. • Allows utilization of categorical data, which is the data type provided by most airport authorities.

Additionally, all of the marketing research techniques can assist in a better understanding of the passengers' perception of the level of service provided at an airport passenger terminal. *Cross tabulations* and *analysis of variance* would help understand the association of variables of the nominal type, like gender, purpose of trip or type of flight. *Discriminant analysis* could be used to evaluate airport choice (in case of multiple-airport cities or regions) as a function of overall LOS of each airport. *Factor analysis* would permit identifying the most important attributes for passengers out of a bundle of many possible attributes. *Cluster analysis* might assist on whether to implement new retail areas in the airport passenger terminal or how passengers are clustered in terms of shopping consumption in the terminal. *Conjoint analysis* would indicate what are the most important factors affecting the passengers' perceptions of LOS at the airport and determine the relative weights. *Multiple Regression Analysis* would allow us to determine how much of the variation in the characteristics of the airport facilities would influence the LOS' ratings; we could then finally determine the structure of the relationship between these two variables.

If there were not so many parameters (there are 17 attributes, e.g. check-in waiting time, lounge number of seats, etc), we could apply *Conjoint Analysis* to determine the relative weights of these parameters. Usually, this technique has been applied in cases having no more than 5 attributes (Aaker et. al (1998), Proctor (2000)). A great number of parameters would confuse the mind of the interviewed passenger when choosing between the hypothetical alternatives presented.

Multiple Regression Analysis is employed by the Utility Theoretic Approach and the Psychometric Technique previously described. Both theories can be successfully employed in our research. We will make use of the psychometric scaling theoretical framework. Its main advantage over the other approaches is the transformation of qualitative data into quantitative data; that is a very important pre-requisite for LOS evaluation at airports, since most existing data in current airports are of a qualitative nature (categorical), while regression analysis application assumes that the data is quantitative (interval). The psychometric technique method data demands are the proportion of responses between the categories. There is no additional numerical input necessary. When using the utility theoretic approach, Omer and Khan (1998) assumed that the various LOS categories (1-7) are evenly distributed within the 0-1 scale; such assumption is not necessary when using the psychometric scaling technique. Finally, one of the main difficulties associated with the fuzzy set theory and the utility theory is that they rely on a 0-1 scale. Unfortunately, most service measures (such as waiting time) do not have natural upper bounds. In this case, they cannot be converted by a linear transformation to a 0-1 scale.

3.9. Theoretical Framework

3.9.1. Introduction

The methodology adopted for LOS evaluation is based on the psychometric scaling technique developed by Bock and Jones (1968) and further applied by Muller (1987) and Ndoh and Ashford (1993).

Psychometrics and psychological scaling theory has given extensive consideration to the behavior of subjects, sampled from a specific population, in choosing among alternatives (Bock and Jones, 1968). These ideas can be applied to passenger level of service evaluation of an airport terminal by considering passengers as subject to the experience of being processed at the terminal during the transition between their access and egress mode (whether by ground or air), and then being asked to choose a rating for the quality of that experience (Muller and Gosling, 1991). Most of the studies on this subject are developed from the work of Thurstone (1959). He introduced the fundamental concept of a sensory continuum, which remains an essential part of current psychological theory.

There are many methods available based on psychometric scaling theory. We could divide them into two categories. There are the methods where judges assess a stimulus directly in terms of other objects, in which categories are included the constant, paired comparisons and rank order methods. In the other category, successive-categories judgments, however, depends upon passenger evaluations of the stimulus as a function of rating categories. For the purpose of measuring terminal LOS, it is supposed that the passenger will experience a stimulus only once during his/her trip experience, which is being measured; in this case constant, paired comparisons and rank order methods are not useful for measuring performance variables LOS of different terminal components. Considering this, the successive categories method will be employed, since it is the most

58

suitable for measuring airport passenger terminal LOS. The method has been mathematically developed by Bock and Jones (1968), as presented below.

3.9.2. The Method of Successive Categories

The following methodology for obtaining LOS quantitative values will be illustrated with a practical example consisting of a survey applied to 119 passengers at the check-in counter at São Paulo/Guarulhos International Airport.

In the following paragraphs, a simplified version of the methodology will be presented. The detailed derivation is given in Appendix B.

Consider a sample of air passengers that have been serviced at a check-in counter. All of them have experienced a "waiting time" in the queue. They are asked to rate this experience into five ordered level of service categories. In general these categories will be defined by k, which is described as follows: unacceptable ($k = 1$), poor ($k = 2$), fair ($k = 3$), good ($k = 4$) or excellent ($k = 5$). Table 3.5 illustrates the distribution of responses for a survey at São Paulo/Guarulhos International Airport.

Table 3.5: Distribution of Responses Between Categories

Group	WT Range (min)	Average WT (min)	(1) Unaccep.	(2) Poor	(3) Fair	(4) Good	(5) Excellent	Total
1	WT = 0	0.0	0	0	1	8	7	16
2	WT = 1	1.0	0	0	1	4	4	9
3	WT = 2	2.1	0	0	1	0	4	5
4	WT = 3	3.0	0	0	2	5	6	13
5	WT = 4	4.0	0	0	2	3	1	6
6	WT = 5	5.0	0	0	0	4	1	5
7	$5 < WT \leq 10$	7.9	0	1	2	11	0	14
8	$10 < WT \leq 15$	13.4	0	1	5	6	2	14
9	$15 < WT \leq 25$	20.4	0	1	4	9	1	15
10	$25 < WT \leq 35$	33.4	0	5	5	1	0	11
11	$35 < WT \leq 55$	49.1	2	4	1	0	0	7
12	$55 < WT \leq 75$	68.8	3	1	0	0	0	4

For the survey illustrated in Table 3.5, waiting times (WT) were measured for each passenger, prior to the interview. To facilitate the calculation, the 119 observed passengers have been separated into 12 groups of similar waiting times.

From the data presented in Table 3.5, it is possible to obtain the proportion of responses where the waiting time is assigned at or below category k. Let us denote these proportions of responses as p_{jk}, where j represents the group number, and k represents the category. Table 3.6 presents the proportions for the surveyed passengers at São Paulo/Guarulhos International Airport.

Table 3.6: Proportions (p_k) of Responses at or Below Category k

Group	WT (min)	k - category 1 - Unac.	2 - Poor	3 - Fair	4 - Good	5 - Exc.
1	0.0	0.000	0.000	0.063	0.563	1.000
2	1.0	0.000	0.000	0.111	0.556	1.000
3	2.1	0.000	0.000	0.200	0.200	1.000
4	3.0	0.000	0.000	0.154	0.538	1.000
5	4.0	0.000	0.000	0.333	0.833	1.000
6	5.0	0.000	0.000	0.000	0.800	1.000
7	7.9	0.000	0.071	**0.214**	1.000	1.000
8	13.4	0.000	0.071	0.429	0.857	1.000
9	20.4	0.000	0.067	0.333	0.933	1.000
10	33.4	0.000	0.455	0.909	1.000	1.000
11	49.1	0.286	0.857	1.000	1.000	1.000
12	68.8	0.750	1.000	1.000	1.000	1.000

The proportion of responses represents a simplified LOS measure. It indicates the level of user satisfaction in each group. In group 7, only 21.4% of passengers rate the waiting time (7.9 minutes) as fair, poor or unacceptable; the great majority (78.6%) rate the waiting time as good or excellent. This LOS measure might be used by the management of an airport to asses the level of user satisfaction, however, it is not useful to precisely determine a quantitative LOS measure.

Let us define a level of service quantitative continuum ranging from $-\infty$ to $+\infty$. Values on the far negative side represent a "bad" level of service. Values on the far positive side represent "good" level of service. Zero represents a neutral position. Suppose this continuum can be divided into five regions, which represent each individual level of service category (Figure 3.4).

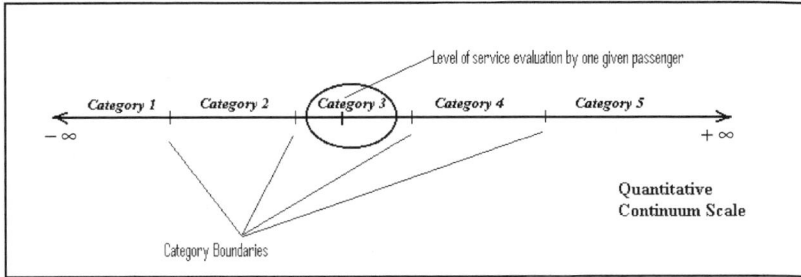

Figure 3.4: Illustration of Quantitative Continuum Scale

Each category has a lower and an upper boundary. In Figure 3.4 for instance, a given passenger has evaluated the level of service of a facility between the lower and upper boundaries of category 3. In the following paragraphs, only the upper boundary of each category will be considered as far as it concerns the methodology development.

Suppose it is possible to obtain a quantitative LOS rating for the waiting time experienced. Consider that this rating v_{ji}^{LOS} can be defined as follows for a given passenger i:

$$v_{ji}^{LOS} = \mu_j^{LOS} + \varepsilon_{ji} \qquad (3.5)$$

where μ_j^{LOS} represents the mean LOS rating common to all passengers in group j, and ε_{ji} represents a quantitative rating associated with a randomly selected passenger i in group j.

The position of a given category boundary is also assumed to be perceived at different points on the continuum by different passengers. Its location is also defined by a probability distribution with its own mean and dispersion. Thus the perceived location of the upper boundary of category k is given by:

$$v_{ki}^{UB} = \mu_k^{UB} + \varepsilon_{ki} \tag{3.6}$$

where μ_k^{UB} represents the mean quantitative rating associated with category k. The component ε_{ki} is random based on passenger i.

Figure 3.5 illustrates the position of v_{ji}^{LOS}, as defined by a given passenger i. In this illustration, the passenger i has rated the waiting time experienced as fair (category 3) by choosing a value between v_{2i}^{UB} and v_{3i}^{UB}. He/she has also interpreted the category boundaries at v_{1i}^{UB}, v_{2i}^{UB}, v_{3i}^{UB} and v_{4i}^{UB}, as shown. It is worth noting that the upper boundary of category 5 is $+\infty$.

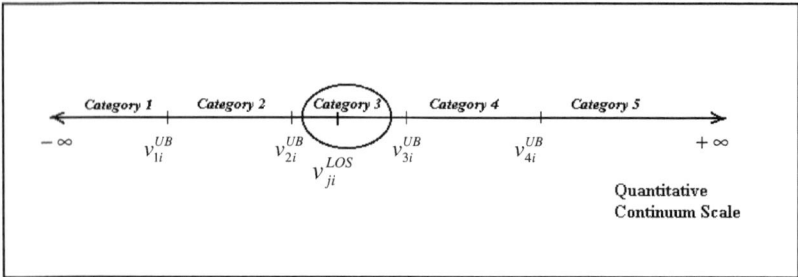

Figure 3.5: Location of category upper boundaries and LOS rating for passenger i

We assume the joint distribution of ε_{ji} and ε_{ki} to be bivariate normal, with means of zero, variances δ_j^2 and γ_k^2, and intercorrelation zero. In the absence of information to the contrary, it is usual to consider the variance γ_k^2 to be constant across all categories k; so we will assume that $\gamma_k^2 = \gamma^2$ for all k. Figure 3.6 illustrates the assumptions of normality for the distributions of v_{ji}^{LOS} and v_{ki}^{UB}.

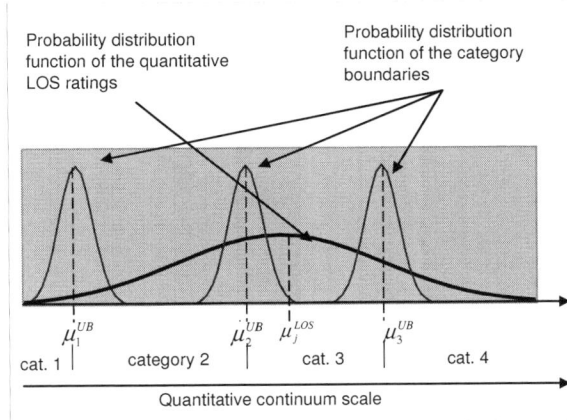

Figure 3.6: Illustration of the Successive Categories Method for all Passengers

The response of passenger i is assumed to be determined as follows. WTj (waiting time for passengers in group j) will be rated at or below point k for passenger i if:

$$v_{jki}^{\Delta} = v_{ji}^{LOS} - v_{ki}^{UB} = \mu_{j}^{LOS} - \mu_{k}^{UB} + \varepsilon_{ji} - \varepsilon_{ki} \leq 0 \qquad (3.7)$$

Clearly, v_{jki}^{Δ} is normally distributed, with mean

$$\mu(v_{jk}^{\Delta}) = \mu_{j}^{LOS} - \mu_{k}^{UB}, \qquad (3.8)$$

and variance

$$V(v_{jk}^{\Delta}) = \delta_{j}^{2} + \gamma^{2} = \sigma_{j}^{2} \qquad (3.9)$$

Equation (3.7) can be illustrated using Figure 3.5. We note that v_{ji}^{LOS} is smaller than v_{3i}^{UB}. In this case $v_{jki}^{\Delta} = v_{ji}^{LOS} - v_{3i}^{UB} < 0$. So, WTj is rated under category 3. Although it is very obvious, this equation will be very useful to the development of the model. The application of this equation to an integral of probability distribution, considering the mentioned assumptions, and after change of variables, can provide the following relation:

$$P_{jk} = \Phi\left[(\mu_k^{UB} - \mu_j^{LOS})/\sigma_j\right] \tag{3.10}$$

Equation (3.10) represents the probability that a passenger will judge WT_j at or below category k.

The inverse of this function is

$$(\mu_k^{UB} - \mu_j^{LOS})/\sigma_j = \Phi^{-1}(P_{jk}) \tag{3.11}$$

Data from experimental design may be cast in the form of observed proportions p_{jk}, the proportions of judgments of WT_j at or below category k. Then according to the model,

$$(\mu_k^{UB} - \mu_j^{LOS})/\sigma_j \cong \left[\Phi^{-1}(p_{jk})\right]$$
$$\cong (y_{jk}) \tag{3.12}$$

y_{jk} is the normal deviate corresponding to the proportion p_{jk} in the lower tail of the unit normal distribution.

Bock and Jones showed that the estimate of μ_k^{UB}, $\underline{\mu}_k^{UB}$, can be determined as the average of the kth value of the standard normal deviates over all passenger groups j, that is:

$$\underline{\mu}_k^{UB} = \frac{1}{n}\sum_{j=1}^{n} y_{jk} \tag{3.13}$$

According to the normal distribution, $\underline{\mu}_k^{UB}$ will vary linearly with y, and so the estimate of μ_j^{LOS} and σ_j can be obtained by the regression line defined using these values of $\underline{\mu}_k^{UB}$ as the dependent variables, and the y_{jk}, $k = 1, 2, ..., (m-1)$, for each j as the independent variables. The slope will be σ_j and the intercept on the $\underline{\mu}_k^{UB}$ axis will be the value of μ_j^{LOS}. This last value is the mean LOS quantitative rating for group j.

Before proceeding with the calculations to obtain μ_j^{LOS}, let us summarize the necessary steps:

1) Separate the passengers into groups of similar waiting times. In the example, they were divided into 12 groups. Each of them has an average waiting time, denoted by WTj, where j is the group number ($j = 1, 2, ..., 12$).

2) Obtain the number of responses for each category in each group.

3) Calculate the proportions p_{jk}.

4) Calculate the normal deviates y_{jk}.

5) Calculate $\underline{\mu}_k^{UB}$ as the average of y_{jk} over all groups for each category k.

6) Perform a regression analysis to obtain the μ_j^{LOS}. For the regression, the independent variable should be y_{jk}; the dependent variable should be $\underline{\mu}_k^{UB}$.

In the example proposed, steps 1-3 have been already undertaken. We now proceed to the calculation of the normal deviates y_{jk}. The procedure to calculate the normal deviates is presented in Appendix B. Table 3.7 shows the normal deviates for the case of the survey conducted at São Paulo/Guarulhos International Airport.

Table 3.7: Normal Deviates – Waiting Time at the Check-in Counter - SP

Group	WT (min)	1	2	3	4	Sum
1	0.00	-4.287	-2.653	-1.534	0.158	-8.316
2	1.00	-3.974	-2.340	-1.221	0.140	-7.394
3	2.10	-3.594	-1.960	-0.841	-0.841	-7.238
4	3.00	-3.773	-2.139	-1.020	0.097	-6.835
5	4.00	-3.184	-1.550	-0.431	0.967	-4.198
6	5.00	-3.161	-1.527	-0.408	0.841	-4.253
7	7.90	-3.099	-1.465	-0.792	0.457	-4.898
8	13.40	-3.099	-1.465	-0.180	1.067	-3.677
9	20.40	-3.135	-1.501	-0.431	1.501	-3.566
10	33.40	-1.748	-0.114	1.335	2.584	2.057
11	49.10	-0.566	1.067	2.186	3.435	6.123
12	68.80	0.674	2.308	3.427	4.676	11.087
	Sum	-33.620	-15.647	-3.336	10.407	-42.195
$\underline{\mu}_k^{UB}$		-2.802	-1.304	-0.278	0.867	
	(-1.304 - 0.278) / 2 = -0.791					
$\underline{\mu}_k^{UB}$ (normalized)		-2.011	-0.513	0.513	1.658	

The $\underline{\mu}_k^{UB}$'s have been calculated as the average of the y_{jk}'s over all groups. The second last row of Table 4 calculates the mean of $\underline{\mu}_k^{UB}$'s for the lower and upper bounds of category 3. Its value (-0.791) represents the quantitative rating corresponding to the neutral position or indifference (mean of category 3). This value has been subtracted to the values of the originals $\underline{\mu}_k^{UB}$'s for obtaining the "normalized" $\underline{\mu}_k^{UB}$'s (last row of Table 4).

There is now enough data for obtaining the μ_j^{LOS} 's. We will illustrate the procedure for obtaining μ_7^{LOS}, which is the mean LOS rating for group 7 (waiting time = 7.9 minutes). In this case, a regression analysis must be performed between the two variables presented in Table 3.8.

Table 3.8: Necessary data for performing a regression analysis.

Upper Bound of Category	Dependent Variable $\underline{\mu}_k^{UB}$	Independent Variable y_{7k}
1 - Unacceptable	-2.011	-3.099
2 – Poor	-0.513	-1.465
3 – Fair	0.513	-0.792
4 – Good	1.658	0.457

The regression analysis provides the intercept of the curve, which is (1.20). This is the value of μ_7^{LOS}. The remaining μ_j^{LOS} (j = 1 to 6, 8 to 12) are presented in Table 3.9.

Table 3.9: μ_j^{LOS} 's for each group (j).

Group (j)	μ_j^{LOS}	WTj (min)
1	1.64	0.00
2	1.57	1.00
3	1.97	2.10
4	1.52	3.00
5	0.84	4.00
6	0.89	5.00
7	1.20	7.90
8	0.71	13.40
9	0.62	20.40
10	(0.52)	33.40
11	(1.49)	49.10
12	(2.63)	68.80

From Table 3.9 it can be seen that the mean quantitative LOS ratings become more negative as the waiting time increases; this represents the decreasing user satisfaction as the waiting time assumes greater values. It is possible to obtain a numeric function depicting the relationship between LOS and waiting times. The function obtained from a regression analysis performed using data from Table 3.9 is provided below:

$$LOS = 1.597 - 0.06\ (WT) \qquad\qquad (3.14)$$
$$R^2 = 0.96\ \ F = 262.30$$

The curve corresponding to equation 3.14 is represented by the line in Figure 3.7. The data points are represented by the dots. Equation 3.14 can be used to determine the level of service standards associated with the boundaries of categories. Table 3.10 shows the upper boundaries of categories 1-4.

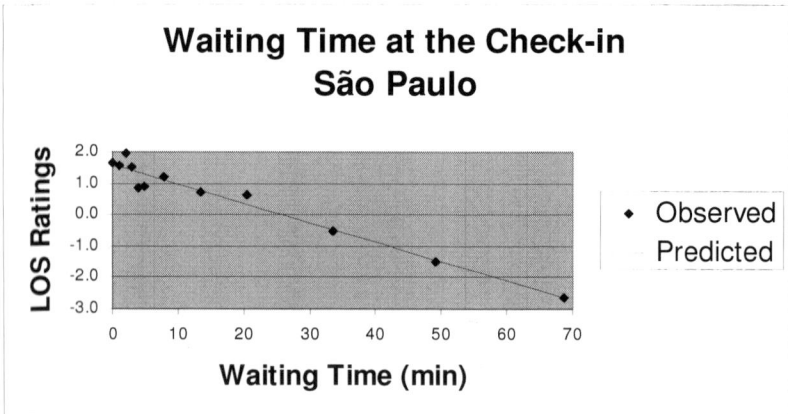

Figure 3.7: Data for Waiting Time at the Check-in Counter

Table 3.10: Category boundaries

Upper Bound of Category	μ_k^{UB}
1 - Unacceptable	-2.011
2 – Poor	-0.513
3 – Fair	0.513
4 – Good	1.658

The substitution of the μ_k^{UB} values of Table 3.10 into Equation 3.14 provides the WT values corresponding to the upper boundaries of the categories. Table 3.11 shows the LOS standards calculated using this procedure:

Table 3.11: Proposed LOS Standards

LOS	WAITING TIME (min)
A	< 1
B	$1 - 17$
C	$17 - 34$
D	$34 - 58$
E	> 58

For instance, LOS B was defined using waiting times corresponding to upper bounds of categories 3 and 4.

Finally, the conformity of the observed proportions of response in each category, designated $p_{jk} - p_{j,k-1}$ with those derived from the model designated $P_{jk} - P_{j,k-1}$, may be tested by computing a total χ^2 (Chi-Square) for the discrepancies between them:

$$\chi^2 = \sum_{j=1}^{n} \sum_{k=1}^{m-1} \frac{\{[(p_{jk} - p_{j,k-1}) - (P_{jk} - P_{j,k-1})]N_j\}^2}{(P_{jk} - P_{j,k-1})N_j} \qquad (3.15)$$

To determine the degrees of freedom for the total χ^2, we note that there are $n(m-1)$ independent observed proportions (according to the assumptions stated before). From this total $2(n-1)$ degrees of freedom are consumed by the estimates of μ_j^{LOS} and σ_j not determined by the estimates of μ_k^{UB}, and $m-1$ are consumed by the estimates of μ_k^{UB}. Thus, the residual variation is on $(n-1)(m-3)$ degrees of freedom, and it is necessary to use not less than four categories and two objects if the model is to be tested.

(n is the number of groups (12) and m is the number of categories (5))

Equation 3.15 was applied and the chi-square value resulting was 13.476. The degrees of freedom are (12-1) (5-3) = 22. In this case the chi-square value (13.476) is compared to 33.429 at 5% significance level (22 degrees of freedom). By this comparison we see that the model can be used for the LOS modeling.

3.9.3. Composite Evaluations

Considering the simplicity and usefulness of the additive approach method, this research will employ it for obtaining the composite equations representing the overall level of service of a component or for the airport passenger terminal. Using this approach, the composite equation for the check-in facility can be developed as follows:

$$LOS(Check-in) = \sum w_i LOS(X_i) \qquad (3.16)$$

where w_i are positive scaling constants (or weights) between the different check-in characteristics, X_i (e.g. waiting time, processing time, and availability of space). That function allows us to add the separate contributions of the different attributes to obtain the total level of service measure. It is the best known of the multiattribute functions and it is important both because of its relevance to some real problems and its relative simplicity (Keeney and Raiffa, 1976).

It should be mentioned, that the use of the weighting scheme is possible if certain relations are held. These are known as the concept of worth independence and are defined by the following statements (Rand, 1969):

- The relative importance of satisfying separate attributes does not depend upon the various degrees to which each attribute has itself been satisfied. Rather, their relative importance is conceived as being constant in this respect.

- The rate at which increased satisfaction of any given attribute contributes to overall worth is independent of the level of satisfaction already achieved on that and other attributes. Such rates are considered constant.

- The rate at which decision makers would be willing to trade off decreased satisfaction on one attribute for increased satisfaction on other attributes, so as to preserve the same overall worth, is independent of the level of satisfaction already achieved by any or all of the attributes.

There are some procedures that can be applied to verify whether the explanatory variables are additive independent and if either attribute is independent of the other. We will make use of analysis of correlation between variables to determine the degree of multicollinearity between them. The details of this method are found on most statistical books (see Miles and Shevlin, 2001). If it has been found that the variables are not independent of the other, then the analyst must work on reducing the dimensionality of the problem (Keeney and Raiffa, 1976).

3.9.4. Weighting Values

Weighting functions have been used in the past through a great variety of available methods, including:

1. Ranking.

2. Rating.

3. Pairwise Comparisons.

The ranking method is a useful method for obtaining the most important attribute in a given set. Nevertheless, it can not provide the quantitative preferences for the other attributes. The application of this method to LOS evaluation has been criticized elsewhere (Muller and Gosling, 1991). An alternative to solve this issue could be the application of the rating method, but the main deficiency of the application of rating method on the LOS evaluation is that it is not clear that passengers can meaningfully answer questions asking them to assign relative values to widely different metrics. The pairwise comparison scheme is more complete and can overcome the difficulties associated with the ranking and rating methods, being the traditional approach (Taylor III, 1999; Taha, 1997). The pairwise comparison scheme is best known by AHP (analytical hierarchy process). The crux of AHP is the determination of the relative weights. Assuming that we are dealing with n criteria, the procedure establishes an n x n pairwise comparison matrix that reflects the decision maker's judgment of the relative importance of the different criteria. These comparisons are made using a preference scale, which assigns numerical values to different levels of preference.

From the analysis of the three methods it is clear that the pairwise comparison scheme is the most suitable one for obtaining components' importance relative weights. Nevertheless its data needs are so great that its application in an airport passenger terminal is practically impossible. Based on that, we propose an alternative approach, which is capable of obtaining weights without necessarily directly inquiring passengers about them. It can be explained through the following example.

In an attitudinal survey, users are asked to declare LOS ratings for each of the four measures proposed (waiting time, processing time and availability of space) alongwith an overall check-in LOS measure. A regression analysis can be fitted as follows:

$$LOS(check\text{-}in) = w_1 * LOS(WT) + w_2 * LOS(PT) + w_3 * LOS(AS) \qquad (3.17)$$

Where

LOS(check-in) =overall check-in LOS measures

LOS(WT), LOS(PT, and LOS(AS) = LOS ratings for each individual measure

w_1, w_2 and w_3 = measures' relative importance weights.

w_1, w_2 and w_3 are the parameters of the regression equation, which can be obtained through least squares method. In this case, the weights are obtained, reflecting the passengers' perceptions of components' relative importance. Although in this example we have calculated component (check-in) LOS in function of LOS measures (waiting time, processing time, etc), the airport passenger terminal LOS can be evaluated as a function of individual components' LOS (see Chapter 7).

3.10. Conclusions

The successive categories method has been illustrated and has proven to be useful for determining the quantitative level of service measures. Regression analysis can be useful to obtain a relationship these measures and the characteristics of the facilities. Finally, multiple regression analysis can determine the weights associated with individual measures to obtain a composite measure for a component or the overall airport passenger terminal. The next chapters will apply these concepts using Brazilian airports and the Calgary International Airport as case studies.

CHAPTER FOUR: SURVEY APPLICATION

The main objectives of this chapter are to describe the survey method employed, the questionnaire format, the airports and its components being studied, and the summary of responses. A complete statistical analysis for individual components and the overall terminal will be presented in subsequent chapters.

The survey described in this chapter was applied to three Brazilian airports and to the Calgary International Airport - Canada. The interviews and observations occurred in a period of five complete weeks, being performed by four trained professionals.

4.1. Case Study I: Brazilian Airports

Permission was requested from INFRAERO (a Governmental Company that owns and manages the most important Brazilian Airports) for surveying passengers at the following Brazilian airports:

- Rio de Janeiro/Galeão International Airport: June, 11th to 15th, 2003
- São Paulo/Guarulhos International Airport: June, 16th to 22nd, 2003
                                                                                May, 10th to 16th, 2004
- São Paulo/Congonhas International Airport: June, 23rd to 29th, 2003

The administrations of these airports approved the surveys for all areas of the terminal.

These airports handle a significant portion of the Brazilian air passenger traffic and are important gateways to South American countries. Regular non-stop direct flights are served to several important locations in the world: this fact is very interesting, because the survey will get comments from local and international passengers. Because the interviews were done during the Summer/03 and the Summer/04, we had the opportunity to interview several tourists, in addition to business passengers. All these facts will make the survey very representative, catching the perception of various kinds of passengers.

4.1.1. Air Transport in Brazil

Brazil is a big country, larger than the continental United States, being ranked as fifth in the world in territorial extension. It is also ranked as fifth in population, with about 180 million inhabitants. The Brazilian economy is the largest in all Latin America and the ninth largest in the world. In the face of this, air transportation development is a strategic factor in the country's economy.

There are approximately 5,500 airports in Brazil (Caves and Gosling, 1999). The small airports are administered by the relevant municipal or state authority. The 65 larger or more strategically important ones, which include 20 international airports and which process 97% of the country's total traffic, are administered by a federal agency created in 1972 with the title INFRAERO (Empresa Brasileira de Infra-Estrutura Aeroportuária), reporting to the Department of Civil Aviation, with 20,000 in-house and external employees. The INFRAERO share of traffic represented about 75 million passengers or 2 million aircraft movements in 2002 and 1.2 million tons of cargo.

Table 4.1 provides detailed information about the five busiest airports in Brazil. They represent about 50% of all air traffic in Brazilian Airports.

Table 4.1: Passenger Volumes of Top Five Brazilian Airports

Airport	Passengers		
	2001	**2002**	**Dif.**
São Paulo/Congonhas International Airport	11,707,169	12,446,415	6.3
São Paulo/Guarulhos International Airport	13,098,609	11,902,990	(9.1)
Brasilia International Airport	6,205,864	6,503,720	4.8
Rio de Janeiro Domestic Airport	4,946,542	5,626,328	13.7
Rio de Janeiro/Galeão International Airport	5,987,053	5,269,842	(12.0)

Source: Infraero, 2002

Caves and Gosling (1999) presented a portrait of the situation of the Brazilian Air Transportation industry; some important information from their analyses are given below:

- There are 46 airlines, with a total turnover of US$ 5.2 billion. Brazilian airlines have a 60% share of their international market, which may reflect the fact that almost twice as many Brazilians fly out as foreigners fly in. There is, however, an almost unlimited opportunity for tourism, from beach holidays to ecotourism, once the infrastructure is in place and the tourist is made to feel secure.
- One third of the traffic is with other South American countries, most of the rest being with either the US or Europe.
- The domestic market accounted for over 80% of the 51 million passengers handled at Brazilian airports in 1995. There is only a limited competition from other modes for interstate travel, due to the distances and the lack of a quality rail network, though the cheap and efficient coach services provide well for the low value of time market.

4.1.2. São Paulo/Guarulhos International Airport

Construction of the São Paulo/Guarulhos International Airport started in 1980, with the start of operations in 1985. It has an area of 14 square-km with two terminals, which were initially designed to operate only domestic flights; at that time, the majority of international flights to Brazil were handled by the Rio de Janeiro International Airport. During the last two decades, many airlines transferred their operations to São Paulo, which in 2000 handled 13 million passengers, which made it the airport with the busiest passenger traffic in South America.

Not only is the passenger traffic considerable, but there is a daily circulation of 100 thousand people in this airport, including passengers, employees and visitors. 28 countries are joined to this airport. There are 370 companies operating and 41 airlines. The parking garage has 3,500 parking slots. The schematic view of the airport is presented in Figure 4.1.

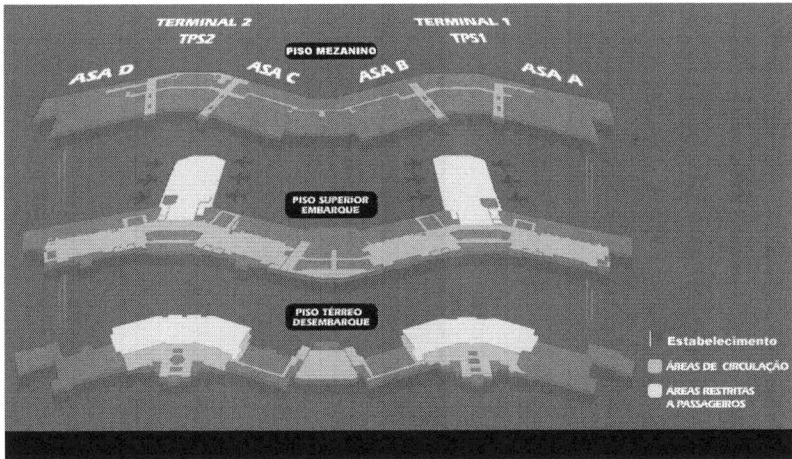

Figure 4.1: Layout of São Paulo/Guarulhos International Airport - Source: www.infraero.gov.br

In the main floor (*piso térreo*) the deplaning operations are processed, while the enplaning operations are processed on the upper floor (*piso superior*). The terminals are designed as pier-fingers. In the Figure above, are the circulation areas (*áreas de circulação*) highlighted in yellow, and the areas restricted to passengers (*áreas restritas a passageiros*) in light yellow. On the mezzanine floor are located some minor commercial stores and services like post office, pharmacy and banks.

Construction of the new terminal (Terminal 3) was planned for 2001, when INFRAERO expected the traffic of 15 million passengers during this year. Nevertheless the project is pending. This forecast has not been reached; on the contrary, in 2002 the passenger movement has declined to less than 12 million passengers a year.

4.1.3. São Paulo/Congonhas Domestic Airport

On April, 12th, 1936 the first flights landed in São Paulo/Congonhas Domestic Airport for testing. After that the land was acquired and the airport construction was started. After more than 60 years, the airport, which is located very close to downtown is surrounded by skyscrapers, making its expansion almost impossible. INFRAERO transferred all regular international flights to São Paulo/Guarulhos International Airport in an attempt to alleviate traffic in that Airport. Even then, its traffic is growing every year; in 2002 it soared above 12 million passengers a year, being the busiest airport in Latin America in that year. Most flights are domestic.

The Airport operates 9 regular airlines, transporting 29 thousand passengers per day, to/from 90 locations in Brazil. It has a big commercial area, which receives not only passengers but also many visitors each day.

The airport is clearly operating beyond its capacity. One of the most important competitive factors compared to São Paulo/Guarulhos International Airport is its location. It is located 10 min away from most business areas, while Guarulhos airport is very far from downtown (about 1 hour drive, in average traffic conditions).

4.1.4. Rio de Janeiro/Galeão ao International Airport

The Rio de Janeiro/Galeão International Airport was supposed to be the busiest airport in Brazil. It was constructed in 1975 for a terminal capacity of 6 million passengers a year. Just two years later, its capacity was practically reached: 5.7 million. In 1990 a large expansion was performed in this airport, but during the last decade, its traffic has declined. For instance, in 2002, its traffic was a little bit more than 5 million passengers a year. INFRAERO affirms that the construction was strategic and air traffic is supposed to grow on next years motivated by tourism. A large amount of domestic traffic was transferred from Rio de Janeiro Domestic to Rio de Janeiro International Airport on September/2004; that would add 6,000 passengers/day to the movement of that airport. This procedure was aimed to alleviate operations at the Rio de Janeiro Domestic airport, whose demand surpassed the capacity many years ago.

4.2. Case Study II: Calgary International Airport - Canada

The air transport network is a fundamental piece of Canada's infrastructure. Some trips within the country are usually performed by air, given the great distances. One trip from Vancouver to Toronto could take several days if done by surface transportation. Surface trips are also not recommended during certain months of the year, due to severe weather. Additionally, Canada has one of the highest per capita incomes in the world, and usually Canadians can afford to travel by air.

The role of airports is changing with the creation of the free trade area between Canada, the United States and Mexico which has liberalized cross-border routes, which has allowed Canadian carriers to obtain equal shares of the cross-border market. The federal authorities own or subsidize 150 airports. A further 300 airports are both owned and operated by the provinces or municipalities. Another 600 airports are owned and operated privately (Caves and Gosling, 1994). Under a new National Airports Policy (NAP), the federal government is now encouraging corporate status and privatization. It is retaining ownership but moving from being an operator to a landlord. The 26 largest airports, forming the newly designated National Airport System (NAS), are being leased for 60 years to Canadian Airport Authorities (CAAs) under enhanced accountability principles.

Calgary International Airport is the fourth busiest airport in Canada and is an important component of the Canadian Civil Air Transport System. The airport functions as an important hub for domestic, transborder and international passengers and air cargo, and is a vital contributor to the economic prosperity of Calgary and the surrounding region.

The control of the airport was transferred to the Calgary Airport Authority in July 1992 under the terms of a Ground Lease agreement with Transport Canada. It is a not-for-profit corporation established under the Alberta Regional Airports Authorities, RSA, 2000 c. R-9. Under the act, the purposes of an airport authority are to:

- manage and operate the airports for which it is responsible in a safe, secure and efficient manner;
- advance economic and community development by means that include promoting and encouraging improved airline and transportation service and an expanded aviation industry.

Calgary's population is approaching 1,000,000 people, although Calgary's market has a population of almost 2,000,000 people. Beyond regional, domestic and transborder routes, international service is provided to countries in Europe and Latin America. Table 4.2 shows the passenger forecasts for the next 20 years.

Table 4.2: Passenger Forecasts for Calgary International Airport

Year	Domestic	Trans-border	Other Int'l	Total Revenue	Non-Revenue	Total
2002	5,532,400	1,436,300	302,300	7,571,000	356,255	7,927,255
2007	6,717,472	1,794,831	795,144	9,307,447	437,900	9,745,347
2012	7,741,472	2,197,716	969,294	10,908,995	513,100	11,422,095
2017	8,731,200	2,618,070	1,156,963	12,506,232	589,100	13,095,332
2022	9,639,950	3,064,640	1,360,900	14,065,490	663,200	14,728,690

Source: Calgary Airport Authority (2004)

The airport just released its Master Plan 2004, where they are planning to build a new parallel runway and expand the terminal to cope with the forecasted demand.

Calgary Airport Authority has approved the conduction of surveys with the air passengers that occurred on January, 19th-23rd, 2004.

4.3. Questionnaires

A questionnaire is a data-collection instrument. It formally sets out the way in which the research questions of interest should be asked. Even simple questions need proper wording and organization to produce accurate information. Consideration needs to be given to how questions should be worded, in the light of objectives of the research, and the target group of respondents who are to be questioned. Attention also needs to be given to the organization of the questionnaire and to its pretesting (Proctor, 2000).

Aaker et al. (1998) suggest a sequence of logical steps that every researcher must follow to develop a good questionnaire:

1. Plan what to measure.
2. Formulate questions to obtain the needed information.
3. Decide on the order and wording of questions and on the layout of the questionnaire.
4. Using a small sample, test the questionnaire for omissions and ambiguity.
5. Correct the problems (and pretest again, if necessary).

These steps were applied to develop the questionnaire. After a long period of planning and thinking about the structure of the questionnaire, it was applied to a preliminary survey at the three Brazilian airports during the Summer/03. Some corrections were made and it was finally applied at the São Paulo /Guarulhos International airport during the Summer/04 and at the Calgary International Airport during the Winter/04. The basic changes were the inclusion of some variables that need to be present in the LOS evaluation. These variables were suggestions made by the users to the interviewers: they are orientation, walking distance, and security environment. Some changes were also made in function of the preliminary statistical analysis. Some variables presented high degree of correlation and should be taken out of the analysis. That was the case for the curbside evaluation. The three variables were very correlated (space available for cars, walking distance, and waiting time). That is why it was decided to evaluate the curbside by the space available for cars only.

The questionnaires were planned with the following guidelines:

1. Use simple language, avoiding technical jargon, ambiguity, and vague words. Even after three applications, it was realized that some words did not prove to be very objective. And in this case, they were removed from the final analysis. One example

of this is the word "circulation". Many interviewees did not know exactly what that meant and needed further explanation.

2. Avoid leading questions and presuming words. We intended to show the users that the survey was being led by the University of Calgary, for academic purposes. That helped to alleviate the pressure on the interviewee.

3. Refrain from relying on the users' memory. The degree of accuracy with which information is recalled is a basic determinant of the quality of the response. One example of this is asking the passenger about precise information, such as the precise time they arrived at the airport, distance they walked, etc.

4. Avoid hypothetical questions. People are not good at predicting their behavior in a hypothetical situation. Example of such a question: how would you rate the level of service if the space available were $2m^2$ per passenger? As opposed to this, it was planned to just ask passengers about the actual level of service, and then measure the space available per passenger, which is more precise.

In this case, the questionnaires were developed with the purpose of getting the following specific information:

- Type of flight: international or domestic. This information is very important, as LOS may be different in each situation.
- Trip purpose: business or non-business. Passengers' expectations are very different depending on the trip purpose. In this case, the LOS evaluations will also be different in each case.
- Movement type: arriving or departing.
- Gender: Male or Female
- Airline. Although most services are performed by the airport administration, the airline has an influence on the level of service proposed. For this reason, LOS analyses must be separated between different airlines.

84

- User opinions about LOS: Five categories are proposed for passengers' ratings: excellent, good, fair, poor, and unacceptable.
- Performance measurement: there is a space in the questionnaire for information on physical measures, which will be taken by an official person assigned by the University of Calgary.

At Appendix A, we present the format of questionnaires. A questionnaire written in Portuguese was also developed for interviewing Brazilian passengers. Attention was paid to provide an accurate translation but still being clear to local passengers.

4.4. Survey Method

One drawback of the simple survey method is that much of the information obtained is based on the interviewees' statements describing what they have done or expect to do in the future. With respect to past actions, the interviewees can make mistakes in trying to recall what has happened, particularly when some time has elapsed since the event. The same kind of problem also applies to their intended actions, since these may also differ markedly from what actually happens. On the other hand, observation involves the personal or mechanical monitoring of selected activities. It records actions as they occur and thus there is no lack of accuracy caused by a respondent's faulty recollection of their past actions or inadequate estimate of future ones. Proctor (2000) affirms that three conditions usually exist if the observation method is to be effectively carried out:

1. The event must be observable: attitudes, motives and other mental activities are difficult to record with the observation method.
2. The event must occur frequently or be predictable.
3. The event must be completed over a short period of time.

The modeling of level of service assumes there is a causal relationship between passenger perceptions (ratings obtained from questionnaire application) and actual physical measures experienced by the passenger. For this reason, before the interview process, several variables will be measured from the curbside to the departure lounge. Simultaneously, the surveyor observes the service performance measurement of the passenger, for instance, waiting time, service processing time, and availability of space. In this idea, a passenger is acting as a 'client' in timing his or her own sequential movements and the surveyor is acting as 'monitor'. Finally, at the departure lounge, surveyors carry on asking the questions using a questionnaire about the passenger subjective perception of the provision of service level through each facility including ground access to airport. The respondent and monitored passenger at each service facility are the same person.

The advantages of the method are: (1) detailed information can be obtained by the tracing and monitoring of the passenger movements at each service activity facility, (2) the respondent for questionnaire and monitored passenger are one, so the reliability of data can be maximized, (3) it is possible to compare the passenger perception of the provided service with actual measures of service performance.

This complete survey method was successfully employed at the three Brazilian airports. A simplified version was applied to Calgary International Airport. In this airport, the users were observed and measured at each individual facility (curbside, check-in, departure lounge, and baggage claim). In this case, it was not possible to get overall measures, like walking distance, walking time, total waiting time, and total processing time. The adoption of this simplified version was due to security procedures existing at that airport.

4.5. Description of Components

The terminal area is the major interface between the airfield and the rest of the airport. It includes the facilities for passenger and baggage processing, cargo handling, and airport maintenance, operations, and administration activities. The passenger terminal system has three major components. These components and the activities that occur within them are as follows (Horonjeff & McKelvey, 1994):

1. The *access interface* where the passenger transfers from the access mode of travel to the passenger processing component. Circulation, parking, and curbside loading and unloading of passengers are the activities that take place within this component.
2. *Processing*, where the passenger is processed in preparation for starting, ending, or continuation of an air transportation trip. The primary activities in this component are ticketing, baggage check-in, baggage claim, seat assignment, federal inspection, services, and security.
3. The *flight interface* where the passenger transfers from the processing component to the aircraft. The activities that occur here include assembly, conveyance to and from the aircraft, and aircraft loading and unloading.

We summarize below all the components, for which LOS will be evaluated within the scope of this research:

Departing Passengers:
- Enplaning Curbside
- Ticket Counter and Baggage Deposit
- Security Screening.
- Departure Lounge
- Circulation and Orientation
- Total Time

- Concessions

Arriving Passengers:

- Baggage Claim Area

A brief description of these components is presented in this section. A complete description and an explanation of why particular variables have been selected for analysis will be presented on subsequent chapters.

4.5.1. Curbside

The curbside element is the interface between the terminal building and the ground transportation system. Increasing traffic volumes in association with its peaking characteristics, and the complicated situation of people and vehicles merging, may result in extensive traffic congestion at the curbside area. This in turn causes inconvenience, frustration, and delay to passengers at large airports. Because of arbitrary standards applied in many airports, oversized or undersized facilities might be provided at an airport, resulting in unbalanced operations of the components of that facility. The airport community is therefore interested in a methodology that could lead to rational standards (Siddiqui, 1994).

Passengers were asked to rate (1 to 5) the space available for cars, walking distance at the curbside, waiting time to find a parking position and the overall curbside. In turn, the interviewer was supposed to measure the total virtual length of cars, the length of the curbside, the walking distance the passenger walked from car to entrance door, and the time cars had to wait to find a parking position. The total virtual length of cars eventually may be longer than the actual curbside length. That is due to double or triple car lines. That may happen in cases where the cars are parked beyond the actual curbside area.

88

4.5.2. Ticket Counter and Baggage Deposit

The airline ticket counter is where the airline and passenger make final ticket transactions and check in baggage for a flight. The ticket transaction takes place at the ticket counter, which is a stand-up desk. To the left and right of the ticket counter position, a low shelf is provided to deposit, check in, tag, and weigh baggage, if necessary, for the flight. Subsequently, the baggage is passed back by the agent to an outbound baggage conveyance device located near the counter. The check-in counters located in Brazil and at the Calgary International Airport operate with a single line for each individual airline.

Passengers were asked to rate (1 to 5) the waiting time at the queues, the processing time at the counter, the space available at the queue and the overall check-in. The interviewer was supposed to measure the waiting time, processing time, area available at the queue divided by the number of people standing in line, number of hand bags, checked-in bags, baggage carts, and party size.

4.5.3. Security Screening

Not long ago, security problems at airports were confined mainly to the "conventional" crimes associated with other high activity centers of the transportation modes: vandalism, theft, breaking and entering, and even crimes against the person. Since the late 1960s, airports and civil aviation have also become the focus of politically motivated crimes of general terrorism and the phenomenon of aircraft hijacking (Ashford et. al, 1984). Security screening of all airline passengers is an extremely important function in an airport terminal. Security screening of passengers and of hand-carried articles is required prior to boarding airline aircraft (Horonjeff & McKelvey, 1994).

This component was surveyed at the three Brazilian airports, but not at the Calgary International Airport. That was not allowed for security procedures existing at that airport. The processing of passengers at security screening counters located in Brazilian

89

airports is very fast, when compared to airports located in North America. In most of the cases, the waiting and processing times were shorter than 60 seconds. For instance, the longer waiting during all survey periods was 8 minutes. Passengers were asked to rate (1 to 5) the waiting time, processing time, and space available at the queue. In turn the interviewer measured the actual times, and space available per passenger at the queue.

4.5.4. Departure Lounge

The departure lounge serves as an assembly area for passengers waiting to board a particular flight and as the exit passageway for deplaning passengers. It is generally sized to accommodate the number of boarding passengers expected to be in the lounge 15 min prior to the scheduled departure time, assuming this is the time when aircraft boarding begins. The space should accommodate seating for these passengers (although not all need to be seated), space for airline processing plus passengers queues, and an exitway for deplaning passengers. It is customary to allow ticketed passengers only to enter the departure lounge. That was the procedure adopted at the four surveyed airports.

Passengers were asked to rate (1 to 5) the waiting time, number of seats available, area size, and the overall departure lounge. The interviewer measured the waiting time and the number of passengers in the lounge at the moment at the interview. Additionally, the number of seats and the size of the lounge was taken for each departure lounge.

4.5.5. Circulation and Orientation

In general, the terminal circulation component is considered a pedestrian circulation problem and analyzed by using procedures and standards such as those suggested in TRB's Highway Capacity Manual (1985). The length of the passenger's pathway, the passenger's walking speed, number of level changes, and the degree of interference the passenger encounters along the way are key variables in the assessment.

Orientation can be defined as a person's perception of his position, relative to the surroundings, while walking, using mechanical systems, or driving a vehicle (Hart, 1985). When an airport provides poor orientation systems, this might cause unfamiliar passengers to walk more than necessary, causing inconvenience, frustration, and delays in some extreme cases.

The passengers were asked to rate (1 to 5) the circulation component, walking distance, and orientation. In turn, the interviewer measured the total waking distance, the minimum walking distance, and walking time for each interviewed passenger. A pedometer was used to obtain these distances. The total walking distance was defined as the actual distance the interviewer walked to get from curbside to gate. The minimum walking distance was defined as the real attainable distance from curbside to the assigned gate of the interviewed.

4.5.6. Total Time

The main advantage of air transport is to reduce the travel time from origin to destination. To achieve this objective, the processing time at the airport should be minimized. For this reason, passengers were asked to rate (1 to 5) the total waiting + processing time at the airport. The interviewer measured the total waiting time (the sum of waiting time at check-in, security screening and departure lounge) and total processing time (the sum of processing time at check-in, security screening and boarding gate).

4.5.7. Concessions

The factors that influence the extent of passenger amenities include the passenger volume, community size, location and extent of off-airport services, interests and abilities of potential concessionaires, and rental rates. These generally include (Horonjeff & McKelvey, 1994):

- food and beverage services, newsstands, and tobacco stands;

- drugstores; gift, clothing, and florist shops;
- barber shops and shoe shine stands;
- counters for car rental and flight insurance companies;
- public lockers and public and courtesy telephones;
- staffed or automated post offices;
- amusement arcades and vending machines;
- public rest rooms and nursery.

An earlier passenger survey by Seneviratne and Martel (1991) revealed that accessibility to concessions and services is the second most significant characteristic, or indicator, of performance in waiting areas. The concessions in that study included rest rooms, communication facilities (i.e., phones and facsimile), retail outlets, and restaurants.

Passengers were asked to rate (1 to 5) the concessions at the Brazilian airports. No physical measure was recorded in this case, due to the subjective characteristic of this component.

4.5.8. Baggage Claim

This component was surveyed at the Calgary International Airport. Passengers were asked to rate (1 to 5) the processing time, claim frontage, area size, and the overall baggage claim. The interviewer measured the processing time (time the passenger stands at the carrousel waiting for all bags), length of the carrousel divided by the number of people in the room, and the area size of the room (minus the carrousel area) divided by the number of people in the room.

4.5.9. Overall Terminal

Passengers were asked to rate (1 to 5) the overall experience at the terminal. This variable will be used to get overall LOS measures for an airport passenger terminal.

4.6. Summary of Responses

400 passengers have been observed and interviewed at the four airports. 14 questionnaires were discarded for lacking important information. In this case, 386 surveys have been considered good for analysis. The number of surveys for each airport is shown in Table 4.3:

Table 4.3: Number of Complete Interviews Performed at the Four Airports

Airport	Domestic Passengers	International Passengers	Total
Rio de Janeiro International	23	12	35
São Paulo/Congonhas International	30	0	30
São Paulo/Guarulhos International	56	63	119
Calgary International Airport	109	93	202
Total	**218**	**168**	**386**

Although São Paulo/Congonhas Airport operates some international flights, it does not operate regular international flights. That is why all surveys in that airport were realized with domestic passengers.

4.6.1. Trip Purpose

Table 4.4 shows the distribution of respondents as a function of trip purpose and airport.

93

Table 4.4: Distribution of Responses by Trip Purpose

Airport	Business	Non-Business	Combined
Rio de Janeiro International	18	17	0
São Paulo/Congonhas International	23	7	0
São Paulo/Guarulhos International	57	53	9
Calgary International Airport	96	102	4
Total	194	179	13

These numbers show a good balance between business and non-business passengers.

4.6.2. Gender

Table 4.5 shows the distribution of passengers by gender.

Table 4.5 - Distribution of Responses by Gender

Airport	Male	Female
Rio de Janeiro International	22	13
São Paulo/Congonhas International	20	10
São Paulo/Guarulhos International	86	33
Calgary International Airport	136	66
Total	264	122

4.6.3. Airlines

Tables 4.6 and 4.7 provide information on the airline utilized by interviewed passengers:

Table 4.6: Airlines at Brazilian Airports

Airline	Country of Airline	Respondents
Aero Mexico	Mexico	3
Aerolineas Argentinas	Argentina	3
Air Canada	Canada	5
Air France	France	3
Alitalia	Italy	5
American Airlines	United States	2
British Airways	England	2
Copa	Panama	2
Delta Airlines	United States	4
Gol	Brazil	14
Iberia	Spain	3
Lanchile	Chile	1
Lufthansa	Germany	8
South African	South Africa	2
Swiss	Switzerland	8
TAM	Brazil	30
TAP	Portugal	10
United Airlines	United States	4
Varig	Brazil	69
Vasp	Brazil	6
	Total	**184**

Table 4.7: Airlines at the Calgary International Airport

Airline	Country of Airline	Respondents
Air Canada	Canada	63
Air Transat	Canada	5
America West	United States	6
American Airlines	United States	19
Canadian North	Canada	1
Jazz	Canada	4
Northwest	United States	7
Sky Service	Canada	4
United Airlines	United States	19
Westjet	Canada	70
Zip	Canada	4
	Total	**202**

There are other airlines operating at these airports; they are not represented in the chart above because the passengers that utilize them were not interviewed in this survey.

4.6.4. Space Available for Cars

This variable provided the perceptions of the passengers, regarding the space available for cars at the curbside. Table 4.8 and Figure 4.2 provide the distribution of responses for the rating of this variable.

Table 4.8: Rating of Space Available for Cars: Distribution of Responses

Rating Category	Responses							
	Rio de Janeiro Intl.		São Paulo Guarulhos		São Paulo Congonhas		Calgary International	
1	0	0.0%	0	0.0%	3	10.0%	1	3.3%
2	1	2.9%	11	9.2%	5	16.7%	5	16.7%
3	3	8.6%	26	21.8%	13	43.3%	8	26.7%
4	20	57.1%	67	56.3%	8	26.7%	11	36.7%
5	11	31.4%	15	12.6%	1	3.3%	5	16.7%
Total	35	100.0%	119	100.0%	30	100.0%	30	100.0%

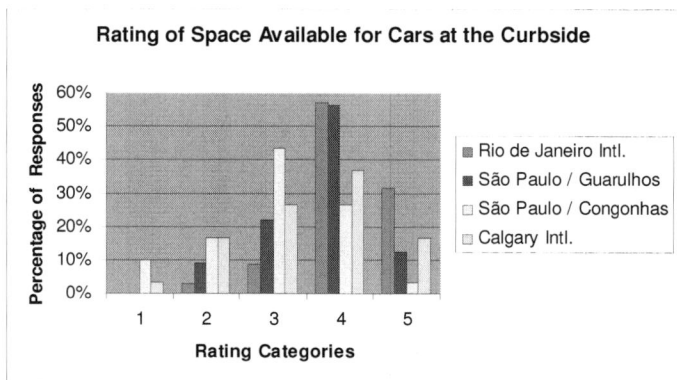

Figure 4.2: Rating of Space Available for Cars

4.6.5. Walking Distance at the Curbside Area

This variable represents the rating passengers attribute for the distance they walk from the car parked at curbside to the front door. No respondent passenger has rated this variable as unacceptable. Table 4.9 and Figure 4.3 provide the distribution of responses for the rating of this variable.

Table 4.9: Rating of Walking Distance at the Curbside: Distribution of Responses

Rating Category	Responses							
	Rio de Janeiro Intl.		São Paulo Guarulhos		São Paulo Congonhas		Calgary International	
1	0	0.0%	0	0.0%	0	0.0%	0	0.0%
2	0	0.0%	1	2.5%	4	13.3%	3	10.0%
3	4	11.4%	6	15.0%	2	6.7%	9	30.0%
4	18	51.4%	20	50.0%	21	70.0%	11	36.7%
5	13	37.1%	13	32.5%	3	10.0%	7	23.3%
Total	35	100.0%	40	100.0%	30	100.0%	30	100.0%

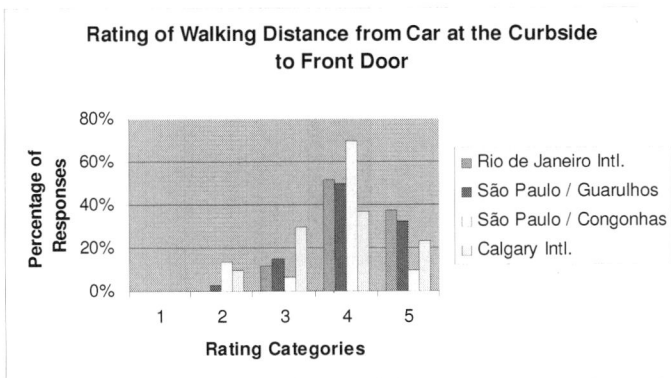

Figure 4.3: Rating of Walking Distance from Curbside to Front Door

4.6.6. Waiting Time at the Curbside

This variable represents the time drivers have to wait to find a parking spot at the enplaning curbside. In very busy periods this time is supposed to be very high, decreasing the level of service provided at this facility. Table 4.10 and Figure 4.4 provide the distribution of responses for the rating of this variable.

Table 4.10: Rating of Waiting Time at the Curbside – Distribution of Responses

Rating Category	Responses							
	Rio de Janeiro Intl.		São Paulo Guarulhos		São Paulo Congonhas		Calgary International	
1	0	0.0%	0	0.0%	3	10.0%	0	0.0%
2	1	2.9%	0	0.0%	2	6.7%	2	6.7%
3	3	8.6%	5	12.5%	4	13.3%	7	23.3%
4	20	57.1%	19	47.5%	16	53.3%	15	50.0%
5	11	31.4%	16	40.0%	5	16.7%	6	20.0%
Total	**35**	**100.0%**	**40**	**100.0%**	**30**	**100.0%**	**30**	**100.0%**

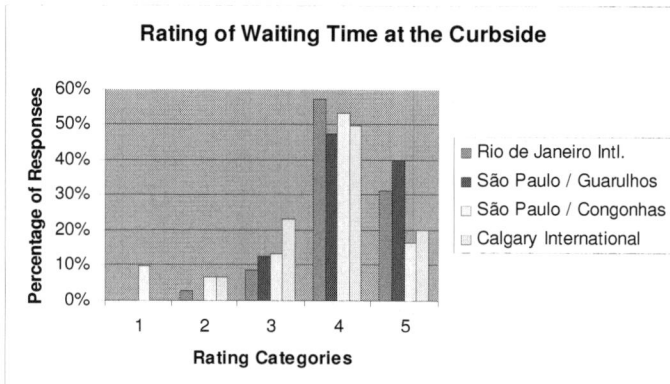

Figure 4.4: Rating of Waiting Time at the Curbside

4.6.7. Overall Rating of the Curbside

After rating individual performance measures of the curbside, the passengers were finally asked to provide a rating for the curbside as a whole. Table 4.11 and Figure 4.5 provide the distribution of responses for the rating of this variable.

Table 4.11: Overall Curbside Ratings: Distribution of Responses

Rating Category	Responses							
	Rio de Janeiro Intl.		São Paulo Guarulhos		São Paulo Congonhas		Calgary International	
1	0	0.0%	0	0.0%	3	10.0%	0	0.0%
2	0	0.0%	0	0.0%	4	13.3%	3	10.0%
3	3	8.6%	4	10.0%	4	13.3%	7	23.3%
4	19	54.3%	27	67.5%	18	60.0%	15	50.0%
5	13	37.1%	9	22.5%	1	3.3%	5	16.7%
Total	35	100.0%	40	100.0%	30	100.0%	30	100.0%

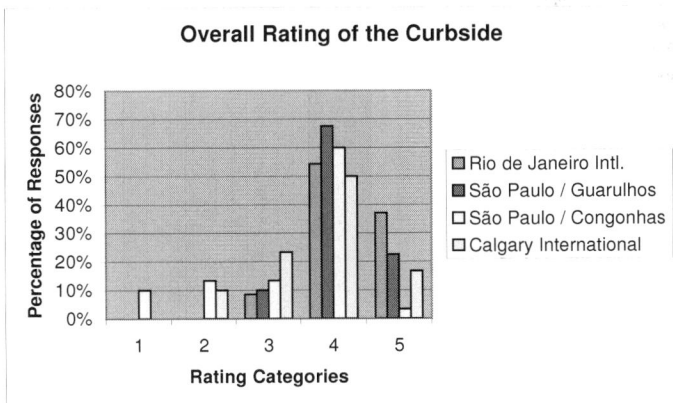

Figure 4.5: Overall Curbside Ratings

100

4.6.8. Waiting Time at the Check-in Counter

The time passengers have to wait in queue until getting to the check-in counter is represented by the Waiting Time variable. During this time the passenger stays in a line with his/her bags, sometimes with baggage carts. Table 4.12 and Figure 4.6 provide the distribution of responses for the rating of this variable.

Table 4.12: Rating of Waiting Time at the Check-in: Distribution of Responses

Rating Category	Responses							
	Rio de Janeiro Intl.		São Paulo Guarulhos		São Paulo Congonhas		Calgary International	
1	0	0.0%	5	4.2%	0	0.0%	0	0.0%
2	0	0.0%	13	10.9%	0	0.0%	3	4.8%
3	2	5.7%	24	20.2%	5	16.7%	16	25.8%
4	10	28.6%	51	42.9%	14	46.7%	22	35.5%
5	23	65.7%	26	21.8%	11	36.7%	21	33.9%
Total	35	100.0%	119	100.0%	30	100.0%	62	100.0%

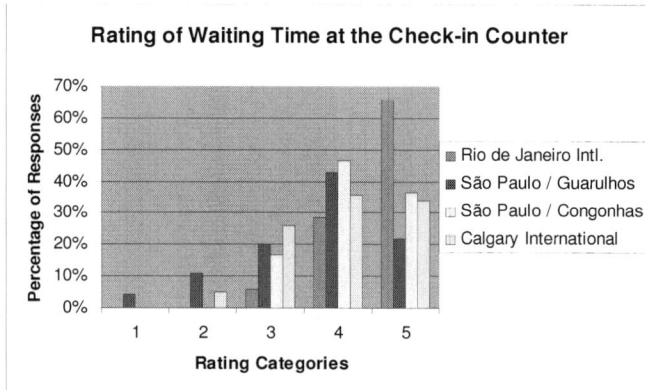

Figure 4.6: Rating of Waiting Time at Check-in Counter

4.6.9. Processing Time at the Check-in Counter

After waiting in the line, the passengers are ready to be processed at the check-in counter. During this time, passengers are checked-in, documents are checked and luggage is deposited (except hand baggage). Usually this processing time is dependable on the number of checked bags, passengers checked-in and airline procedures. Table 4.13 and Figure 4.7 provide the distribution of responses for the rating of this variable.

Table 4.13: Rating of Processing Time at the Check-in: Distribution of Responses

Rating Category	Responses							
	Rio de Janeiro Intl.		São Paulo Guarulhos		São Paulo Congonhas		Calgary International	
1	1	2.9%	2	1.7%	0	0.0%	0	0.0%
2	0	0.0%	4	3.4%	0	0.0%	2	3.2%
3	2	5.7%	10	8.4%	0	0.0%	1	1.6%
4	12	34.3%	69	58.0%	17	56.7%	25	40.3%
5	20	57.1%	34	28.6%	13	43.3%	34	54.8%
Total	35	100.0%	119	100.0%	30	100.0%	62	100.0%

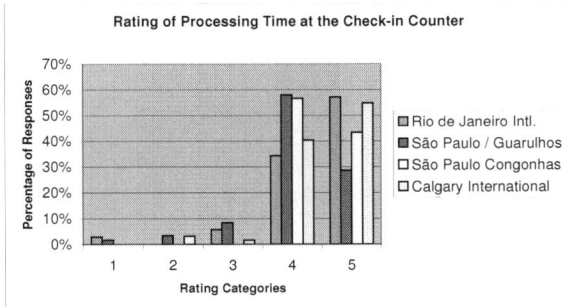

Figure 4.7: Rating of Processing Time at the Check-in Counter

4.6.10. Availability of Space at the Check-in Counter

This variable represents the space available for passengers while in the line. This space should be capable of accommodating the passengers, bags, baggage carts and people accompanying the passengers. There are some cases where this space is not enough and people invade the circulation area, making the check-in area very confusing and very crowded. Table 4.14 and Figure 4.8 provide the distribution of responses for the rating of this variable.

Table 4.14: Rating of Space at the Check-in Line: Distribution of Responses

Rating Category	Responses							
	Rio de Janeiro Intl.		São Paulo Guarulhos		São Paulo Congonhas		Calgary International	
1	0	0.0%	0	0.0%	0	0.0%	0	0.0%
2	0	0.0%	3	2.5%	1	3.3%	0	0.0%
3	0	0.0%	18	15.1%	6	20.0%	7	11.3%
4	8	22.9%	74	62.2%	15	50.0%	30	48.4%
5	27	77.1%	24	20.2%	8	26.7%	25	40.3%
Total	35	100.0%	119	100.0%	30	100.0%	62	100.0%

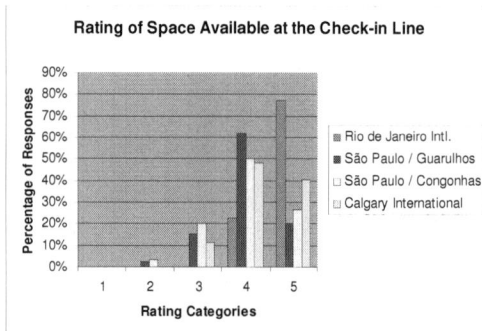

Figure 4.8: Rating of Availability of Space at Check-in Counter Line

103

4.6.11. Overall Rating of the Check-in Counter

This variable measures the passenger overall perception about the level of service provided at the check-in facility. Rio de Janeiro Airport has been highly rated, when the majority of passengers rate it as excellent (65.7%). Even the other surveyed airports have the majority of passengers rating the check-in facility as good or excellent. In all airports, no passenger has rated the check-in as unacceptable and only 4 passengers rated it as poor. Table 4.15 and Figure 4.9 provide the distribution of responses for this variable.

Table 4.15: Overall Rating of the Check-in Counter: Distribution of Responses

Rating Category	Responses							
	Rio de Janeiro Intl.		São Paulo Guarulhos		São Paulo Congonhas		Calgary International	
1	0	0.0%	0	0.0%	0	0.0%	0	0.0%
2	0	0.0%	4	3.4%	0	0.0%	0	0.0%
3	1	2.9%	18	15.1%	5	16.7%	7	11.3%
4	11	31.4%	75	63.0%	18	60.0%	31	50.0%
5	23	65.7%	22	18.5%	7	23.3%	24	38.7%
Total	35	100.0%	119	100.0%	30	100.0%	62	100.0%

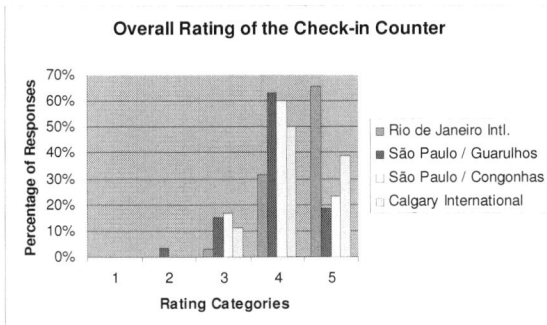

Figure 4.9: Overall Rating of the Check-in Counter

4.6.12. Waiting Time at the Security Screening

This variable represents the time passengers have to stand in line before being processed at the security screening. The distribution of responses shows that the three airports have similar data with high concentration of responses between rating categories 4 and 5. Only 2 interviewed passengers have rated the waiting time at security screening as unacceptable or poor and only 9 passengers have rated it as fair. Table 4.16 and Figure 4.10 provide the distribution of responses for the rating of this variable.

Table 4.16: Rating of Waiting Time at Security: Distribution of Responses

Rating Category	Responses					
	Rio de Janeiro Intl.		São Paulo Guarulhos		São Paulo Congonhas	
1	0	0.0%	1	0.8%	0	0.0%
2	0	0.0%	1	0.8%	0	0.0%
3	1	2.9%	7	5.9%	1	3.3%
4	10	28.6%	59	50.0%	14	46.7%
5	24	68.6%	50	42.4%	15	50.0%
Total	**35**	**100.0%**	**118**	**100.0%**	**30**	**100.0%**

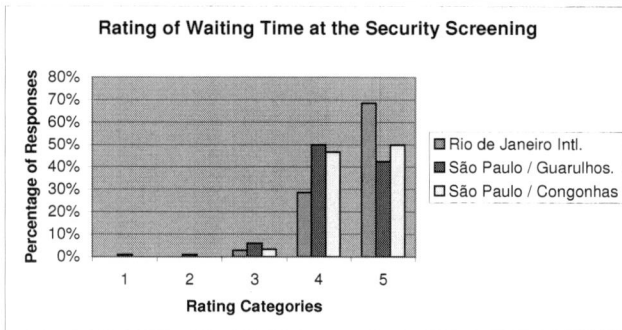

Figure 4.10: Rating of Waiting Time at the Security Screening

4.6.13. Processing Time at the Security Screening

This variable represents the time passengers stay at security screening while being processed. In most of the cases one single inspection is enough, but there are situations where the passenger is asked to proceed again through the metal detector. Once again the responses present a very high concentration of answers between categories 4 and 5 and only 2 interviewed passengers have rated the service as unacceptable or poor. Table 4.17 and Figure 4.11 provide the distribution of responses for the rating of this variable.

Table 4.17: Rating of Processing Time at Security - Distribution of Responses

Rating Category	Responses					
	Rio de Janeiro Intl.		São Paulo Guarulhos		São Paulo Congonhas	
1	0	0.0%	1	0.8%	0	0.0%
2	0	0.0%	1	0.8%	0	0.0%
3	1	2.9%	8	6.8%	0	0.0%
4	9	25.7%	58	49.2%	18	60.0%
5	25	71.4%	50	42.4%	12	40.0%
Total	35	100.0%	118	100.0%	30	100.0%

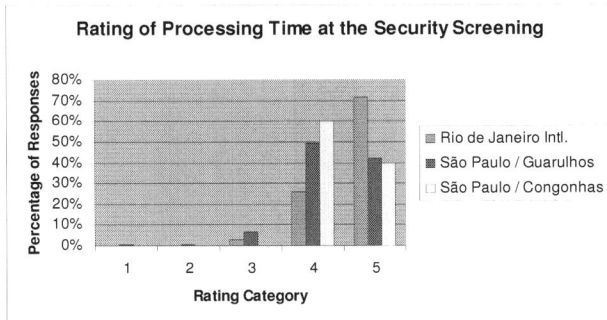

Figure 4.11: Rating of Processing Time at the Security Screening

4.6.14. Space Available at the Security Screening

Differently from waiting time and processing time, the variable availability of space has shown different results for each airport evaluated. As we can see by the Table and chart below, Rio de Janeiro International presented the better performance and São Paulo / Congonhas the worst performance according to passenger perceptions. Even then, most of the responses qualify the service as good or excellent in all airports. Table 4.18 and Figure 4.12 provide the distribution of responses for the rating of this variable.

Table 4.18: Rating of Space at Security - Distribution of Responses

Rating Category	Responses					
	Rio de Janeiro Intl.		São Paulo Guarulhos		São Paulo Congonhas	
1	0	0.0%	1	0.8%	0	0.0%
2	0	0.0%	2	1.7%	2	6.7%
3	1	2.9%	12	10.2%	8	26.7%
4	10	28.6%	61	51.7%	11	36.7%
5	24	68.6%	42	35.6%	9	30.0%
Total	**35**	**100.0%**	**118**	**100.0%**	**30**	**100.0%**

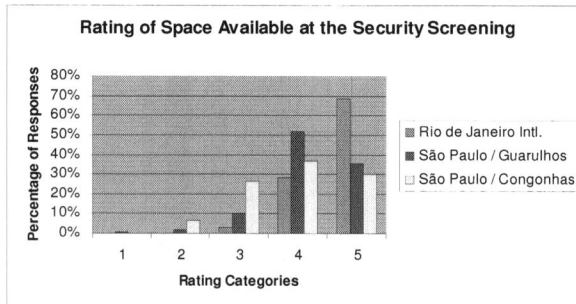

Figure 4.12: Rating of Space Available at the Security Screening

4.6.15. Overall Rating of the Security Screening

The overall rating of security screening is evaluated by the majority of passengers as good or excellent. In Rio de Janeiro, the majority of passengers rate it as excellent while in São Paulo Airports that does not happen. A greater concentration of fair category responses is observed for the overall rating, as opposed to waiting time, processing time and availability of space evaluations. Table 4.19 and Figure 4.13 provide the distribution of responses for the rating of this variable.

Table 4.19: Overall Rating of Security - Distribution of Responses

Rating Category	Responses					
	Rio de Janeiro Intl.		São Paulo Guarulhos		São Paulo Congonhas	
1	0	0.0%	2	1.7%	0	0.0%
2	0	0.0%	4	3.4%	2	6.7%
3	2	5.7%	12	10.2%	4	13.3%
4	11	31.4%	64	54.2%	17	56.7%
5	22	62.9%	36	30.5%	7	23.3%
Total	**35**	**100.0%**	**118**	**100.0%**	**30**	**100.0%**

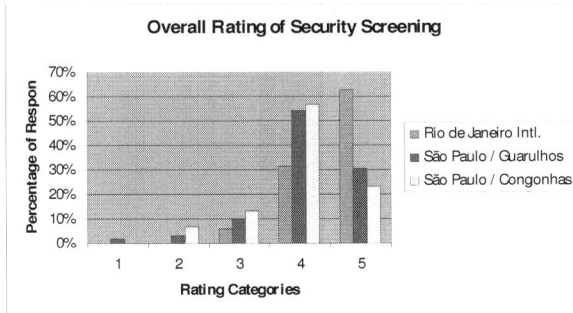

Figure 4.13: Overall Rating of the Security Screening

4.6.16. Waiting Time at the Departure Lounge

This amount of time prior to departure that passengers must arrive at the departure lounge varies from 30 minutes to 1 hour depending if the flight is domestic, international and country that passengers are flying to. The majority of respondents rated it as good or excellent at Rio de Janeiro. It is interesting to note that 13.3% of interviewed passengers at São Paulo / Congonhas rate the waiting time as unacceptable or poor, meaning that this considerable amount of passengers are very dissatisfied with the time they have to wait. Table 4.20 and Figure 4.14 provide the distribution of responses for the rating of this variable.

Table 4.20: Rating of Waiting Time at the Lounge: Distribution of Responses

Rating Category	Responses							
	Rio de Janeiro Intl.		São Paulo Guarulhos		São Paulo Congonhas		Calgary International	
1	1	2.9%	1	0.9%	1	3.3%	2	3.9%
2	0	0.0%	7	6.0%	3	10.0%	2	3.9%
3	4	11.4%	32	27.4%	10	33.3%	21	41.2%
4	16	45.7%	58	49.6%	13	43.3%	24	47.1%
5	14	40.0%	19	16.2%	3	10.0%	2	3.9%
Total	35	100.0%	117	100.0%	30	100.0%	51	100.0%

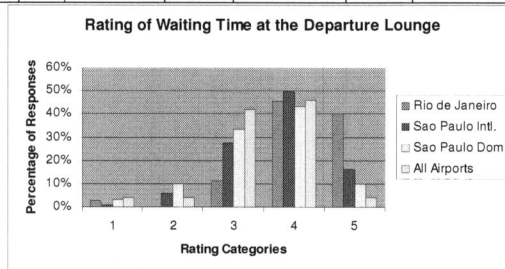

Figure 4.14: Rating of Waiting Time at the Departure Lounge

109

4.6.17. Number of Seats at the Departure Lounge

Considering that passengers will stay a considerable time at the departure lounge, it is important that seats be provided as close as possible to the boarding gates. Passengers were asked to rate the level of service according to number of seats at departure lounge. Rio de Janeiro has been evaluated as excellent by the majority of respondents and no passengers rating the service as unacceptable or poor. This figure is a lot different on the remaining surveyed airports. Table 4.21 and Figure 4.15 provide the distribution of responses for the rating of this variable.

Table 4.21: Rating of Number of Seats at the Lounge: Distribution of Responses

Rating Category	Responses							
	Rio de Janeiro Intl.		São Paulo Guarulhos		São Paulo Congonhas		Calgary International	
1	0	0.0%	5	4.3%	1	3.3%	3	5.9%
2	0	0.0%	21	17.9%	3	10.0%	6	11.8%
3	1	2.9%	30	25.6%	5	16.7%	11	21.6%
4	13	37.1%	41	35.0%	16	53.3%	25	49.0%
5	21	60.0%	20	17.1%	5	16.7%	6	11.8%
Total	35	100.0%	117	100.0%	30	100.0%	51	100.0%

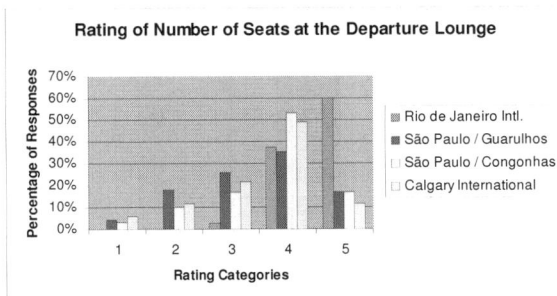

Figure 4.15: Rating of Number of Seats at the Departure Lounge

4.6.18. Space Available at the Departure Lounge

The third variable passengers have been asked to rate is the availability of space at the departure lounge. That space must be enough for passengers to circulate and wait (stand or sited). Since most passengers have hand luggage, that space must be able to accommodate these bags. Table 4.22 and Figure 4.16 provide the distribution of responses for the rating of this variable.

Table 4.22: Rating of Space Available at the Lounge: Distribution of Responses

Rating Category	Responses							
	Rio de Janeiro Intl.		São Paulo Guarulhos		São Paulo Congonhas		Calgary International	
1	0	0.0%	3	2.6%	1	3.3%	2	3.9%
2	0	0.0%	7	6.0%	4	13.3%	5	9.8%
3	1	2.9%	31	26.5%	5	16.7%	9	17.6%
4	14	40.0%	48	41.0%	17	56.7%	29	56.9%
5	20	57.1%	28	23.9%	3	10.0%	6	11.8%
Total	**35**	**100.0%**	**117**	**100.0%**	**30**	**100.0%**	**51**	**100.0%**

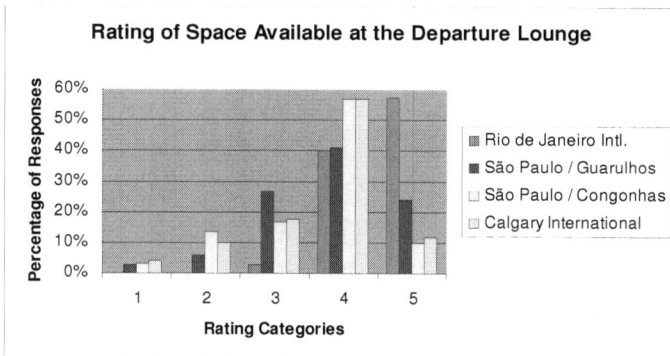

Figure 4.16: Rating of Space Available at the Departure Lounge

4.6.19. Overall Rating of the Departure Lounge

This variable provides an overall perception of passengers concerning the level of service provided at the departure lounge. Since passengers were interviewed a few minutes prior to boarding time, they had time to experience the quality at this facility. The answers are very reasonable to what should be expected compared to the ratings of the three variables: waiting time, number of seats and availability of space. Table 4.23 and Figure 4.17 provide the distribution of responses for the rating of this variable.

Table 4.23: Overall Rating of the Departure Lounge: Distribution of Responses

Rating Category	Responses							
	Rio de Janeiro Intl.		São Paulo Guarulhos		São Paulo Congonhas		Calgary International	
1	0	0.0%	3	2.6%	1	3.3%	2	3.9%
2	0	0.0%	8	6.8%	2	6.7%	1	2.0%
3	3	8.6%	34	29.1%	8	26.7%	16	31.4%
4	16	45.7%	54	46.2%	16	53.3%	28	54.9%
5	16	45.7%	18	15.4%	3	10.0%	4	7.8%
Total	35	100.0%	117	100.0%	30	100.0%	51	100.0%

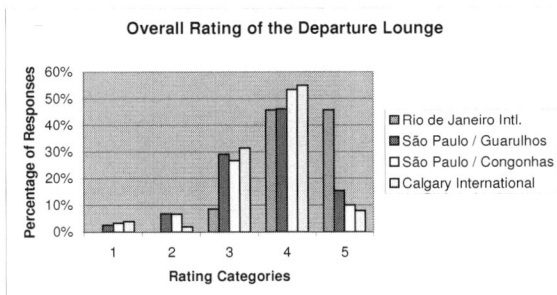

Figure 4.17: Overall Rating of the Departure Lounge

112

4.6.20. Access Facilities

Passengers were asked to rate the level of service according to access to the airport. For this variable, Rio de Janeiro Airport presented the worst performance when compared to the previous variables; 37.2% of passengers interviewed rate the access facilities as unacceptable, poor or fair. In addition, only 31.4% rate the access to the airport as excellent, the lowest value for the excellent category in this survey. Although the majority of respondents in Sao Paulo Domestic rate the access facilities as good, no passenger has rated it as excellent. Table 4.24 and Figure 4.18 provide the distribution of responses for the rating of this variable.

Table 4.24: Rating of Access Facilities: Distribution of Responses

Rating Category	Responses							
	Rio de Janeiro Intl.		São Paulo Guarulhos		São Paulo Congonhas		All Airports	
1	1	2.9%	2	5.0%	0	0.0%	3	2.9%
2	5	14.3%	5	12.5%	2	6.7%	12	11.4%
3	7	20.0%	9	22.5%	11	36.7%	27	25.7%
4	11	31.4%	17	42.5%	17	56.7%	45	42.9%
5	11	31.4%	7	17.5%	0	0.0%	18	17.1%
Total	**35**	**100.0%**	**40**	**100.0%**	**30**	**100.0%**	**105**	**100.0%**

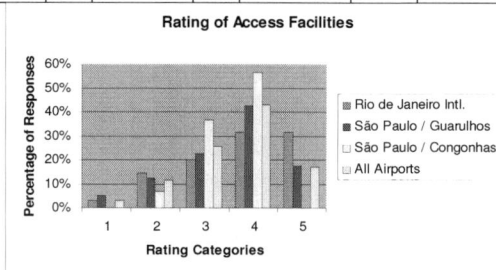

Figure 4.18: Rating of Access Facilities

4.6.21. Circulation

This variable represents all facilities that provide circulation within the airport: corridors, stairs, elevators and circulation area. Table 4.25 and Figure 4.19 provide the distribution of responses for the rating of this variable.

Table 4.25: Rating of Circulation: Distribution of Responses

Rating Category	Responses					
	Rio de Janeiro Intl.		São Paulo Guarulhos		São Paulo Congonhas	
1	0	0.0%	1	0.8%	3	10.0%
2	0	0.0%	4	3.4%	3	10.0%
3	6	17.1%	20	16.9%	10	33.3%
4	13	37.1%	75	63.6%	11	36.7%
5	16	45.7%	18	15.3%	3	10.0%
Total	**35**	**100.0%**	**118**	**100.0%**	**30**	**100.0%**

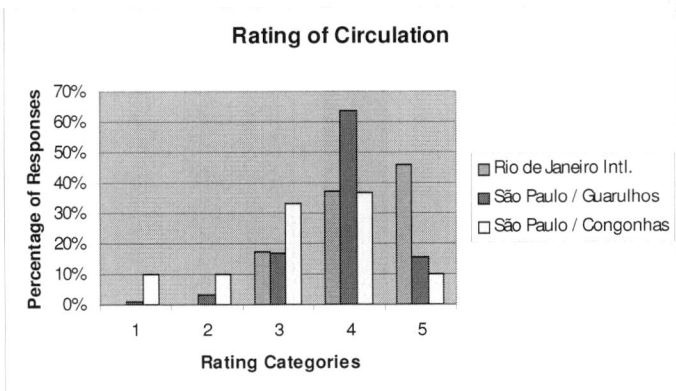

Figure 4.19: Rating of Circulation

4.6.22. Concessions

The concessions variable represents the level of service provided at the airport as per the commercial areas inside the airport terminal. Since the passengers were interviewed inside the departure lounge, they had time to visit the shops or at least pass by them. In Sao Paulo Domestic, 43.3% of respondent passengers rate the concessions as unacceptable, poor or fair; in Rio de Janeiro International and São Paulo / Guarulhos these numbers are 25.7% and 40.7% respectively. Table 4.26 and Figure 4.20 provide the distribution of responses for the rating of this variable.

Table 4.26: Rating of Concessions: Distribution of Responses

Rating Category	Responses					
	Rio de Janeiro Intl.		São Paulo Guarulhos		São Paulo Congonhas	
1	0	0.0%	1	0.8%	1	3.3%
2	2	5.7%	8	6.8%	5	16.7%
3	7	20.0%	39	33.1%	7	23.3%
4	17	48.6%	53	44.9%	15	50.0%
5	9	25.7%	17	14.4%	2	6.7%
Total	**35**	**100.0%**	**118**	**100.0%**	**30**	**100.0%**

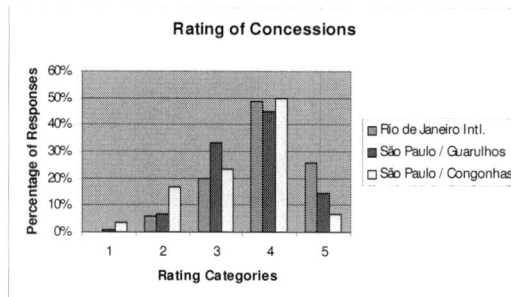

Figure 4.20: Rating of Concessions

4.6.23. Walking Distance, Orientation, and Total Time.

These three overall measures were collected during the second survey at São Paulo / Guarulhos International Airport. Table 4.27 and Figure 4.21 present the distribution of responses.

Table 4.27: Rating of overall measures: São Paulo / Guarulhos Airport

Rating Category	Responses					
	Walking Distance		Orientation		Total Time	
1	0	0.0%	2	2.6%	0	0.0%
2	9	11.7%	9	11.7%	4	5.1%
3	21	27.3%	14	18.2%	18	23.1%
4	38	49.4%	41	53.2%	43	55.1%
5	9	11.7%	11	14.3%	13	16.7%
Total	77	100.0%	77	100.0%	78	100.0%

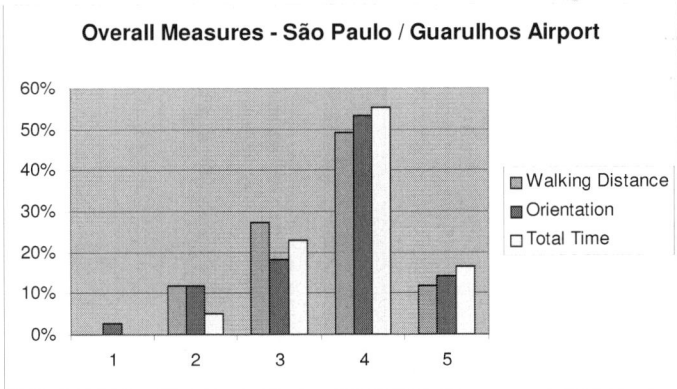

Figure 4.21: Rating of Overall Measures at São Paulo / Guarulhos International Airport

4.6.24. Baggage Claim

Passengers were asked to provide the opinion about the baggage claim services at Calgary International Airport. Table 4.28 and Figure 4.22 provide the distribution of responses.

Table 4.28: Ratings of Baggage Claim - Calgary International Airport

Rating Category	Responses							
	Processing Time		Claim Frontage		Availability of Space		Overall Bag. Claim	
1	0	0.0%	0	0.0%	0	0.0%	0	0.0%
2	8	13.6%	1	1.7%	0	0.0%	2	3.4%
3	10	16.9%	1	1.7%	2	3.4%	6	10.2%
4	32	54.2%	38	64.4%	36	61.0%	37	62.7%
5	9	15.3%	19	32.2%	21	35.6%	14	23.7%
Total	59	100.0%	59	100.0%	59	100.0%	59	100.0%

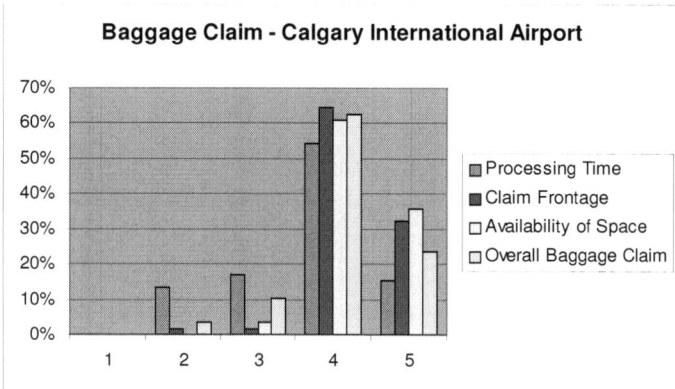

Figure 4.22: Ratings of Baggage Claim - Calgary International Airport

4.6.25. Overall Terminal Rating

Finally passengers were asked to provide a rating for the whole airport passenger terminal. This rating should be based on the experience the passenger had through all the terminal components, from curbside to the departure lounge. Table 4.29 and Figure 4.23 provide the distribution of responses for the rating of this variable.

Table 4.29: Overall Terminal Rating: Distribution of Responses

Rating Category	Responses					
	Rio de Janeiro Intl.		São Paulo Guarulhos		São Paulo Congonhas	
1	0	0.0%	1	0.8%	1	3.3%
2	0	0.0%	4	3.4%	2	6.7%
3	5	14.3%	22	18.6%	10	33.3%
4	22	62.9%	76	64.4%	14	46.7%
5	8	22.9%	15	12.7%	3	10.0%
Total	35	100.0%	118	100.0%	30	100.0%

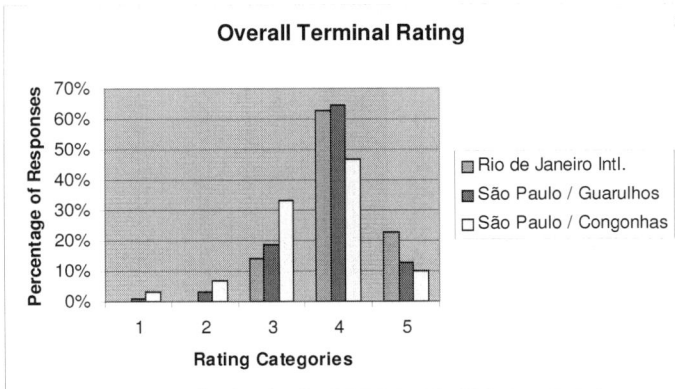

Figure 4.23: Overall Terminal Rating

4.7. Conclusions

The distribution of responses between LOS categories (1 to 5) provides fundamental information for application of the methodology presented at the Chapter 3. Likewise, the physical measures collected (waiting time, processing time, space available, number of seats, walking distance, etc) will be useful for generating LOS standards. Chapter 5 will present the statistical analyses for individual components, while Chapter 6 will present the analyses for overall measures.

CHAPTER FIVE: ANALYSIS OF INDIVIDUAL COMPONENTS

5.1. Introduction

The methodology presented in Chapter 3 is now applied to analyze several individual components of the airport passenger terminal. The objective of the analysis is to obtain LOS standards as a function of the physical measures taken for each individual passenger.

Five components will be the object of study in this chapter: Curbside, Check-in Counter, Security Screening and Departure Lounge for departing passengers, and Baggage Claim fir arriving passengers. Data from São Paulo / Guarulhos International Airport and Calgary International Airport will be analyzed. Data from São Paulo / Congonhas International Airport and Rio de Janeiro International Airport will not be analyzed in this Chapter. They will be treated in Chapter 7, in the section called Benchmarking. The reason for this is that the data for these two airports is insufficient to apply the complex methodology presented in Chapter 3.

All steps of the methodology have been presented in Chapter 3. Thus, the details of the application will be presented in Appendix C.

The statistical calculations were performed using SPSS 13.0. MathCAD was used to calculate the Chi-Square values when it was necessary to perform advanced calculations (e.g. complex integrals).

The LOS standards proposed in this chapter are applicable to the surveyed airports, and reflect the traffic characteristics, mix of passengers, and cultural characteristics of the passengers. Application of these standards at airports that have different characteristics might not be suitable. Nevertheless, the methodology can be applicable to any airport if sufficient data is collected.

5.2. Summary of the Methodology Proposed

The steps in the methodology are summarized in the following. They will be employed for the analysis of each measure of individual components.

1) Separate the passengers into groups of similar characteristics (waiting time, processing time, space available, etc).

2) Obtain the number of responses for each category in each group.

3) Calculate the proportions of responses (p_{jk}).

4) Calculate the normal deviates y_{jk}.

5) Calculate $\underline{\mu}_k^{UB}$ as the average of y_{jk} over all groups for each category k.

6) Perform a regression analysis to obtain the μ_j^{LOS}. For the regression, the dependent variable should be $y_{jk;}$ the independent variable should be $\underline{\mu}_k^{UB}$.

7) Perform a regression analysis to obtain an equation providing a relationship between μ_j^{LOS} and the characteristics of facilities.

8) Substitute $\underline{\mu}_k^{UB}$ (k = 1, ... 5) in the equation to get the characteristics of facilities corresponding to categories 1 to 5. These numbers will be the proposed LOS standards.

A complete and detailed explanation of these steps was presented at Chapter 3, illustrated with data from Waiting Time at the check-in counters at São Paulo / Guarulhos International Airport.

5.3. Emplaning Curbside

5.3.1. Introduction

The function of the curbside is to provide an interface between ground access and the airport passenger terminal. It is the first airport component that most passengers pass through for their departing trip. For this reason, the LOS of this facility can influence the first impression passengers have regarding the whole airport. In addition to that, because the main function of a curbside is to transfer passengers from the ground transportation system to the terminal building, the entire ground/air linkage will be unbalanced if this area does not operate properly.

For many years, approaches to LOS and capacity problems have dealt with vehicles rather than people (Siddiqui, 1994). Most of the past studies dealt primarily with the length of curbside areas, not considering passengers' perceptions of other attributes that might influence the LOS evaluation of these facilities.

5.3.2. State of the Art

The principal demand and operating factors influencing service level and capacity for the terminal curb are summarized in Table 5.1 (TRB, 1987):

Table 5.1: Demand and Operating Factors Influencing

Service Level and Capacity of the Terminal Curb

Factor	Description
Available frontage	length of curb frontage modified by presence of obstructions and assigned uses (e.g., airport limousines only, taxi only), separation of departures and arrivals
Frontage roads and pedestrian paths	Number of traffic lanes feeding to and from frontage area; pedestrians crossing vehicle traffic lanes
Management policy	Stopping and dwell regulations, enforcement practices, commercial access control, public transport dispatching
Passenger characteristics and motor vehicle fleet mix	Passenger choice of ground transport mode, average occupancy of vehicles, dwell times at curb, passenger patterns of arrival before scheduled departure, baggage loads
Flight schedule	Basic determinant of number of people arriving and departing at given time in given area

Source: TRB, 1987

According to Martel and Seneviratne (1990), the most important factors that passenger consider when evaluating LOS of parking and curbside are:

- direct access (minimum walking distance);
- level changes (going up or down);
- space available for circulation;
- more weather protection;
- better visual information (comprehensible);
- lighting;
- aesthetics (beauty, cleanliness).

Mandle et. al (1982) adopted definitions of LOS for airport curbside planning and design, on the range from A to E, as follows:

- Level A: no traffic queues, no double parking.
- Level B: effective curb utilization equal to 1.1 times actual curb frontage.

- Level C: effective curb utilization equal to 1.3 times actual curb frontage.
- Level D: effective curb utilization equal to 1.7 times actual curb frontage.
- Level E: operational breakdowns, effective curb utilization equal to 2.0 times actual curb frontage.

The effective curb utilization is defined as the effective length of the area occupied by vehicles. This definition states that actual curb length may differ from effective curb length, due to double or triple parking or undesirable loading/unloading areas. In this viewpoint, effective length of curb is directly related to the LOS provided at the curb.

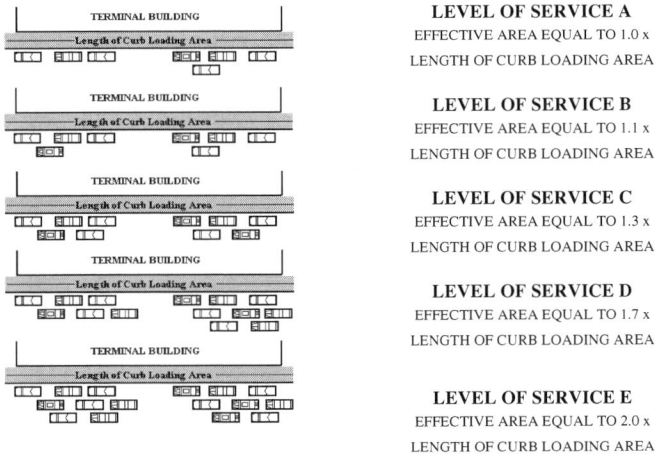

LEVEL OF SERVICE A
EFFECTIVE AREA EQUAL TO 1.0 x
LENGTH OF CURB LOADING AREA

LEVEL OF SERVICE B
EFFECTIVE AREA EQUAL TO 1.1 x
LENGTH OF CURB LOADING AREA

LEVEL OF SERVICE C
EFFECTIVE AREA EQUAL TO 1.3 x
LENGTH OF CURB LOADING AREA

LEVEL OF SERVICE D
EFFECTIVE AREA EQUAL TO 1.7 x
LENGTH OF CURB LOADING AREA

LEVEL OF SERVICE E
EFFECTIVE AREA EQUAL TO 2.0 x
LENGTH OF CURB LOADING AREA

Figure 5.1: Airport Curbside Levels of Service (Mandle et al, 1982)

Siddiqui (1994) developed utility equations, dependent on two variables: time (TME) and walking distance (DIS). The equations (5.1 and 5.2) are shown below, for departure and arrival curb, respectively:

$$U = -0.00792 \cdot TME - 0.00464 \cdot DIS + 1.095 \qquad (5.1)$$
$$R^2 = 0.439; \ F = 116.7; \ F_{CR} = 3.07$$

$$U = -0.00842 \cdot TME - 0.00524 \cdot DIS + 1.0976 \qquad (5.2)$$
$$R^2 = 0.441; \ F = 84.4; \ F_{CR} = 3.07$$

The definition of the two variables is given below:
- TME: the time each vehicle requires to find an unloading/loading position in the curb area, measured from the moment of passing the entrance ramp, and
- DIS: the distance that a user travels by foot, between the unloading/loading position and entrance door.

The association of utility values and LOS standards can be found in the following Tables:

Table 5.2: Suggested LOS standards (departure curb)

Performance Measures	A to B	B to C	C to D	D to E	E to F
Time (seconds)	13.9	26.3	38.7	51.0	63.4
Distance (meters)	26.6	40.2	63.3	67.3	80.9

Source: Siddiqui (1994)

Table 5.3: Suggested LOS standards (arrival curb)

Performance Measures	A to B	B to C	C to D	D to E	E to F
Time (seconds)	16.9	28.1	42.3	55.1	67.9
Distance (meters)	13.9	29.7	45.5	61.4	77.1

Source: Siddiqui (1994)

5.3.3. LOS Factors

Based on the above studies the following objective factors could be applied for curbside LOS evaluation:

- Effective curb utilization - ECU (it will be further correlated to the ratings of space available for cars).

- Walking distance from unloading position to entrance door.

- Time each vehicle requires to find an unloading position in the curb area.

These three variables were used in the questionnaire applied for the three Brazilian Airports during the Summer/03. Table 5.4 presents the correlation between the responses (1 to 5) passengers provided for each of these three variables.

Table 5.4: Correlation between Variables at Curbside

	ECU	WD	WT
ECU	1		
WD	0.51	1	
WT	0.71	0.57	1

There is a strong relationship between ratings of Effective Curb Utilization, Waiting Time and Walking Distance concerning curbside level of service evaluation. These correlations are due to the fact that passengers experiencing a very busy curbside (high ECU), face long delays (WT) and usually cannot park very close to the front door, having to walk long distances (WD).

In the face of the high correlation values, it was decided to evaluate the curbside component by the space available for cars (ECU) only. This variable was picked because it is more suitable for infra structure planning, as opposed to the other two variables. ECU was the only variable (concerning curbside LOS evaluation) included on the

126

questionnaire applied in the second survey at São Paulo / Guarulhos International Airport
(Summer/04).

5.3.4. Effective Curbside Utilization (ECU)

Passengers have been asked to rate the curbside facilities according to space available for
cars. At the same time, the surveyor measured the 'length' of vehicles presently at the
curbside; with the length of the curbside area, it would be possible to calculate the
effective curb utilization (ECU).

After careful analysis of a sample of 119 passengers at São Paulo / Guarulhos
International Airport, it was possible to split this sample into 10 groups of similar ECU
values. Table 5.5 shows the range of ECU values, average ECU values, number of
respondents, and μ_j^{LOS} values for each group j.

Table 5.5: Curbside Data for São Paulo / Guarulhos Airport

Group (j)	Range	Average Value (ECU)	#	μ_j^{LOS}
1	$0.20 \leq ECU < 0.30$	0.25	13	0.96
2	$0.30 \leq ECU < 0.40$	0.33	16	1.17
3	$0.40 \leq ECU < 0.50$	0.42	15	1.03
4	$0.50 \leq ECU < 0.60$	0.51	23	1.34
5	$0.60 \leq ECU < 0.70$	0.62	14	1.16
6	$0.80 \leq ECU < 0.90$	0.82	15	0.47
7	$1.00 \leq ECU < 1.50$	1.19	14	0.54
8	$1.50 \leq ECU < 2.00$	1.68	4	0.00
9	$2.00 \leq ECU \leq 2.50$	2.33	3	(0.02)
10	$ECU > 2.50$	2.67	2	(0.45)
		Total:	**119**	

A regression analysis was performed using μ_j^{LOS} as the dependent variable and the ECU
values (column 3 of Table 5.5) as the independent variable. The linear relationship has

shown the best fit to the data. The parameters obtained from application of the regression provide Equation 5.3. Figure 5.2 shows a plot of the data and the regression line.

$$\mu_{S\tilde{a}oPaulo}^{LOS} = 1.245 - 0.536 \ (ECU) \hspace{2cm} (5.3)$$

$$(t = 10.3) \quad (t = -6.8)$$

$R^2 = 0.85$
$F = 46.697$
Chi-Square = 22.201
Chi-Square critic: 28.869 (5% signif. - 18 d.f.)

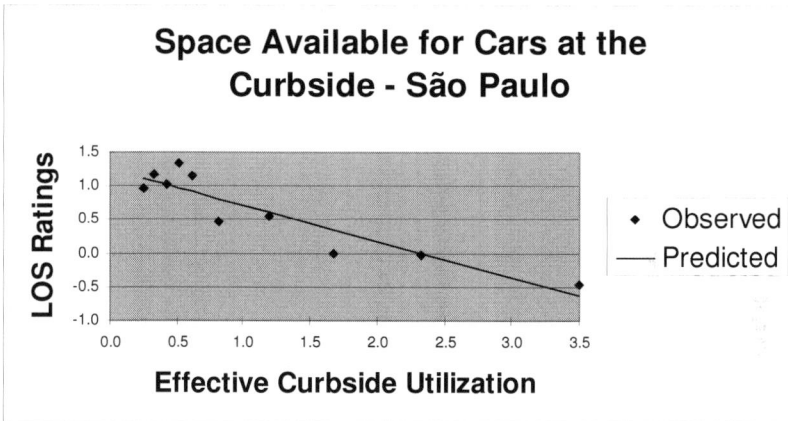

Figure 5.2: Plot of the Data and the Regression Line - Space Available for Cars at Curbside

The μ_k^{UB} values corresponding to the upper boundary of categories k can be substituted into equation 5.3 as the μ_j^{LOS} values. This substitution will provide A-B LOS standards, as shown in Table 5.6.

Table 5.6: Suggested LOS standards for the Curbside

LOS	ECU
A/B	0.0 - 1.5
C	1.5 - 3.2
D/E	>3.2

LOS A and B were joined because LOS A values were negative. LOS D and E were also joined because there was no respondent that rated the space available for cars at the curbside as unacceptable (LOS E). That is why it was not appropriate to include a LOS merely based on projections of Equation 5.3 using hypothetical values.

According to the suggested LOS standards provided in Table 5.6, the curbside will have an excellent (A) or good (B) evaluation if the utilization of the curbside is lower than 150% (ECU < 1.5). This indicates that it is not necessary to provide space at the curbside for all cars, because during short peak periods, some double line is acceptable for the surveyed passengers. However, it is necessary to verify that this double line will not provide additional disturbance to the road traffic. If that is the case, a more conservative provision of space for all cars (100% - ECU = 1.0) would be more appropriate.

5.4.   Check-in Counter

5.4.1. Introduction

Check-in counter LOS evaluations have been previously undertaken by many researchers and perhaps it is the most studied airport passenger terminal component. The check-in counter is the first processing component in the terminal, through which passengers pass

129

during the enplaning trip. In this facility, passengers get their seats assigned, check the baggage, and receive a boarding pass which includes the gate number.

The level of service provided at the check-in counter reflects both the airport and airline images. In addition to that, because it is one of the first components in the passengers pathway, it can cause delay to other activities and finally to the departing flight. Not only can a poor level of service cause operational problems to airlines and airport administration, it can add to passenger stress, when they are trying to get to the airplane as soon as possible.

Despite a number of studies dealing with check-in counter LOS, we have found many opportunities to improve the LOS evaluation. To proceed with the methodology proposed, we first start by reviewing previous approaches of check-in LOS evaluation.

Some airport passenger terminals offer a express check-in in addition to the traditional check-in. In these circumstances the check-in level of service will have two components: the express check-in LOS and the traditional check-in LOS. Demand choice models could be applied in these cases to model the choice of check-in type as a function of some parameters as service time, convenience, etc. Even though these automated check-in facilities have not been studied in this thesis research, a similar methodology can be applied to evaluate their level of service.

5.4.2. State of the Art
The principal demand and operating factors influencing service level and capacity of ticket counter and baggage check are (TRB, 1987):
- number and type of positions;

- airline procedures and staffing;
- passenger characteristics;
- space and configuration;
- flight type, schedule, and load;
- airline lease agreement and airport management practices.

Mumayiz and Ashford (1986) defined three LOS according to passenger perception of delay. The levels for check-in subsystems for scheduled long-haul flights, for example, are defined as:

- Level A (good): T < 15 min;
- Level B (tolerable): 15 min < T < 25 min;
- Level C (bad): T > 25 min.

where T is the time spent on check-in (including waiting).

Omer (1990) proposes the following composite utility Equation (5.4) for the LOS measurement at check-in counters in some Canadian airports:

$$U = 75.489 + (1.430)NSAPP + (-0.864)WTIME + (-1.30)STIME \qquad (5.4)$$

where,

NSAPP = net space available per person,

WTIME = waiting time at the queue, and

STIME = service time at the counter.

In that research, LOS ranges and utility values followed a linear correlation, as can be shown below:

- LOS A: 76.60 < U < 100.00;
- LOS B: 70.15 < U < 76.60;
- LOS C: 58.94 < U < 70.15;

- LOS D: 42.02 < U < 58.94;
- LOS E: 28.80 < U < 42.02;
- LOS F: U < 28.80.

Müller and Gosling (1991) used calibrated causal relationship equations to estimate the effect on passenger perception of the check-in lobby quality of service due to changes in the average waiting time and occupancy. The causal relationship between the waiting time and crowding and the resulting perceived quality of service was assumed to be given by:

$$LQ = \ln(c + aT + bD) \qquad (5.5)$$

where:

LQ = mean perceived check-in lobby quality of service (psychometric scaling theory);
c = constant;
a = average waiting time parameter;
T = average waiting time (minutes);
b = average occupancy parameter;
D = average occupancy (square feet per passenger).

The logarithmic function was explored following Fechner's law, which according to the authors is the main element of a strong line of thinking on psychophysical experiments. It was mentioned that opposition to the logarithmic transformation of stimulus intensity into subjective sensation has been growing stronger, however, and alternative transformations have been suggested, mainly the power transformation. According to the author though, this transformation is not appropriate to the passenger quality perception modeling since it restricts the domain of the dependent variable.

Considering a given passenger average value of time, they proposed perceived value of improved LOS in dollars. The results could, when compared with costs of possible improvement alternatives, assist in making better decisions on how to allocate effectively resources at the terminal.

Seneviratne and Martel (1991) suggest the following two measures (equations 5.6 and 5.7) that can be applied for check-in activities or any other processing component at the passenger terminal building (PTB), applying waiting time (WT) calculations:

$$WT = \frac{\text{mean waiting time per passenger at activity } i}{\text{mean total time a passenger spends in PTB}} \qquad (5.6)$$

$$WT = \frac{\text{mean processing time at activity } i}{\text{mean waiting time per passenger at activity } i} \qquad (5.7)$$

According to the authors, the sum of all WTs over all activities would give a global impression of the performance of processing elements at an airport.

Yen et. al. (2001) applying the fuzzy set theory concept and evaluations of perceived versus observed time, estimated thresholds for different service levels at check-in facilities. The following Table presents the results of their research:

Table 5.7: Estimated Thresholds of Different Service Levels

Service levels		**A**	**B**	**C**	**D**	**E**	
Thresholds		**0**	x_1	x_2	x_3	x_4	**f**
Check-in waiting	Actual	0	4.4	9.9	13.4	15.5	f
time (min)	Perceived	0	3.4	9.2	14.5	18.5	f
Check-in service	Actual	0	2.1	2.8	4.5	5.9	f
time (min)	Perceived	0	3.6	6.2	10.4	12.2	f

Source: Yen et. al. (2001) - NOTES: The upper bounds "f" are not shown in the Table.

The methodologies developed by Müller and Gosling (1991) and Omer (1990) are the most complete of all, allowing the evaluation of LOS considering the interaction of space and time. Not only so, it allowed the evaluation of actual data as opposed to perceived data, which in some cases have proved to be very different from real data (Park, 1994; Yen et. al, 2001).

5.4.3. LOS Factors

As shown, the research on LOS for check-in facilities has concentrated itself mainly on service times and space available for passengers. The ACI survey (ACI, 2000) shows that this practice has been widely used within the airport industry. Among the airports surveyed, the only objective criteria used for check-in facilities are the check-in waiting time/queue and check-in transaction time. Nonetheless, Martel and Seneviratne (1990) provide some factors that have a bearing on the LOS passenger perception of check-in facilities:

(i)   shorter waiting time
(ii)   convenience (counter space, ease of baggage handling)
(iii)   space for circulation
(iv)   aesthetics

An objective measurement of the aesthetics variable is difficult to undertake. Obviously any passenger could provide his/her perception about the terminal aesthetics, expressing it by a linguistic variable as good or excellent; however, it is difficult to propose any performance variable relative to aesthetics, which could be correlated to the aesthetics LOS passengers ratings. Aesthetics is not regarded so importantly as the other factors (waiting time and space for circulation). On the other hand, counter space and ease of baggage handling are clearly correlated to space for circulation. It is easy to see that counter space increases proportionally with space for circulation; the same can be said about baggage handling, since more space for circulation certainly provides more convenience for baggage handling.

In addition to waiting time, the processing time variable is always present in any check-in LOS evaluations. For this reason, it will be included in our analysis.

In summary, this research will apply three variables for LOS evaluation of check-in facilities:

- WT: waiting time.
- PT: processing time.
- AS: availability of space.

The availability of space per passenger will be measured as the crowding level during the surveys. These two variables might be different, depending on the utilization level of the check-in counter line. Figure 5.3 will help to illustrate the difference between them.

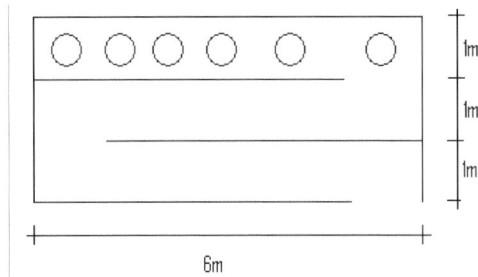

Figure 5.3: Crowding Level at the Check-in Counter Line

According to Figure 5.3, the crowding level experienced by these six passengers is $1m^2$/passenger. On the other hand, the availability of space is $3m^2$/passenger. The crowding level will be taken as opposed to the availability of space because it reflects the real experience of the passenger. Nevertheless, in the cases where the check-in line is full (Figure 5.4), the crowding level coincides with the availability of space (1m2/passenger).

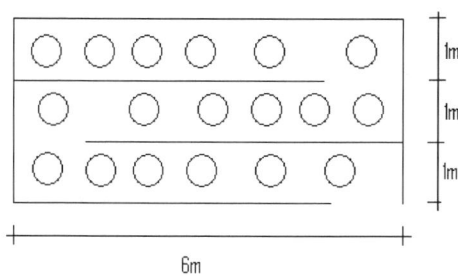

Figure 5.4: Crowding Level at the Check-in Counter Line (Full)

This difference between the variables will not represent any problem, because the check-in counter facilities are designed to operate at full capacity. In this case, the two variables will have the same value. For simplification, availability of space per passenger (AS) will be used to denote the crowding level at the check-in counter line in the subsequent analyses.

5.4.4. Waiting Time

The analysis of waiting time at the check-in counter for São Paulo / Guarulhos was previously demonstrated in Chapter 3 to illustrate the methodology. In this case we will present the analysis for Calgary International Airport.

136

Table 5.8 presents passengers split into 6 groups. Equation 5.8 represents the relationship obtained by the regression analysis using columns 3 and 5 of Table 5.8 as input data. Figure 5.5 shows the plot of the data and the regression line.

Table 5.8: Check-in Waiting time Data for Calgary

Group	Range (min)	Value (min)	#	μ_j^{LOS}
1	$0 < WT \le 2.5$	1.25	10	3.66
2	$2.5 < WT \le 5.0$	4.00	8	3.05
3	$5.0 < WT \le 10.0$	8.07	15	2.13
4	$10.0 < WT \le 15.0$	12.61	14	0.80
5	$15.0 < WT \le 20.0$	18.88	8	0.05
6	$20.0 < WT \le 27.5$	23.64	7	0.44
		Total:	62	

$$\mu_{Calgary}^{LOS} = 3.51 - 0.16\,(WT) \qquad (5.8)$$

$$(t = 8.47)\ (t = -5.35)$$

$R^2 = 0.88$
$F = 28.613$
Chi-Square = 5.403
Chi-Square$_{critic}$ = 18.307 (5% signif. - 10 d.f.)

Waiting Time at the Check-in Calgary

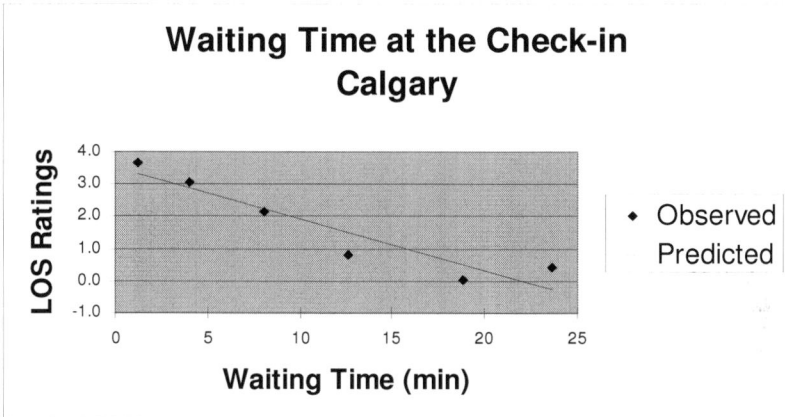

Figure 5.5: Plot of the Data and the Regression Line - Waiting Time at Check-in - Calgary

Table 5.9 represents the suggested LOS standards obtained from application of the methodology. The range of waiting time values from LOS A to LOS E at São Paulo is greater than the range at Calgary. That might be due to the fact that in São Paulo there is more variability of flight types than in Calgary. Most of the flights from Calgary have destinations in North America, as opposed to flights from São Paulo that have domestic destinations, as well as inter-continental flights to Europe, Africa, Asia, North America and Australia. Considering this fact, a direct comparison between LOS standards for these two airports is not appropriate. Nonetheless, even considering all airport differences, the standards are roughly closed together. This similarity is interesting, since the data analysis have been performed individually. That indicates that the employed technique has consistency for providing practical results.

Table 5.9: Suggested LOS Standards

LOS	Waiting Time (min)	
	São Paulo	Calgary
A	< 1	< 7
B	1 – 17	7 - 18
C	17 - 34	18 - 26
D	34 - 58	26 - 34
E	> 58	> 34

5.4.5. Processing Time

Passengers split into groups of similar processing time values is provided in Tables 5.10 and 5.11, along with the respective PT ranges, PT average values, number of respondents, and μ_j^{LOS} for each group j.

Table 5.10: Check-in Processing Time Data for São Paulo / Guarulhos

Group	Range (min)	Average Value (min)	#	μ_j^{LOS}
1	PT = 1	1.00	14	1.61
2	PT = 2	2.00	19	1.59
3	PT = 3	3.00	24	1.74
4	PT = 4	4.00	12	1.58
5	PT = 5	5.00	18	1.23
6	PT = 6	6.00	08	0.76
7	PT = 7 OR PT = 8	7.71	07	0.94
8	PT = 9	9.00	03	1.18
9	PT = 10	10.00	05	1.11
10	10 < PT ≤ 15	12.57	07	1.07
11	15 < PT	28.33	03	(1.34)
		Total:	119	

Table 5.11: Check-in Processing Time Data for Calgary

Group	Range (min)	Value (min)	#	μ_j^{LOS}
1	$0 < PT \leq 1.0$	1.00	4	2.32
2	$1.0 < PT \leq 2.0$	1.80	14	1.64
3	$2.0 < PT \leq 3.0$	2.50	15	2.07
4	$3.0 < PT \leq 5.0$	4.20	17	2.19
5	$5.0 < PT \leq 10.0$	8.40	9	0.92
6	$10.0 < PT \leq 20.0$	15.30	3	0.44
		Total:	62	

A regression analysis was performed using μ_j^{LOS} as the dependent variable and the PT values (column 3 of Tables 5.10 and 5.11) as the independent variable. The linear relationship have shown the best fit to the data. The parameters obtained from application of the regression provide Equations 5.9 and 5.10. Figures 5.6 and 5.7 show the plot of the data and the regression line.

$$\mu_{S\tilde{a}oPaulo}^{LOS} = 1.89 - 0.11 \text{ (PT)} \qquad (5.9)$$

$$(t = 13.87) \ (t = -8.37)$$

$R^2 = 0.89$
$F = 70.065$
Chi-Square = 12.832
Chi-Square$_{critic}$ = 31.410 (5% signif. - 20 d.f)

$$\mu_{Calgary}^{LOS} = 2.30 - 0.13 \text{ (PT)} \qquad (5.10)$$

$$(t = 10.77) \quad (t = -4.42)$$

$R^2 = 0.83$
$F = 19.536$
Chi-Square = 8.088
Chi-Square$_{critic}$ = 18.307 (5% signif. - 10 d.f)

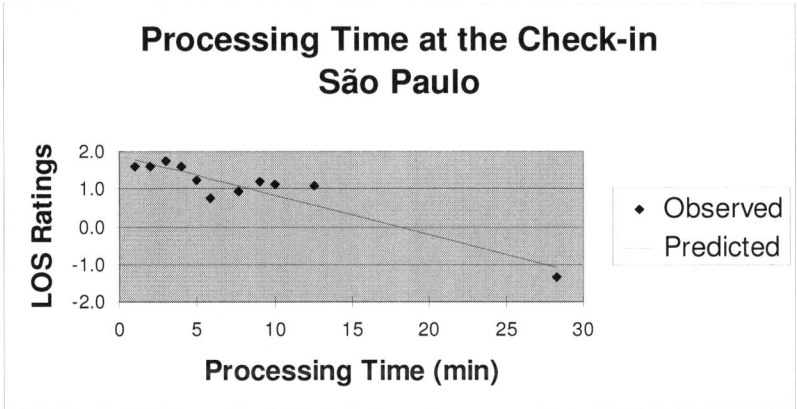

Figure 5.6: Plot of the Data and the Regression Line - Processing Time at the Check-in Counter - São Paulo

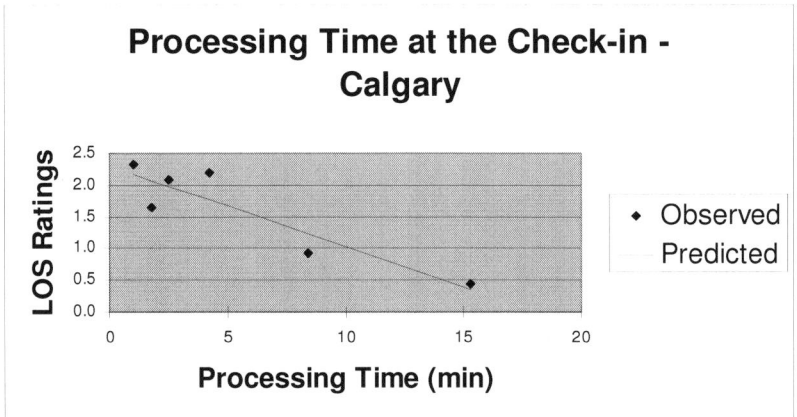

Figure 5.7: Plot of the Data and the Regression Line - Processing Time at Check-in - Calgary

Table 5.12 shows the suggested LOS standards. Once again, it is important to realize that direct comparisons between standards from São Paulo and Calgary cannot be made, since the airport characteristics are very different.

Table 5.12: Suggested LOS Standards

LOS	Processing Time (min)	
	São Paulo	Calgary
A	< 1	< 5
B	1 – 14	5 - 17
C	14-20	17 - 19
D	20-25	19 – 20
E	> 25	> 20

5.4.6. Space Available

Passengers split into 10 groups is presented in Table 5.13, alongwith the characteristics of each group. Equation 5.11 presents the relationship between μ^{LOS} and AS. In this particular case, the log curve presented the best fit as opposed to linear functions. Figure 5.8 presents the plot of the data and the regression line. Table 5.14 presents the suggested LOS standards.

Table 5.13: Space Available Data - Check-in - São Paulo

Group	Range (m^2)	Average Value (m^2)	#	μ_j^{LOS}
1	$0.25 < AS \leq 0.50$	0.42	03	0.01
2	$0.50 < AS \leq 0.75$	0.70	06	0.35
3	$0.75 < AS \leq 1.00$	0.99	11	1.30
4	$1.00 < AS \leq 1.25$	1.24	07	0.17
5	$1.25 < AS \leq 1.50$	1.48	15	1.76
6	$1.50 < AS \leq 1.75$	1.60	29	1.30
7	$1.75 < AS \leq 2.00$	1.97	24	1.40
8	$2.00 < AS \leq 2.50$	2.36	07	1.10
9	$2.50 < AS \leq 3.00$	2.98	09	1.49
10	$AS > 3.00$	3.50	09	1.73
		Total:	**119**	

$$\mu_{S\tilde{a}oPaulo}^{LOS} = 0.781 + 0.756 \text{ LN (AS)} \qquad (5.11)$$

$$(t = 4.819) \qquad (t = -3.383)$$

$R^2 = 0.59$
$F = 11.446$
Chi-Square $= 15.681$
Chi-Square$_{critic} = 28.869$ (5% signif. - 18 d.f.)

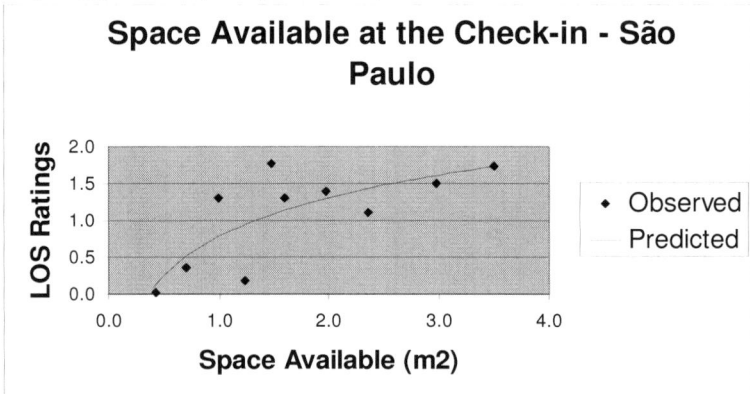

Figure 5.8: Plot of the Data and the Regression Line - Availability of Space at the Check-in - São Paulo

Table 5.14: Suggested LOS Standards - São Paulo

LOS	SPACE AVAILABLE (m²/pax)
A	> 6.2
B	0.6 - 6.1
C	0.2 - 0.6
D/E	< 0.2

LOS D and E were joined because there was no respondent that rated the availability of space at the check-in counter line as unacceptable (LOS E). That is why it was not appropriate to include a LOS merely based on projections of the Equation 5.11 using hypothetical values. LOS A (6.2 m²/pax) is obviously anti-economical and can only exist during periods of low movement. That happened during some hours of the afternoon at the São Paulo / Guarulhos International Airport.

Development of LOS standards for the Calgary International Airport was not undertaken, because the range of AS (m²/pax) values was not enough to provide a reasonable number of different groups. In most cases, the space available per passenger was very close to 2.0m². The values were different from this only in a few cases. In São Paulo/Guarulhos there was a greater variability of situations, where the space available per passenger varied from 0.25m² to more than 3.0 m² (Table 5.13).

5.4.7. Correlation Between Variables

There is a moderate correlation between the variables waiting time, processing time and availability of space as shown in Table 5.15. That is due to the fact that if the waiting time is longer, the amount of space for passengers decreases, and so does its rating. The rating of processing time is also directly correlated to the rating of waiting time. It means that if the processing time goes up, passengers have to stay more time in the line, and that affects the ratings for waiting time. These same ideas can be used to explain the correlation between PT and AS.

Table 5.15: Correlation Between Variables at the Check-in Counter

	WT	PT	AS
WT	1.00		
PT	0.41	1.00	
AS	0.33	0.43	1.00

The correlation between these three variables is not so strong as was the case concerning the correlation between the variables of the curbside.

5.4.8. Collinearity Diagnostics for the Three Independent Variables

Table 5.16 shows the results from a regression analysis between one independent variable and the other remaining ones. For instance the correlation (R^2) between WT and the other two variables (PT and AS) is 0.198. As we can see, there is no evidence of collinearity between those three variables.

Table 5.16: Collinearity Between Variables

Variables	R^2
WT	0.198
PT	0.050
AS	0.063

5.4.9. Composite Evaluation

The main condition for a composite evaluation to be performed according to the weighted average method, is the independence between variables. Although for the check-in case there is a certain correlation between the variables waiting time, processing time and availability of space, they are not so strong as to hinder the composite evaluation calculations.

The variables' ratings can be weighted and then combined, according to the following equation (5.12):

$$LOS(check\text{-}in) = w_1 * LOS(WT) + w_2 * LOS(PT) + w_3 * LOS(AS) \qquad (5.12)$$

Where

$LOS(check\text{-}in)$ = overall check-in LOS ratings

$LOS(WT), LOS(PT), and\ LOS(AS)$ = LOS ratings for each individual measures

$w_1, w_2,$ and w_3 = measures' relative importance weights.

Substituting the LOS ratings of the above equation by the survey responses and performing a regression analysis will provide the values w_1, w_2, and w_3 as the parameters of the regression equation, which can be obtained through least squares method. In this case, the weights reflecting the passenger perceptions of components' relative importance are obtained.

The results of the regression analysis are shown below:

R Square = 0.63

F = 42.943

$w_1 = 0.204$ t Stat = 3.820   P-value = 0.0003

$w_2 = 0.288$ t Stat = 4.181   P-value = 7.69 E-05

$w_3 = 0.506$ t Stat = 6.927   P-value = 1.21 E-09

The intercept was not very significant (P-value = 0.09) and was removed from the analysis.

Rounding the parameters to the first decimal point, the Equation (5.13) can then be written as follows:

$$LOS(check\text{-}in) = 0.2 * LOS(WT) + 0.3 * LOS(PT) + 0.5 * LOS(AS) \qquad (5.13)$$

These three rounded parameters are still within the confidence intervals (lower and upper 95%).

The LOS ratings vary from 1 to 5 corresponding to the LOS ranges, A to E: A-5, B-4, C-3, D-2, and E-1.

According to the weightings, availability of space is the most important factor; processing time is the second most important and waiting time is the least important.

The above equation can be utilized for performing a composite evaluation of a check-in facility as a function of the individual measures formerly presented.

5.5. Security Screening

5.5.1. Introduction

All airline passengers are required to pass through a security screening. This is an important measure to warrant the safety of aircraft. This procedure is required prior to departure both for passengers and for hand luggage. Security screening is done before passengers enter the departure lounge. In some airports it is done at the entrance to a concourse. In others, it is done at each gate. The equipment used for this process are x-ray screening and magnetometers. A more rigid inspection is performed for some specific destinations, like New York or Washington D.C. In this case, all hand luggage is opened and thoroughly inspected.

5.5.2. State of the Art

The principal demand and operating factors influencing service level and capacity of passenger security areas are (TRB, 1985):

- Number of channels, space, personnel;
- Type, equipment sensitivity, and airport/airline/agent policy and practice;
- Passenger characteristics;
- Building layout and passenger circulation patterns;
- Flight schedule and load.

Mumayiz and Ashford (1986) defined three levels for evaluation of performance of processing activities of an airport passenger terminal, proposed as: good, tolerable and bad. The results of the application of a passenger's survey on Birmingham International Airport, using this evaluation framework is given below for the security check:

- Good: T < 6.5 minutes;
- Tolerable: 6.5 < T <10.5 minutes;
- Bad: T > 10.5 minutes.

where T = time spent in security check (include waiting).

Although they have used time spent as the only representative variable, according to the authors, other variables could be included for evaluation. Inclusion of the occupancy variable will be explored in this work. We are going to use the space-time interaction concept for the security screening facilities, as in the case of ticket counter and baggage deposit.

5.5.3. LOS Factors

As suggested by Seneviratne and Martel (1990), the most important factors that have a bearing on the LOS passengers' perception of security screening facilities are:

(i)   waiting time
(ii)   space available for circulation
(iii)   convenience
(iv)   simplicity of procedure

As was the case for check-in LOS measurement, it is easy to see that the convenience variable is highly correlated to the other variables proposed. Considering this, it will not be included in our study. The 'simplicity of procedure' variable is very difficult to be measured objectively; based on this fact and considering the low importance attributed to that criteria, we will disregard this variable in this study.

Similar to the check-in counter study, this research would apply three variables to the LOS evaluation of check-in facilities:

- WT: waiting time.
- PT: processing time.
- AS: availability of space.

Some characteristics of the security screening procedure performed at São Paulo/Guarulhos International Airport encouraged a modification of these variables. The processing time for the surveyed passengers was usually just a few seconds; in some cases it was so fast that the surveyors had difficulty measuring it. This speed provided a smooth flow of passengers, where the waiting line was very short and the space available per passengers was generous. In the face of this, it makes no sense to evaluate the level of service as a function of the space available, because we would not have a reasonable range of different values enough to split the passengers into different groups. It also makes more sense to add the waiting and processing times to provide a single and more expressive unit, which we will denote service time. In summary, the level of service of the security screening at São Paulo / Guarulhos International Airport will be evaluated by the waiting + processing time. The adoption of the three previously mentioned variables could still be employed for analysis of security screening at airports that have a more rigid and longer inspection.

5.5.4. Service Time

Table 5.17 presents the splitting of passengers into 8 groups of similar service times. Equation 5.14 shows the relationship between μ^{LOS} and the service time. Figure 5.9 presents the plot of the data and the regression line.

Table 5.17: Service Time Data - Security - São Paulo / Guarulhos

Group (j)	Range (min)	Value (min)	#	μ_j^{LOS}
1	0 - 0.4	0.3	16	2.14
2	0.5 - 0.9	0.7	11	2.73
3	1.0	1.0	31	2.04
4	1.1 - 1.5	1.4	10	2.09
5	2.0 - 2.5	2.1	21	1.54
6	3.0 - 3.5	3.1	13	0.44
7	4.0	4.0	7	1.35
8	≥ 5.0	7.9	9	0.41
		Total:	**118**	

$$\mu_{S\tilde{a}oPaulo}^{LOS} = 2.296 - 0.275 \ (WT + PT) \qquad\qquad (5.14)$$

$$(t = 8.50) \qquad (t = -3.52)$$

$R^2 = 0.67$
$F = 12.391$
Chi-Square $= 21.350$
Chi-Square$_{critic} = 23.685$ (5% signif. - 14 d.f.)

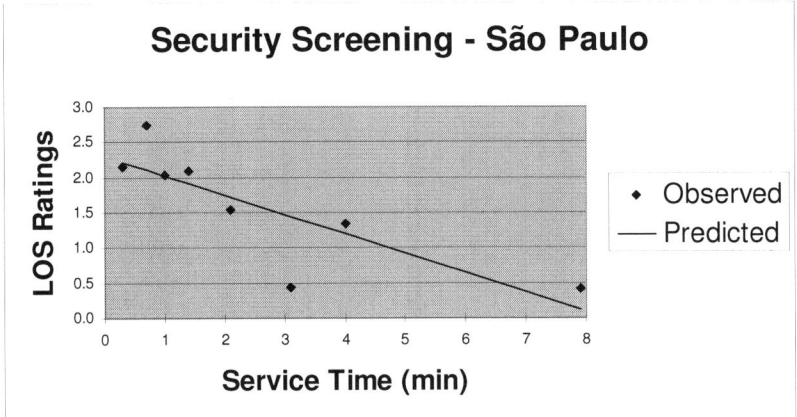

Security Screening - São Paulo

♦ Observed
— Predicted

Figure 5.9: Plot of the Data and the Regression Line - Service Time at Security Screening - São Paulo

The suggested LOS standards for service time at the security screening are demonstrated in Table 5.18. According to that, passengers will rate the security screening component as good if the service time falls between 2 and 7 minutes.

Table 5.18: Suggested LOS Standards

LOS	Service Time (min)
A	< 2
B	2 - 7
C	7 - 10
D	10 - 12
E	> 12

5.6. Departure Lounge

5.6.1. Introduction

The main purposes of the departure lounge are to assemble passengers that are waiting to board the flight and in some airports, to serve as a passageway for deplaning passengers. People accompanying passengers are not allowed into this area. It is also usual to separate international from domestic passengers. There are airports where airlines have exclusive departure lounges; in other cases the airlines have to share the same area (as is the case for São Paulo / Guarulhos International Airport). Most airports provide lounges for business and first class passengers. In these particular places, comfortable seats, appetizers, newspapers, TV's, ambient music are provided, and access is limited.

Usually the airlines stipulate the time before departure when passengers are supposed to arrive at the departure lounge. Of course there are some passengers who arrive later, but they take the risk of missing the flight, especially because of today's long security check queues. There are others who prefer to enter the lounge in advance just so sit and relax before the flight. As we can see, the airline procedures and human behavior are very important factors when planning the space and facilities to be available in the departure lounge.

The LOS evaluation of holding components is very particular and subjective, because we have to deal with parameters as comfort, convenience and aesthetics. In the processing components, there are not so many things the airport and airlines can do to improve the quality the passenger experience while he/she waits. Conversely, in holding components, many factors can influence the passenger perception of LOS as for example the availability of seats or concessions in the area.

5.6.2. State of the Art

Passengers waiting in areas serving aircraft gates and terminal lobbies may be subjected to crowding and congestion if facilities are inadequate. The principal demand and operating factors influencing service level and capacity of passenger areas are (TRB, 1987):

- Waiting and circulation area;
- Seating and waiting-area geometry;
- Flight schedule, aircraft type, passenger load, and gate utilization;
- Boarding method;
- Passenger behavioral characteristics.

Muller (1987) proposed the following formulation for the evaluation of quality of service at a departure lounge facility:

$$BQ = \ln(C_{BQ} + b_{BQ} \cdot D_{BQ}) \qquad (5.15)$$

where:

BQ = the mean boarding lounge quantitative quality of service perception,

C_{BQ} = a constant parameter,

b_{BQ} = the occupancy rate parameter, and

D_{BQ} = the boarding lounge occupancy rate given in square feet per passenger.

The mean boarding lounge quantitative quality of service perception was calculated using the psychometric scaling theory formerly proposed by the author. The equation was calibrated with data obtained through two surveys applied at the San Francisco International Airport during the year of 1987, whose parameters are presented as follows:

Table 5.19 - Parameters for Equation 5.15

Parameter	Estimation	t-Statistic
C_{BQ}	0.5511	1.5982
b_{BQ}	0.0292	1.8276
R^2 (adj) = 43.82%		

Source: Muller (1987)

Omer (1990) proposed the following composite utility equation for the LOS measurement at departure lounges:

$$U = 102.16 + (0.0024)NSAPP + (-3.732)CTIME \qquad (5.16)$$

where,

NSAPP = net space available per person,

CTIME = waiting time.

The correlation of LOS ranges and utility values is shown as follows:

- LOS A: $86.2 < U < 100.0$;
- LOS B: $71.2 < U < 86.2$;
- LOS C: $56.1 < U < 71.2$;

- LOS D: $41.2 < U < 56.1$;
- LOS E: $26.3 < U < 41.2$;
- LOS F: $U < 26.3$.

A survey conducted by Seneviratne and Martel (1990) considered the availability of seats the most significant performance indicator of waiting areas in airport passenger terminals. The other relevant factors are:

- good seating arrangements;
- space available for circulation;
- lighting;
- comfort;
- proximity of concessions and amenities;
- aesthetics.

Wirasinghe and Shehata (1988) defined and obtained an equation for the optimal number of seats as that which minimizes the sum of the cost of the lounge (proportional to its area), the cost of seats and a penalty for compulsory standing time. Using this concept, Seneviratne and Martel (1994) defined a seating availability index for the evaluation of LOS in departure lounges, as follows:

$$PI_{as} = \frac{N_a}{N_o} \qquad (5.17)$$

where,

N_a = number of available seats in area considered at a given time;

N_o = optimal number of seats;

PI_{as} = performance index for availability of seats.

Thus, LOS in relation to availability of seats was defined as:

- Level A: $PI_{as} \geq 1.0$.
- Level B: $0.9 > PI_{as} > 0.7$.
- Level C: $0.6 > PI_{as} > 0.4$.
- Level D: $0.3 > PI_{as} > 0.2$.
- Level E: $0.2 > PI_{as} > 0.1$.
- Level F: $PI_{as} < 0.1$.

One alternative formulation proposed by Seneviratne and Martel (1991) suggested the following performance measure (5.18) for seat availability (SA) in relation to the standard design criterion – typical peak-day peak-hour passengers:

$$SA = \frac{\text{total number of seats available}}{\text{typical peak day peak hour passengers}} \tag{5.18}$$

5.6.3. LOS Factors

In the brief review of departure lounge LOS evaluation, as presented in this section, we have identified the following LOS factors, which have been considered in the analyses:

- Space available for circulation.
- Number of available seats.
- Waiting time.

The above three variables present a good set of attributes for LOS evaluation at departure lounges. We will employ all of them in this research. Some considerations must be taken, however, before applying them:

- Space Available for Circulation will be considered relative to the number of passengers in the room. The output scale will be then m^2/passenger. The area considered will be taken as the total lounge area.

- The number of seats per passenger must be considered as a function of the number of passengers in the lounge. In practice, when passengers are interviewed to rate the departure lounge LOS according to existing seats, the number of passengers in the lounge at the interviewing time will be taken to get the following correlation:

  Number of existing seats / number of passengers inside the lounge

- Waiting time must be considered as the duration of the passengers' stay in the lounge. This duration is strongly influenced by airline procedures, type of flight (international/domestic), flight class (economy, first class, business class), security procedures that might exist at the airport, and availability of other locations such as VIP lounges and restaurants where early passengers may choose to wait.

Other factors could be considered when evaluating departing lounge LOS. Availability of concessions is a very important LOS factor, since passengers could use their free time to shop or have some snacks. The objective measurement of this factor is practically impossible though. In the same way, other subjective factors as lighting, comfort and aesthetics present the same problem for practical measurement.

5.6.4. Number of Seats per Passenger

Table 5.20 presents the splitting of passengers into 10 groups of similar NS/P values. Equation 5.19 shows the relationship between NS/P and LOS ratings. Figure 5.10 illustrates the plot of the data and the regression line. Table 5.21 presents the suggested LOS standards.

Table 5.20: Number of Seats Data for São Paulo / Guarulhos Airport

Group (j)	NS/P Range	NS/P Average Value	#	μ_j^{LOS}
1	0.4 - 0.5	0.47	15	(0.30)
2	0.6 - 0.7	0.69	12	0.11
3	0.8 - 0.9	0.83	23	(0.06)
4	1.0 - 1.2	1.07	18	0.38
5	1.3 - 1.5	1.36	12	0.27
6	1.6 - 2.0	1.92	9	1.01
7	2.1 - 3.0	2.52	14	0.87
8	3.1 - 5.0	3.50	5	1.58
9	5.1 - 7.0	5.76	5	1.19
10	> 7.1	8.49	4	2.12
		Total:	**119**	

$$\mu_{S\tilde{a}oPaulo}^{LOS} = 0.268 + 0.777 \text{ LN (NS/P)} \qquad (5.19)$$

$$(t = 2.788) \qquad (t = 8.617)$$

$R^2 = 0.90$
$F = 74.254$
Chi-Square $= 16.127$
Chi-Square$_{critic} = 28.869$ (5% signif. - 18 d.f.)

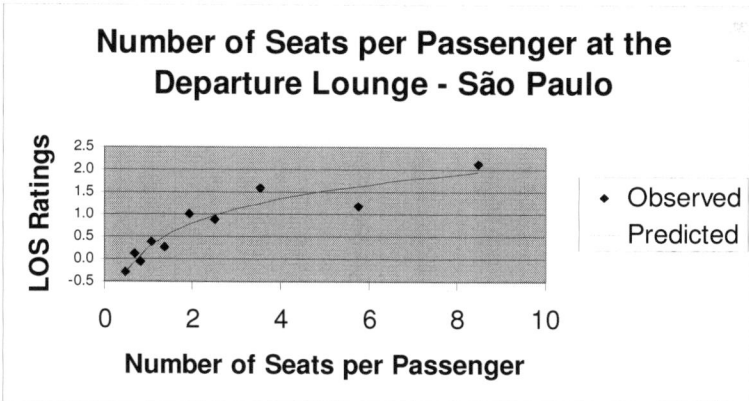

Figure 5.10: Plot of the Data and the Regression Line - Number of Seats per Pax - São Paulo

Table 5.21: Suggested LOS Standards

- Number of Seats per Passenger

LOS	SEATS PER PASSENGER (NS/P)
A	> 4.5
B	1.3 - 4.5
C	0.4 - 1.3
D	0.1 - 0.4
E	< 0.1

According to the suggested LOS standards, the airport has to provide more seats than passengers to obtain a good LOS evaluation. That is due to the fact that some passengers occupy more than one seat, with clothes, bags, etc. In some extreme cases, there are people that sleep on the seats, occupying two or more seats. However, a poor LOS evaluation will happen only when the number of seats per passenger is below 40%, which was not the case at the surveyed airports, even during peak hours.

5.6.5. Availability of Space

Table 5.22 presents the splitting of passengers into 10 groups of similar AS values. Equation 5.20 shows the relationship between AS and LOS ratings. Figure 5.11 illustrates the plot of the data and the regression line. Table 5.23 presents the suggested LOS standards.

Table 5.22: Availability of Space Data for São Paulo / Guarulhos Airport

Group (j)	Range (m²)	Average Value (m²)	#	μ_j^{LOS}
1	AS < 2.0	1.5	25	0.09
2	2.0 ≤ AS < 3.0	2.3	26	0.61
3	3.0 ≤ AS < 4.0	3.4	27	1.11
4	4.0 ≤ AS < 5.0	4.2	9	1.21
5	5.0 ≤ AS < 6.0	5.4	4	1.11
6	6.0 ≤ AS < 7.0	6.5	7	1.62
7	7.0 ≤ AS < 8.0	7.3	3	2.22
8	8.0 ≤ AS < 11.0	9.5	6	1.78
9	11.0 ≤ AS < 14.0	12.3	5	1.53
10	AS > 14.0	18.5	5	2.63
		Total:	117	

$$\mu_{S\tilde{a}oPaulo}^{LOS} = 0.823 \text{ LN (AS)} \qquad (5.20)$$

$$(t = 15.871)$$

$R^2 = 0.83$
$F = 43.981$
Chi-Square = 6.195
Chi-Square$_{critic}$ = 28.869 (5% signif. - 18 d.f.)

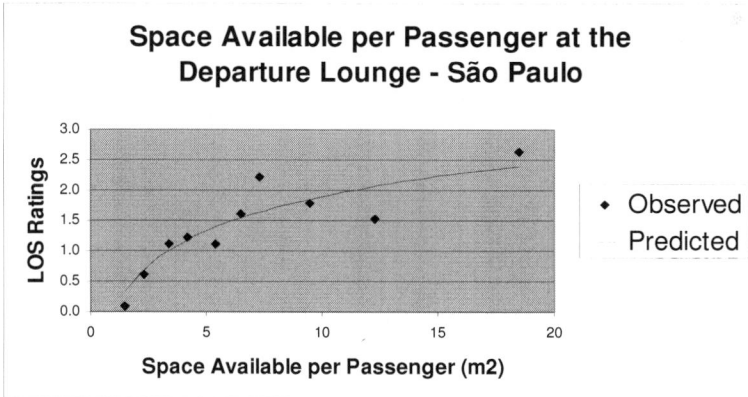

Figure 5.11: Plot of the Data and the Regression Line - Availability of Space - São Paulo

Table 5.23: Suggested LOS Standards

Availability of Space - São Paulo

LOS	SPACE AVAILABLE (m2)
A	> 8.7
B	2.0 - 8.8
C	0.5 - 2.0
D	0.2 - 0.5
E	< 0.2

LOS A values in Table 5.23 are exaggeratedly high. Nevertheless, that usually happens when the movement at the airport is very low, e.g., between 2PM and 4PM. On the opposite side, values between $0.2m^2$ and $0.5m^2$ will only occur during very busy periods.

5.6.6. Waiting Time

Waiting time was originally planned to be an evaluation variable. It was removed from the analysis, however, because the regression analysis did not provide good results Many passengers arrive at the departure lounge even before the stipulated time indicated by the airlines. In this case, a long waiting time could not be associated with a poor level of service. Similarly, a short waiting time would not necessarily represent a high level of service, but actually, that the passenger was delayed for the flight.

5.6.7. Correlation between Variables

There is correlation between the variables at the departure lounge, as the Table 5.24 shows.

Table 5.24: Correlation between Variables of Departure Lounge

	NS/PAX	AS
NS/PAX	1.00	
AS	0.82	1.00

The very strong relationship between number of seats per passenger (NS/Pax) and availability of space (AS) is a major hindrance to apply a composite evaluation for the departure lounge. In this case, an individual LOS evaluation for each measure is recommended.

5.7. Baggage Claim

5.7.1. Introduction

The LOS evaluation of baggage claim facilities is discussed in this last section. There is not too much work regarding this subject, since as we have mentioned in the second chapter of this thesis (literature review) the emphasis of previous studies is concentrated on departing passengers. For this reason, we can affirm that research in this area is needed, as emphasized by many researchers and airport agencies. We start by providing a brief state of the art on baggage claim facilities and then we enumerate the main LOS factors that will be employed in this research. The methodology and theoretical framework employed will be the same as the ones proposed for the other components, which have been studied in previous sections.

5.7.2. State of the Art

Unlike most other modes, in air transport it is customary to separate passengers from their baggage during the line haul portion of the trip. This adds substantially to the complexity of handling the air trip and seriously complicates the design of passenger terminals, since it is essential that the separation and reuniting of passenger and baggage be carried out with maximum efficiency and at an extremely high level of reliability (Ashford and Wright, 1992). That separation imposes a challenge to airport operators, since unloading of passengers is usually processed faster than unloading of baggage.

The baggage claim lobby should be located so that checked baggage may be returned to terminating passengers in reasonable proximity to the terminal deplaning curb. At low-activity airports, checked baggage may be placed on a shelf for passenger claiming. More active airports have installed mechanical delivery and display equipment. The number of claim devices required is determined by the number and type of aircraft that will arrive during the peak hour, the time distribution of these arrivals, the number of terminating passengers, the amount of baggage checked on these flights, and the mechanism used to transport baggage from aircraft to the claim area (Horonjeff & McKelvey, 1994). The distance from baggage claim lobby to terminal curb has been for many years one of the main quality indicators of baggage claim facilities. That is a very important issue, since arriving passengers are supposed to be tired from the air trip, and carrying lots of bags will be a cumbersome task for them. Not only must the distance be short, but also enough orientation must be provided, since many passengers may not be familiar with the terminal.

The inbound baggage area is composed of the following spaces (Hart, 1985):

1. Baggage off-load area, consisting of a cart drive aligned with the section of the claim device assigned for off-loading with 3 ft (0.9 m) of space between the cart and the device for handling off-loading, which can be direct feed or remote feed. Because this area is not open to passengers, it does not directly affect the LOS.
2. The section of the claim device located in the public area.
3. Claim area around the device.
4. Public milling and waiting area.

5. Concessions, mainly car rental counters, service counters, courtesy phones, public telephones.

The principal demand and operating factors influencing service level and capacity in the baggage claim are summarized in Table 5.25:

Table 5.25: Demand and Operating Factors Influencing Service Level and Capacity of the Baggage Claim Area

Factor	Description
Equipment configuration and claim area	Type, layout, feed mechanism, and rate of baggage display; space available for waiting passengers; relation of wait area to display frontage; access to and amount of feed belt available
Staffing practices	Availability of porters (sometimes called "sky caps") and inspection of baggage at exit; rate of baggage loading/unloading from cart to feed belt
Baggage load	Numbers of bags per passengers, fraction of passengers with baggage, time of baggage arrival from aircraft
Passenger characteristics	Rate of arrival from gate, ability to handle luggage, use of carts, number of visitors

Source: TRB, 1987

The TRB group stresses that research on baggage claim LOS is a critical need. According to them additional data are needed on characteristics of bags, passengers, and equipment, as well as on airline and airport procedures. Because of the importance of the baggage claim to the passenger's overall perception of an airport and an airline, research into what levels of delay passengers may tolerate and under what conditions is also needed. These data would be valuable as well in mathematical modeling of baggage handling operations, a necessary tool for exploring consequences of new larger aircraft and changes in flight schedules (de Barros & Wirasinghe, 2004).

Martel and Seneviratne (1990) suggest the following factors as they might influence quality of service of baggage claim facilities:

- Processing time;

- Service variability range;
- Area size;
- Pedestrian density;
- Claim frontage;
- Care of handling;
- Aids to handicapped
- Proximity to curb.

Although this list provides a summary of factors to be considered when evaluating baggage claim LOS, some of them are very subjective making their measurement an impossible task. For instance, care of handling is expected to be very important for passengers, but its measurement is difficult. The same can be said about aids to handicapped travellers.

De Neufville and Odoni (2000) suggest the most important factor for baggage claim areas is claim frontage. According to them baggage claim areas must first provide enough claim presentation length, that is, length along the conveyor belt or race tracks, for people to identify and pick up their bags. The IATA standards recommend about 70 m for wide body, and about 40 m for narrow-body aircraft being served at the same time. This standard implies about 0.3 m of claim presentation per passenger. The FAA alternatively defines the length required in terms of the number of aircraft arriving in the peak 20 min, and assumes that passengers check 1.3 bags per person. Either standard leads to approximately the same results. However, these standards should be modified according to local realities such as the average number of bags checked, and the possibility that passengers are passing previously through another queue such as immigration clearance.

De Barros and Wirasinghe (2004) provided a method to size the baggage claim area for the new large aircraft. According to them, the presence of passengers traveling together, forming clusters, and the correlation between the arrival times of bags belonging to a passenger cluster, have a significant impact on the planning of the design area.

5.7.3. LOS Factors

Considering the literature review presented in the last paragraphs, we will employ the following factors for LOS evaluation:

- Processing time: measured from the time the passenger arrive at the baggage claim area, until the last bag is claimed.
- Claim frontage per passenger.
- Area size per passenger.

The selection of factors is based on the following criteria:

- *Possibility of Measurement*: since we aim to provide a LOS evaluation methodology based on LOS measures, we can not work with very subjective variables, which are impossible to be measured or whose measurement is so complicated that it would make this research impractical.
- *Importance for Passengers:* one of the goals of this research is to provide a LOS evaluation according to passenger perceptions. Considering this, it is important that the factors employed be the most important ones according to passengers' perceptions. That's way we will apply many of the factors provided by Martel and Seneviratne (1990), which is based on a passenger survey applied to Canadian airports.
- *Designers' Point of View:* airport designers are supposed to design airport passenger buildings in a way to satisfy passengers and management needs. In this case their opinion is very important to our research. In the reviews of this chapter we have mentioned their opinions, which are very similar to the results of the passenger survey previously mentioned. The TRB (1987) study, in particular, was developed by a group composed of airport professionals from very different backgrounds.

5.7.4. Correlation between Variables

The correlation between the three study variables are presented in Table 5.26:

Table 5.26: Correlation between Variables
Baggage Claim - Calgary

	PT	CF	AS
PT	1.0		
CF	0.2	1.0	
AS	0.2	0.9	1.0

It was identified that a high correlation exists between the variables claim frontage and area size. That is due to the fact that increasing carrousel length sizes leads to greater claim areas, and that is reflected on the LOS responses. In this case, it was decided to evaluate the baggage claim level of service as function of the processing time and claim frontage. This former variable was chosen as opposed to area size, because it better represents the baggage claim LOS. Passengers are more concerned with space close to the carrousel, than with the total baggage claim area. Conversely, if there is enough claim frontage for passengers, that will indicate that the area size is adequate.

5.7.5. Processing Time

Table 5.27 presents the splitting of passengers into 6 groups of similar PT values. Equation 5.21 shows the relationship between PT and LOS ratings. Figure 5.12 illustrates the plot of the data and the regression line. Table 5.28 presents the suggested LOS standards.

Table 5.27: Processing Time at Baggage Claim Data - Calgary

Group (j)	Range (min)	Average Value (min)	#	μ_j^{LOS}
1	$0 < PT \leq 5.0$	4.70	6	1.46
2	$5.0 < PT \leq 8.0$	6.90	16	0.84
3	$8.0 < PT \leq 11.0$	9.80	17	1.32
4	$11.0 < PT \leq 14.0$	12.30	7	0.27
5	$14.0 < PT \leq 17.0$	15.20	6	0.22
6	$17.0 < PT \leq 20.0$	19.60	7	(0.18)

$$\mu_{Calgary}^{LOS} = 1.88 - 0.11 \ (PT) \qquad\qquad (5.21)$$

$$(t = 5.686) \ (t = -4.053)$$

$R^2 = 0.80$
$F = 16.426$
Chi-Square $= 12.631$
Chi-Square$_{critic} = 18.307$ (5% signif. - 10 d.f.)

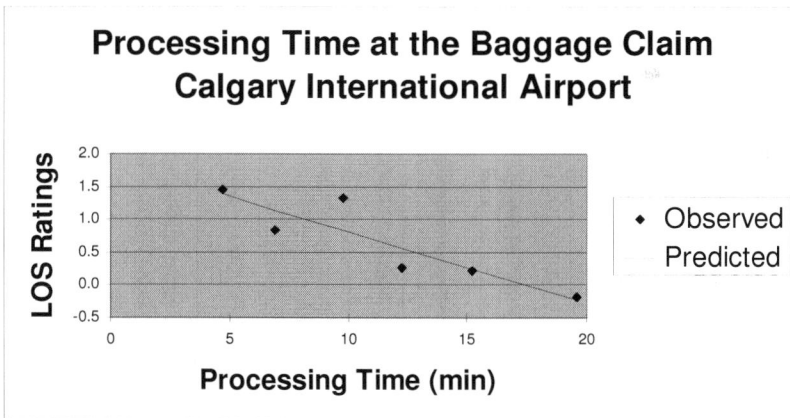

Figure 5.12: Plot of the Data and the Regression Line - Processing Time at Baggage Claim - Calgary

Table 5.28: Suggested LOS Standards
Processing Time - Calgary

LOS	Processing Time at Baggage Claim (min)
A	< 1
B	1 - 14
C	14 - 20
D	20 - 26
E	> 26

According to the suggested LOS standards, it is recommended that a processing time that is lower than 14 minutes be targeted to obtain a good (B) level of service evaluation. Processing times longer than 20 minutes will provide a poor (D) or unacceptable (E) level of service evaluation.

5.7.6. Claim Frontage per Passenger

Table 5.29 presents the splitting of passengers into 6 groups of similar CF values. Equation 5.22 shows the relationship between CF and LOS ratings. Figure 5.13 illustrates the plot of the data and the regression line. Table 5.30 presents the suggested LOS standards.

Table 5.29: Claim Frontage Data - Calgary

Group (j)	Range (m)	Average Value (m)	#	μ_j^{LOS}
1	$0.7 < CF \leq 0.8$	0.73	19	1.61
2	$0.9 < CF \leq 1.0$	0.95	15	1.31
3	$1.1 < CF \leq 1.4$	1.34	10	2.16
4	$1.5 < CF \leq 1.6$	1.56	6	2.85
5	$1.7 < CF \leq 1.8$	1.80	2	2.42
6	$CF > 1.8$	2.50	7	2.60

$$\mu_{Calgary}^{LOS} = 1.81 + 1.10 \; LN \; (CF) \qquad (5.22)$$
$$(t = 9.28) \quad (t = 2.87)$$

$R^2 = 0.67$
$F = 8.25$
Chi-Square $= 2.794$
Chi-Square$_{critic}$ $= 18.307$ (5% signif. - 10 d.f.)

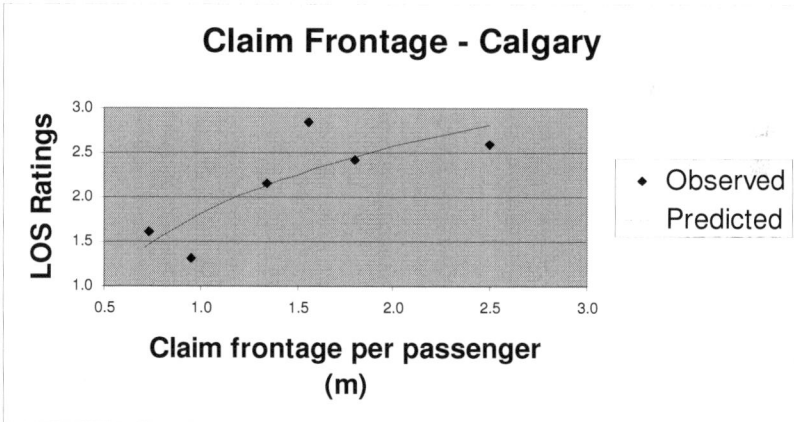

Figure 5.13: Plot of the Data and the Regression Line - Claim Frontage - Calgary

Table 5.30: Suggested LOS Standards
Claim Frontage - Calgary

LOS	Claim Frontage per Passenger (m)
A	> 1.73
B	0.23 - 1.73
C	< 0.23

LOS D and E were not presented, because there was no unacceptable (LOS E) response and only 1 poor (LOS D) response. The LOS standards generated would not be very significant with such a small number of responses.

5.7.7. Composite Evaluation

The ratings of both variables (processing time and claim frontage) can be weighted and then combined, according to the following equation (5.12):

$$LOS(baggage\ claim) = w_1 * LOS(PT) + w_2 * LOS(CF) \qquad (5.23)$$

Where

$LOS(baggage\ claim)$ = overall baggage claim LOS ratings

$LOS(PT)\ and\ LOS(CF)$ = LOS ratings for each individual measures

$w_1\ and\ w_2$ = relative importance weights of individual measures

Substituting the LOS ratings of the above equation by the survey's responses and performing a regression analysis will provide the values w_1 and w_2 as the parameters of the regression equation, which can be obtained through least squares method. In this case, the weights are obtained, reflecting the passenger perceptions of the relative importance of the components.

The results of the regression analysis are shown below:

R Square = 0.48

F = 25.983

$w_1 = 0.51$ t Stat = 7.41   P-value = 6.5 E-10

$w_2 = 0.50$ t Stat = 8.17   P-value = 3.6 E-11

The intercept was not very significant (P-value = 0.10) and was removed from the analysis.

Equation 5.23 can then be written as follows (5.24):

$$LOS(baggage\ claim) = 0.5 * LOS(PT) + 0.5 * LOS(CF) \qquad (5.24)$$

The LOS ratings vary from 1 to 5 corresponding to the LOS ranges, A to E: A-5, B-4, C-3, D-2, and E-1.

According to the weightings, both factors have roughly the same importance.

The above equation can be utilized for performing a composite evaluation of a baggage claim facility as a function of the individual measures formerly presented.

5.8. Conclusions

All the LOS analysis have shown that the methodology proposed can be applied in practice, and is able to generate valuable LOS standards according to the user perceptions. Some conclusions can be drawn from the analysis:

1. Sample Size: 119 passengers have been observed and interviewed at São Paulo / Guarulhos International Airport. It was possible to split these passengers into 10 or more groups for most of the surveyed facilities. The main requisite for application of the methodology proposed is having a reasonable number of different groups. Otherwise, the model application will be very limited. The analysis of check-in counter and the baggage claim for the Calgary International Airport was done with 6 groups, because of the low sample size: 60 passengers. However, it was still possible to split these passengers to get a reasonable model. It is suggested that regression analysis be performed with at least 30 data points (Wright, 1997). Thus, as a rule of thumb, we could define the ideal number of sample passengers as 300 passengers. That sample size would allow passengers split into 30 groups of similar stimulus values.

2. Sensitivity Analysis: it would be interesting to verify the sensitivity of the model as function of other variables like trip purpose, gender, and type of flight. Such analyses would only be possible with collection of more data.

3. Application of the Survey: the survey has to be applied in different periods of the day to provide a representative model. Late morning, and early afternoons are not interesting, because the airport movement will be very low both for arriving and departing. If 100% of the surveys are applied between 9AM and 5PM, most probably all the responses about the level of service will be good/excellent. In this case no modeling can be performed. Usually an airport terminal is busy during the early morning (5-9AM), and evenings (5-8PM); it is necessary to allocate the surveyors at

different periods to get varied LOS responses. That was the procedure employed in this research.

4. Suggested LOS Standards: the LOS standards generated are applicable to the surveyed airports. Application of these standards to other airports is not recommended, because each airport has its own characteristics, procedures, and passenger mix. In these cases, more data should be collected.

5. Inclusion of Other Variables: other variables could be employed. They can be modeled, as long they are measurable and collectable. Very subjective variables are difficult to measure. Examples of these are aesthetics, comfort, and lighting. There are variables for which it is difficult collect data, because of security procedures that exist at airports.

6. Composite Evaluation: variables that have a high degree of correlation cannot be used to obtain a composite evaluation. That was the case for the variables for the curbside (waiting time, space, and walking distance), departure lounge (space available and number of seats), and baggage claim (area size and claim frontage). In all these three cases, it was necessary to reduce the degree of the model to get an overall measure.

7. Normality of Responses: unless the responses follow a normal distribution, the methodology can not be successfully employed. The chi-square was calculated for all models, and the responses follow a normal distribution to a 5% confidence level.

Chapter 6 will apply these same procedures to obtain overall LOS measures (total time, walking distance, and orientation). Chapter 7 will develop a method to combine all these individual measures to obtain a composite evaluation for the airport passenger terminal.

CHAPTER SIX: OVERALL TERMINAL MEASURES

6.1. Introduction

Chapter 5 analyzed the level of service for individual components. All the measures employed were associated with characteristics of those components. Characteristics associated with the airport passenger terminal as a whole will be employed in this chapter. We will call these measures 'overall terminal measures'. Three overall measures will be employed in this analysis: (1) Total waiting + processing time, (2) Walking Distance, and (3) Orientation.

The state of the art of overall measures for level of service evaluation at airport passenger terminals is scarce. Besides, there is no method for overall LOS evaluation according to passenger perceptions.

The three proposed measures are by no means intended to cover all aspects of the operations of an airport passenger terminal. However, Chapter 7 will provide an overall LOS measure based on the addiction of the level of service of individual terminal components.

6.2. Total Waiting + Processing Time

The main advantage of the air transport mode is to reduce the travel time between origin and destination, compared to surface transportation. The total travel time is composed of access time, terminal time and air time. The access time is a matter of major concern. In many cases this time exceeds the air time by a considerable margin. For a journey of 500 km between two large metropolitan areas, the ground time can be as much as twice the air travel time. Similar comparisons can be made between the terminal time and air time. The terminal time can be one of the major components of the total travel time. This fact is especially true when there are many connections along the route.

Although the terminal time can be an important factor to evaluate the terminal LOS, it is important to determine which components of the terminal should be included in the analysis. The terminal time can be divided in waiting time, processing time, and other time. Waiting time is the time spent at the check-in counter line, security screening line, passport inspection line, and at the departure lounge. Processing time is the time spent at the check-in counter desk, security screening processing, passport inspection desk, and at the loading process. Other time is the remaining time where the passenger is walking, or at other non-operational components like toilets, food area, and shops. In this analysis, the other time component has been excluded from the terminal time analysis, for the following reasons:

1. The walking time will be evaluated when the other two overall measures are considered: walking distance and orientation. Including that time in this analysis would provide a duplicate effect.

2. The services and concessions area is not a mandatory component. Even though many passengers could want and need to go to this area, they do it freely. That is not true for the operational components like check-in or security inspection.

3. The analysis presented herein involves only departing passengers. It would be necessary to include the other time when connecting passengers are involved, because the concession time is actually a waiting time for the departing flight.

We will denote the total waiting + processing time as service time in this section. The airport and airline management have the power to reduce the service time. This can be done by improving procedures, implementing new technology, or adding new staff. All these changes have an associated cost, but might be able to improve the level of service offered.

Obtaining the service time for each passenger is a long and cumbersome task. The only way to do that is following the passenger from curbside to loading. This process can take up to 4 hours! That was the case for some passengers traveling overseas from São Paulo / Guarulhos International Airport. It is also virtually impossible for one surveyor to follow two different passengers at the same time, because the travel path would probably be different for each one. Observing passengers in a group is not recommended, because the responses for all passengers in the group are usually the same (they hear the first interviewed passenger and usually repeat the same answers). The productivity of a surveyor on an 8 hour-shift can be as low as 2 passengers/day. However, that is the only way to get accurate overall measures. At the moment of loading, the observed passengers were asked to state their opinion about the level of service concerning the total waiting + processing time.

Table 6.1 shows the splitting of passengers into 8 groups of similar service times. Equation 6.1 presents the relationship between total service time and LOS responses of total service time. Figure 6.1 shows the plot of the data and the regression Line. Table 6.2 presents the suggested LOS standards.

Table 6.1: Total Service Time Data - São Paulo / Guarulhos Airport

Group (j)	Range (min)	Value (min)	#	μ_j^{LOS}
1	0-9	6.4	5	2.99
2	10-29	21.4	16	1.17
3	30-49	35.7	16	1.42
4	50-59	54.4	7	0.57
5	60-69	64.4	12	1.15
6	70-99	83.7	12	0.84
7	100-129	109.3	7	0.63
8	>130	237.7	3	-0.89
		Total:	78	

177

$$\mu_{S\tilde{a}oPaulo}^{LOS} = 4.542 - 0.911 \text{ LN } (T_{WT+PT}) \tag{6.1}$$

$$(t = 7.655) \quad (t = -6.198)$$

$R^2 = 0.86$
$F = 38.420$
Chi-Square $= 6.465$
Chi-Square$_{critic} = 23.685$ (5% signif. - 14 d.f.)

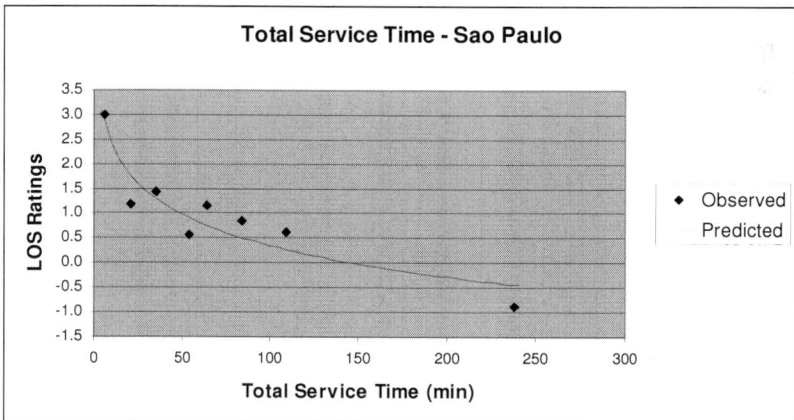

Figure 6.1: Plot of the Data and the Regression Line - Total Service Time - São Paulo

Table 6.2: Suggested Level of Service Standards
Total Service Time - São Paulo

LOS	TOTAL SERVICE TIME (min)
A	0-14
B	14-88
C	88-242
D	>242

According to the suggested LOS standards (Table 6.2), passengers evaluate the LOS of the terminal as good (LOS B) if the total service time is shorter than 88 minutes. If the service time is longer than 242 minutes, the level of service will be evaluated as poor (LOS D). No passenger evaluated the service time as unacceptable (LOS E). In this case, it was impossible to generate the LOS E standard.

These LOS standards might not be applicable to airports that have characteristics that are different from São Paulo / Guarulhos International Airport. The high values of service times corresponding to LOS C and LOS D are due to the following reasons:

- The airport has a great share of inter-continental flights. For these flights, around 300 passengers/flight are processed with only 3 check-in counters (hospitality class). Besides, passengers are asked to arrive at the departure lounge 90 minutes before departure and to arrive at the airport 3-4 hours before departure. For some Europeans flights, the boarding times took more than 30 minutes.
- The ride to the airport from downtown can take around 30-60 minutes. Some passengers do not want to take the risk of missing the flight and arrive very early at the airport. In this case, they have more time to stand in long queues.

6.3.   Walking Distance

Walking in terminals is one of the most important, most controversial, and least understood activities. Walking distances in some terminals, especially for transfers passengers, have become quite long. The walking distance has been used by many researchers as an important measure of the level of service for an airport passenger terminal (Bandara and Wirasinghe (1992), Seneviratne and Martel (1994), Correia (2000), deNeufville et. al (2002), and de Barros & Wirasinghe (2003). Although its importance as a level of service measure is recognized, there has been no study to evaluate the impact of the walking distance on the LOS according to passenger perceptions.

For departing passengers that use the curbside at São Paulo / Guarulhos International Airport, the most common sequence is:

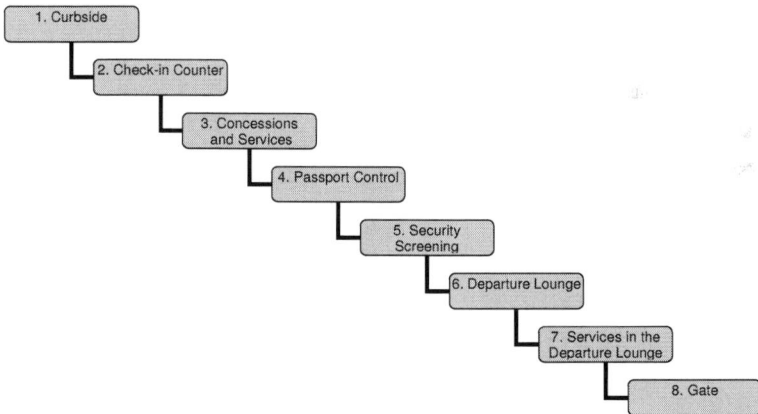

Figure 6.2: Passenger Sequence on a Departing Trip

It is possible to obtain the walking distance from a given curbside origination and a given boarding gate, passing through the mandatory components (1, 2, 4, 5, 6, and 8 of the above list). This distance is called minimum walking distance. This is usually the distance walked by users familiar with the airport, especially the ones that do not have too much time to spend at the airport. The remaining passengers walk more than this minimum distance, which will be called real walking distance. These people might walk more than necessary because they are lost, they want to use the concessions/service area, or just because they want to 'kill' time. Another walking distance definition could be created to identify the actual walking distance between operational components, excluding the walking to the concessions/service areas. This distance will be called real operational walking distance.

Passengers have been asked to rate the walking distance, without any other specification (minimum, real, operational, etc). However, we will try to correlate the responses to the different walking distances previously mentioned. All the details will not be mentioned, but the measure that had the best correlation with the walking distance responses was the real operational walking distance.

The user walking distances have been collected with the use of a digital pedometer. The surveyor (following a given passenger) walked the exact pathway of the passenger. All the distances between components have been recorded in a sheet. At the end of the interview, the surveyor walked again the pathway (from curbside to loading) to identify the minimum walking distance for this passenger.

Table 6.3 shows the splitting of passengers into 8 groups of similar walking distances. Equation 6.2 presents the relationship between walking distance and LOS responses of walking distance. Figure 6.3 shows the Plot of the Data and the Regression Line. Table 6.4 presents the suggested LOS standards.

Table 6.3: Real Operational Walking Distance Data - São Paulo Airport

Group	Wd$_{op}$ Range (m)	Wd$_{op}$ Value (m)	#	μ_j^{LOS}
1	< 100	44.33	9	1.06
2	100-199	165.23	13	0.76
3	200-249	224.08	13	0.61
4	250-349	288.91	23	0.57
5	350-399	363.70	8	0.93
6	400-499	420.00	5	0.45
7	>500	538.50	6	0.01
		Total:	**77**	

$$\mu_{S\tilde{a}oPaulo}^{LOS} = 1.117 - 0.002 \ (Wd_{op}) \qquad (6.2)$$

$$(t = 6.170) \quad (t = -3.045)$$

$R^2 = 0.65$
$F = 9.27$
Chi-Square $= 8.352$
Chi-Square$_{critic} = 21.026$ (5% signif. - 14 d.f.)

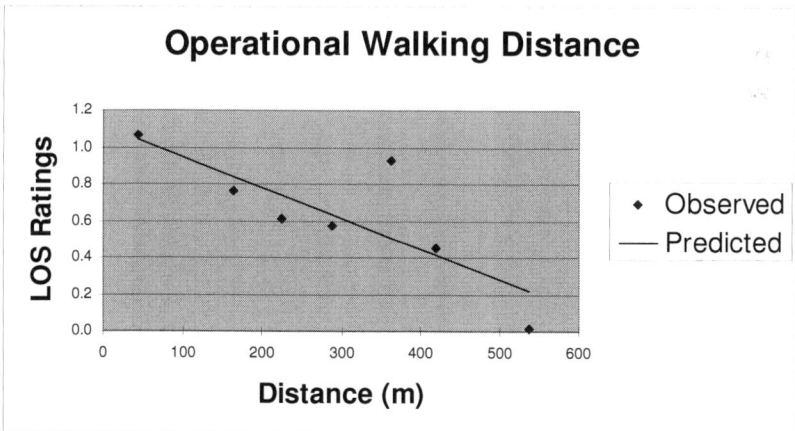

Figure 6.3: Plot of the Data and the Regression Line - Operational Walking Distance - São Paulo

Table 6.4: Suggested LOS Standards
Operational Walking Distance - São Paulo

LOS	Wd_{op} (m)
A/B	0-415
C	415-922
D	> 922

6.4. Orientation

Many people who have been in airport terminals know how difficult it can sometimes be to find some of the places and services that one wants in the terminal building. This difficulty is inversely proportional to the easiness of orientation provided. Disorientation or delays in orientation can be caused by (Hart, 1985):

1. Transition in surroundings, such as leaving an aircraft and entering the concourse, leaving the curb platform and entering the terminal. Transition can also involve scale, such as in leaving the highway system, entering the airport road system, and subsequently entering the terminal road system.

2. Transition in the mode of transportation, such as from walking to riding in a vehicle, from driving to walking, from standing or walking on a mechanical moving device to walking on the floor.

3. Complexity of the terminal plan. For example, a layout that requires a number of signs, multiple decisions at various points, frequent decisions, and short distances between decisions will not give the average person enough time for perception and reaction.

In summary, the main impacts of a bad orientation system at the terminal result in additional walking distance, especially for unfamiliar users of the airport. If the terminal planning provides a good orientation system, the users will be able to get to their desired destinations walking the minimum distance necessary; otherwise, they might walk considerably more than the minimum. This idea suggested the creation of the following orientation index:

$$O_I = \frac{\text{Real Operational Walking Distance}}{\text{Minimum Walking Distance}}$$

A good orientation system would have O_I equaling 1.0. Increasing values of O_I would be associated with a bad orientation system. This orientation index will be correlated to the user opinions on the orientation level of service.

Table 6.5 shows the splitting of passengers into 8 groups of similar O_I values. Equation 6.3 presents the relationship between the orientation index and LOS responses of orientation. Figure 6.3 shows the plot of the data and the regression line. Table 6.6 presents the suggested LOS standards.

Table 6.5: Orientation Data - São Paulo International Airport

Group (j)	Wd_{op}/Wd_{min} Range	Wd_{op}/Wd_{min} Value	#	μ_j^{LOS}
1	1.0	1.00	30	1.14
2	1.1	1.10	10	1.41
3	1.2	1.20	12	1.21
4	1.3-1.4	1.40	10	0.92
5	1.5-1.6	1.60	4	0.38
6	1.7-1.9	1.80	4	-0.01
7	> 2.0	3.40	7	-0.27
		Total:	77	

$$\mu_j^{LOS} = 1.280 - 1.443 \text{ LN } (Wd_{op}/Wd_{min}) \qquad (6.3)$$

$$(t = 7.756) \qquad (t = -4.925)$$

$R^2 = 0.83$
$F = 24.254$
Chi-Square = 11.950
$\text{Chi-Square}_{critic} = 21.026$ (5% signif. - 12 d.f.)

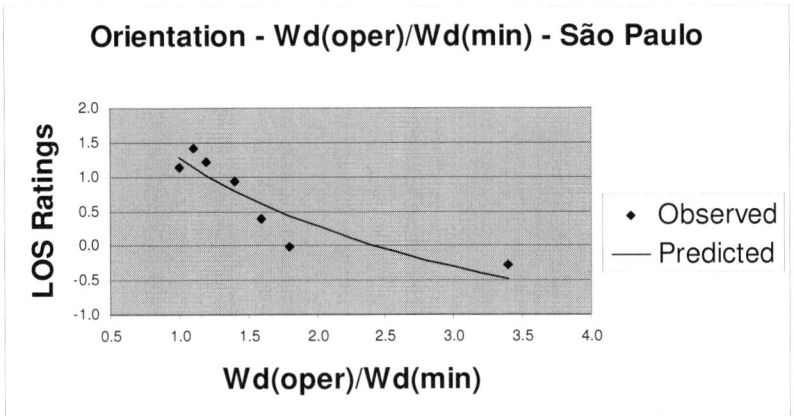

Figure 6.4 - Plot of the Data and the Regression Line - Orientation - São Paulo

Table 6.6 - Suggested LOS Standards
Orientation - São Paulo

LOS	Wd_{op}/Wd_{min}
A	1.0
B	1.0-2.1
C	2.1-3.4
D	3.4-4.5
E	> 4.5

These suggested LOS standards indicate that an excellent level of service (LOS A) will exist when passengers walk just the minimum walking distance. A good level of service (LOS B) will be achieved when people walk up to two times the minimum walking distance. The minimum walking distances for São Paulo / Guarulhos International Airport range from 150m to 350 m (from curbside to gate). Other large international airports around the world may have minimum walking distances much longer than these ones (e.g. Dallas Fort Worth, Frankfurt, Toronto Pearson, etc). In these airports, the acceptable O_I indices might be different, because people would not be happy to walk two times a long distance.

One of the effects of a bad orientation program is that visitors and passengers will remain in the terminal longer than would be necessary, thus causing accumulations that might require additional building space. This additional time was researched by Dada (1997), when he developed an orientation index called tardity differential, defined as walking time difference between experts and novices (T), divided by the route length (D). Higher values of tardity-differential may signify some difficulty in wayfinding. We undertook to correlate this tardity-differential to the user opinions about orientation level of service. The expert walking time was defined as the minimum walking time (walking time of the surveyor). The novices walking time was the user walking time, collected by the surveyor. The results are presented next.

Table 6.7 shows the splitting of passengers into 8 groups of similar T/D values. Equation 6.4 presents the relationship between the orientation index and LOS responses of orientation. Figure 6.5 shows the plot of the data and the regression line. Table 6.8 presents the suggested LOS standards.

186

Table 6.7: Tardity Differential Data - São Paulo / Guarulhos International Airport

Group (j)	T/D Range (s/m)	T/D Average Value (s/m)	#	μ_j^{LOS}
1	< 0.00	-0.04	11	1.29
2	0.01 - 0.10	0.06	11	2.62
3	0.11 - 0.20	0.15	8	1.60
4	0.21 - 0.30	0.26	9	1.56
5	0.31 - 0.60	0.46	12	0.96
6	0.61 - 0.90	0.72	12	0.50
7	0.91 - 1.50	1.13	8	0.79
8	>1.50	1.50	7	-0.24
		Total:	78	

$$\mu_j^{LOS} = 1.820 - 1.294 \, (T/D) \qquad (6.4)$$

$$(t = 7.07) \quad (t = -3.71)$$

$R^2 = 0.70$
$F = 13.733$
Chi-Square = 8.191
Chi-Square$_{critic}$ = 23.685 (5% signif. - 14 d.f.)

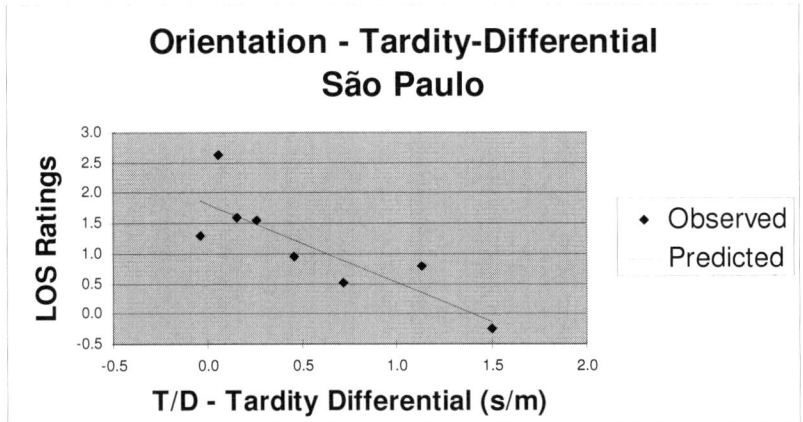

Figure 6.5: Plot of the Data and the Regression Line - Tardity Differential - São Paulo

Table 6.8: Suggested LOS Standards
Tardity-Differential - São Paulo /Guarulhos

LOS	T/D (s/m)
A	< - 0.35
B	-0.35 - 1.08
C	1.08 - 1.73
D	1.73 - 2.42
E	> 2.42

The advantage of using this index is that it may be correlated to physical measures of the building and then be used for planning purposes. Dada (1997) developed an association between the tardity-differential and the number of decision points and number of level changes. A decision point is usually an intersection of corridors, where a user has to choose between two or more routes, or where there is a need for further information on which to base a direction finding decision.

The research for the development of this correlation was done at a complex building in the University of Calgary. Two groups of subjects (31 each) were recruited for this investigation. One group was composed of users familiar with the building. The other group was composed of novices. Five routes were selected for these two groups. The results of this investigation are presented in Table 6.9.

188

Table 6.9: Number of Decision Points, Distance, Time Difference Between Experts and Novices, and Level Changes

Route Number	Number of Decision points	Distance (m)	Time difference (sec)	Number of level changes
1	4	66	16.05	2
2	5	75	10.08	1
3	6	162	31.40	1
4	6	155	48.09	2
5	13	265	27.89	0

Source: Dada (1997)

Using that data, a regression analysis was performed between the tardity-differential (T/D), number of decision points (N), and number of level changes (L_c). Equation 6.5 portraits the relationship:

$$T/D = (8.681N + 107.236\,L_c)10^{-3} \qquad (6.5)$$

Equation 6.5 has the power to identify how the physical measures of the building have an impact on the wayfind easiness. In this case, the two step process to evaluate the level of service of a planned building, would be to define the number of decision points and level changes of a given route. These two measures would provide the tardity-differential through equation 6.5. Finally, Table 6.8 would indicate the LOS associated with this tardity-differential. The only drawback of this process is that equation 6.5 was obtained from an investigation undertaken in Calgary - Canada, but the LOS standards of Table 6.8 were developed with data from São Paulo / Guarulhos International Airport. To solve this deficiency, an investigation should be undertaken to obtain a relationship similar to equation 6.5, but applied to São Paulo / Guarulhos International Airport.

6.5.   Conclusions

The overall measures represent an important step for the overall level of service evaluation for airport passenger terminals. Although the process of obtaining data is complex, a reasonable sample of 100 passengers can be obtained with the participation of 4 trained surveyors collecting data during a week (8 hour shift).

The importance of these new LOS standards is stressed, given the lack of research on this subject. Not only are the standards useful for application at São Paulo / Guarulhos International Airport, but this chapter has indicated how this methodology can be further applied. It would be useful to apply this methodology in other airports located in Brazil and even internationally. This effort would provide a more comprehensive understanding of the relationship between important overall terminal measures and the level of service associated with them.

The next chapter will develop a method to obtain the overall airport passenger terminal level of service as a function of the level of service of individual components.

CHAPTER SEVEN: OVERALL TERMINAL EVALUATION

7.1. Motivation

As it was mentioned in Chapter 6, there is no previous research developed to analyze the overall level of service for airport passenger terminals. However, overall airport LOS standards would be very useful for planning and design, management, and benchmarking purposes. At the planning level, several terminal building improvement alternatives must be evaluated as a function of many criteria, including (Horonjeff & McKelvey, 1994):

1. Processing cost per passenger.
2. Walking distances for various types of passenger.
3. Passenger delays in processing.
4. Occupancy levels and degree of congestion.
5. Construction costs.
6. Administrative, operating, and maintenance costs.
7. Potential revenue sources and the expected level of revenues from each source.

The performance indices presented above indicate that any proposed alternative must be operationally compatible, cost-effective and provide a reasonable level of service for passengers. It is therefore necessary to evaluate the overall level of service of each alternative. This overall level of service is also useful for management purposes, to check if the system is well balanced. In this case, not only is it necessary to verify the existing level of service of individual components, but also the overall level of service. Finally an overall measure is necessary for benchmarking purposes, where the airport administration wants to check its level of service compared with its competitors. That is especially true when there is competition between airports (multiple airport regions, hubs) or competition between modes.

This thesis will provide two methods for overall LOS evaluation:

- *Overall Evaluation from Components' LOS ratings:* in this case the components' LOS ratings are combined to obtain an overall LOS. This method will be presented in details in this Chapter.
- *Overall Terminal Measures:* this evaluation method was presented in Chapter 6; it consists of a correlation between overall terminal measures (total service time, walking distance, and orientation) and level of service user opinions.

7.2. Correlation Between Variables

Chapter 3 presented the methodology that will be employed in this chapter. Basically, a regression analysis will be performed between the overall LOS user ratings (1 to 5) and LOS user ratings for each individual component. A problem often encountered in multiple regression is multicollinearity, or the amount of "overlapping" information about the dependent variable that is provided by several independent variables (Taylor, 1999). This problem usually occurs when the independent variables are highly correlated. The correlation factor measures the relationship between two variables. A correlation of -1 means that there is a perfect (linear) negative relationship. A correlation of +1 means that there is a perfect (linear) positive relationship. A correlation of 0 means that there is no linear relationship. Table 7.1 presents the correlation between the independent variables calculated by SPSS.

Table 7.1: Correlation of Variables at the Overall Level

	Curb	Check-in	Sec. Screen.	Dep. Lounge	Walk. Dist.	Orient.	Total Time	Circ.	Conc.	Sec. Envir.
Curbside	1.0									
Check-in	0.2	1.0								
Security Scr.	0.4	0.2	1.0							
Lounge	0.3	0.2	0.3	1.0						
Walking Dist.	0.3	0.2	0.3	0.2	1.0					
Orientation	0.3	0.4	0.3	0.3	0.4	1.0				
Total Time	0.3	0.4	0.2	0.3	0.6	0.4	1.0			
Circulation	0.5	0.2	0.3	0.2	0.2	0.3	0.2	1.0		
Concessions	0.4	0.3	0.2	0.2	0.1	0.4	0.2	0.5	1.0	
Security Env.	0.4	0.1	0.2	0.3	0.1	0.3	0.1	0.4	0.4	1.0

The highest correlation value was found between the ratings of total time and walking distance. The reason for this is that passengers spend a considerable time walking at the airport to get to the desired destinations (check-in counter, departure lounge, gate, concessions, services, etc). There is also a fairly strong correlation between the total time and check-in and between total time and orientation. Passengers spend a long time at check-in counter lines at São Paulo / Guarulhos International Airport, especially the ones traveling overseas. Some surveyed passengers have spent more than 60 minutes in the check-in counter only. That might be one of the reasons for the correlation value (0.4) between these two variables. The correlation between total time and orientation might be explained by the fact that users that do not receive good orientation at an airport passenger terminal spend more time than necessary on wayfinding. These same ideas might explain the fairly strong relationship between walking distance and orientation (0.4).

It is not convenient to include variables that have a high degree of correlation in a multiple regression model. In this case, it is appropriate to analyze the overall terminal LOS without including the total time variable. Nevertheless, this variable will be indirectly represented by many other variables (curbside, check-in counter, security screening, departure lounge, etc), because a small share of the total time is included in each of these components.

The inclusion or removal of variables must be done in a very responsible manner. A model could become non-representative because important variables were not included or improperly removed. Additionally, each airport may have a different model specification, which will be function of operational, financial, and socio-economic characteristics. The correlation between variables is important, but it is not the only criteria for inclusion/removal of variables in the model.

Two other variables require additional attention. They are the circulation and security

Two other variables require additional attention. They are the circulation and security environment. These variables were originally intended to be part of the overall analysis, but after some thinking and discussion, it was decided to remove them from the evaluation. The respondent passengers found it very difficult to provide a LOS opinion about these two components, because the definitions of circulation and security environment were not clear to them. Besides, just a few passengers (if any) would be able to evaluate the security of the airport. Most probably none of them have had any security concerns at the airport. In this case they have not 'experienced' the security at the airport, as they have experienced the waiting time at the check-in counter or the crowdedness at the departure lounge.

The correlation values for the independent variables (excluding total time, circulation, and security environment) are presented in Table 7.2.

Table 7.2: Correlation of Variables at the Overall Level

	Curb	Check-in	Sec. Screen.	Dep. Lounge	Walking Distance	Orientation	Concessions
Curbside	1.0						
Check-in	0.2	1.0					
Security Screening	0.4	0.2	1.0				
Lounge	0.3	0.2	0.3	1.0			
Walking Distance	0.3	0.2	0.3	0.2	1.0		
Orientation	0.3	0.4	0.3	0.3	0.4	1.0	
Concessions	0.4	0.3	0.2	0.2	0.1	0.4	1.0

All these variables will be employed on the regression analysis to obtain a composite measure because the correlation between these variables is only moderate.

7.3. Composite Evaluation

The ratings of the variables will be combined, according to the following equation:

$LOS(overall) =$

$w_0 + w_1 * LOS(curb) + w_2 * LOS(check-in) + w_3 * LOS(sec. sc.) + w_4 * LOS(lounge) +$

$w_5 * LOS(walking\ dist.) + w_6 * LOS(orientation) + w_7 * LOS(concessions)$ (7.1)

Where

$LOS(overall)$ = overall terminal LOS ratings

$LOS(curb)$, $LOS(check-in)$, $LOS(sec.\ screen.)$, $LOS(lounge)$, $LOS(walk.\ dist.)$, $LOS(orientation)$, and $LOS(concessions)$ = LOS ratings for each individual components

w_0 = intercept

w_1, w_2, w_3, w_4, w_5, w_6, and w_7 = parameters of the equation.

Substituting the LOS ratings of the above equation by the responses (1 to 5) of the survey conducted at São Paulo / Guarulhos International Airport and performing a regression analysis will provide the values w_1, w_2, w_3, w_4, w_5, and w_6 as the parameters of the regression equation, and w_0 as the intercept. In this case, the weights are obtained, reflecting the user perceptions of the relative importance of components.

The results of the regression analysis are shown in Table 7.3:

Table 7.3: Parameters, Standard Error, t Stat, and P-value - Original variables

Component	Parameters	Standard Error	t Stat	P-value
Intercept	0.832	0.533	1.562	0.123
Curbside	0.359	0.102	3.518	0.001
Check-in	0.019	0.108	0.180	0.857
Security Screening	-0.099	0.095	-1.042	0.301
Lounge	0.117	0.077	1.522	0.133
Walking Distance	-0.006	0.083	-0.069	0.945
Orientation	0.196	0.090	2.191	0.032
Circulation	0.183	0.113	1.613	0.111
Concessions	0.027	0.103	0.261	0.795
$R^2 = 0.48$				
F = 7.86				
Observations: 78				

It can be noticed from Table 7.3 that the walking distance has a 94.5% chance of being equal to zero. This motivates us to remove this variable from the analysis. Although this is a very important factor for the overall terminal evaluation, it looks like that passengers at São Paulo / Guarulhos International Airport do not significantly value this factor, as much as they value other factors.

This regression analysis was composed of 78 observations. The 40 observations made at the first survey occurred during the Summer/03 were not included, because walking distance, total time, and security environment were not present in those questionnaires. The subsequent calculations in this chapter will now include these 40 observations, because the absent variables are no more the object of study for the overall LOS.

New regression analyses were performed with the following changes:

- No inclusion of the walking distance variable.

- Addition of the 40 observations made during the Summer/03 survey.

- Removing (stepwise) the variables with high P-values.

The results of the best-fit regression analysis are presented in Table 7.4.

Table 7.4: Parameters, Standard Error, t Stat, and P-value
- Best-fit Regression Analysis

Component	Parameters	Standard Error	t Stat	P-value
Intercept	0.755	0.358	2.108	0.037
Curbside	0.313	0.070	4.504	0.000
Check-in	0.114	0.075	1.513	0.133
Lounge	0.118	0.062	1.889	0.061
Orientation	0.238	0.068	3.517	0.001
Purpose	0.243	0.103	2.365	0.020
$R^2 = 0.443$				
F = 17.799				
Observations: 118				

The variables security screening and concessions presented high P-values. That means they have a high chance of being equal to zero. In addition, security screening had a negative value. That was expected. As it was mentioned in Chapter 5, the security screening process at São Paulo / Guarulhos International Airport is very fast and does not impose any concern to passengers. The concessions component is not mandatory and some users did not have a strong opinion about its level of service because they have not been there to experience it.

One new variable was included in the analysis because it fitted well to the regression equation. That was the 'purpose' variable. It was included as a dummy variable. It is equal to 0 when the trip purpose is business or combined and equal to 1 when the trip purpose is non-business.

The final step to refine the analysis is the detection of possible outliers. The outliers were defined (in this thesis) as responses of passengers that were clearly inconsistent. It might be a passenger that evaluated the overall terminal as excellent, but evaluated all (or most) components as poor or unacceptable. The opposite can also occur: one passenger can evaluate the terminal as poor, but all the components as excellent. Two cases (out of 118 passengers) presented this inconsistency and they were removed from the analysis.

The results of the regression analysis without these two outliers are presented in Table 7.5.

Table 7.5: Parameters, Standard Error, t Stat, and P-value - Final Model

Component	Parameters	Standard Error	t Stat	P-value
Intercept	0.841	0.327	2.575	0.011
Curbside	0.246	0.065	3.809	0.000
Check-in	0.144	0.069	2.094	0.039
Lounge	0.151	0.057	2.643	0.009
Orientation	0.229	0.063	3.656	0.001
Purpose	0.214	0.094	2.291	0.024
$R^2 = 0.47$				
F = 19.538				
Observations: 116				

The parameters of Table 7.5 can be substituted into equation 7.1 to provide the following relation (equation 7.2):

$$LOS(overall) = 0.841 + 0.246 * LOS(curb) + 0.144 * LOS(check\text{-}in) +$$

$$+ 0.151 * LOS(lounge) + 0.229 * LOS(orientation) + 0.214 (purpose) \qquad (7.2)$$

According to equation 7.2, the most important component for passengers is the curbside. The reason for this is that it was the first component for the 118 surveyed passengers. The curbside was the first impression they had about the airport, affecting the evaluation of the terminal as a whole. Orientation is the second most important component. It means that passengers want a terminal that provides easy orientation. A section about orientation level of service was presented in Chapter 6. It includes the main factors that contribute to a good orientation system. The importance of the check-in counter and the departure lounge can be drawn from the fact that usually they spend a considerable time in these two components. The intercept (0.841) indicates that other variables could be included in this analysis. It 'says' that despite the LOS of the curbside, check-in, lounge and orientation, and the purpose of trip, there is a component of the overall LOS that is not represented by these explicative variables.

7.4. Application of the Model

The main purpose of the model is to evaluate the overall LOS as a function of the individual LOS measures. One of the applications would be in terminal building construction or improvements. Usually any airport improvements are done when the LOS of the airport passenger terminal and its components offer a low level of service.

199

The model indicates that some components have a great impact on the overall LOS evaluation. That means they should get priority from the management of the airport. Some factors do not have a great 'importance' on the overall level of service. That does not mean that their individual level of services can be kept low, because the model does not have such elasticity to forecast the overall level of service when the LOS of individual components has extreme values. The analysis is reliable as long as there are observation points to validate the extrapolation of the regression equation curves. However, most components that have been modeled, which do not have a great 'importance' on the overall level of service, received fair, good, and excellent evaluations from the majority of respondent passengers. That was the case for the walking distance, concessions, and security screening.

Chapter 5 and 6 presented the main important measures for LOS evaluation. Table 7.6 provides a summary of these measures.

Table 7.6: LOS Measures for Individual Components

Component	Measures
Curbside	Space Available for Cars (ECU)
Check-in Counter	Waiting Time
	Processing Time
	Space Available for Passengers
Departure Lounge	Number of Seats
	Area Size
Orientation	Tardity-differential

The objective of this section is to provide some actions that could be taken in practice to improve these LOS measures, what will be their impact on the overall LOS evaluation, and what is the cost-benefit associated. The suggested actions were drawn from applications at the surveyed airports and somewhere else. It should be noted however, that they are by no means exhaustive.

7.4.1. Curbside

The measure employed to evaluate the level of service of the curbside was the effective curbside utilization (ECU), which is the virtual length of cars divided by the length of the curbside.

$$ECU = \frac{\text{Virtual Length of Cars}}{\text{Length of Curbside}} \qquad (7.3)$$

Two things can be done to reduce the ECU. (1) Increasing the length of the Curbside or (2) Decreasing the virtual length of cars. The first action is usually adopted at the planning level of a terminal. The length of the curbside required for unloading passengers and baggage is determined by the type and volume of ground vehicle traffic anticipated in the peak period of the design day. The curbside geometry is usually conformed to the geometry of the terminal; any further improvements to this area might not practical. On the other hand, the virtual (total) length of cars can be decreased by reducing the demand on the curbside or reducing the interval that cars stay at the curbside. The virtual (total) length of cars can also be decreased by reducing the size of the vehicles (e.g. segregating the buses in a special remote area).

Calgary International Airport provides a free short-term parking. In this airport, parking is free for the first 30 minutes. In most of the cases, this time is usually enough to drop off or pick up a passenger. And the result of this is that the curbside is rarely operated over its capacity. That procedure was only possible, because the airport constructed a new parkade, which is capable of accommodating the demand for cars. That is not the case for São Paulo / Guarulhos International Airport and São Paulo / Congonhas International Airport, where the parking lots are usually very busy.

Adding new transit alternatives to the airport can alleviate the demand for cars at the airport, and consequently at the curbside. Some airports are also moving in this direction to alleviate the air pollution in its vicinity. However these transit alternatives are usually very expensive and just a few airports have enough traffic to afford them.

The most economical way to improve the efficiency of the curbside at very busy airports is by reducing the time cars stay at the curbside. For instance, if it were possible to reduce the waiting time at the curbside by 50%, this would result in a 100% increase on the ECU. One way to reduce the time cars spend at the curbside is to provide a good orientation system. If drivers are lost, they most probably will spend more time trying to find the best locations and the result of this is increasing curbside utilization.

Enforcement has been applied at some airports to make sure cars do not wait too much time or double park at the curbside. That is the case for the curbside at São Paulo / Congonhas International Airport, where a security guard works at the curbside during busy hours. There is also an anecdotal example from Seattle Airport; the management provided a tower to be parked at the curbside on a permanent basis. That procedure motivated the curbside users to stay a shorter time than usual, in face of the practical possibility of having the car towed away.

7.4.2. Check-in Counter

According to the measures adopted in this research, an airport will offer a good level of service at the check-in counter when the service is fast and reasonable space is available for passengers. These two characteristics are intrinsically dependent on the number and type of check-in counter desks and upon the peak demand.

At the planning level, the number of check-in counter desks required is determined as a function of the peak demand and the waiting time acceptable to the passengers. The demand at the check-in counter is very fluctuating, reflecting user behavioral characteristics. Some arrival curves are provided to facilitate the understanding of the user behavior, like the cumulative arrival distribution in Figure 7.1.

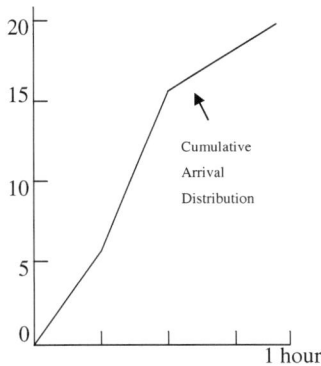

Figure 7.1: Cumulative Arrival Distribution (TRB, 1987)

According to Figure 7.1, during the first 15 min, six passengers arrive at the counter at fairly uniform intervals of 2.5 min apart. The arrival rate then increases, so that by the end of the first half-hour, 10 more people have arrived, a total of 16. All peak-hour passengers, a total of 20 passengers, have arrived by the end of 55 min. No passenger arrivals are expected during the final 5 min of the peak hour. An average service time of approximately 3 min per passenger is maintained during the peak period. As it can be noticed, the arrival of passengers is not uniform. This characteristic influences the design and management of check-in counter facilities. In addition to these cumulative arrival distribution charts, there has been a tendency to apply micro-simulation models to the check-in planning, design and management.

In some markets, a considerable number of passengers may be pre-ticketed, and a higher percentage of express check-in positions may be warranted either within the terminal building or at the curb front. Self-service kiosks are effective at reducing check-in lines; they can also be equipped with a combination of biometrics to perform identity checks for automated 'fast-track' immigration control, self-service check-in or even at security checkpoints (International Airport Review (2003), Issue 1, p. 77, de Barros (2001)). For instance, the adoption of common-use self-service kiosks at Sydney and Melbourne Airports reduced the processing time for check-in to less than one minute (International Airport Review, 2002, Issue 4, p. 11). Shorter processing times result in shorter waiting times, which mean less people in the queues, reducing the need for space provision. The adoption of common use self-service and/or remote kiosks should be adopted in airport passenger terminals that are faced with long check-in lines, like São Paulo / Guarulhos International Airport, especially for inter-continental flights.

7.4.3. Orientation

Some building characteristics may influence the wayfinding easiness. They include the size of the environment, number of decision points, length of the corridors, number of corridors linked to each decision point, and number of level changes (Dada, 1997). All these characteristics must be well planned at the design level of an airport passenger terminal to allow a good orientation system. In addition to this, the planned flow of passengers must be directed and supported by sign programs. A complete program consists of various components and must be considered part of the airport communication systems. Hart (1985) provides the three main purposes of airport sign programs:

1. Direction and orientation - for the direction and guidance of the flow of outbound and inbound traffic of passengers and visitors.

2. Identification of locations - such as those of airlines in ticket lobbies, in baggage claim areas, at gates or in concourses, telephones, restrooms, concessions, such as car rentals, banks, shops, and news stands.

3. Information - to be provided on:
   a. Aircraft arrivals and departures, originations, destinations, and gates.
   b. Baggage delivery by claim device, airline, flight number, and origination.
   c. Governmental regulations, such as security, immigration, and customs.
   d. Special services, such as public ground transportation, hotels, courtesy cars and car rentals.
   e. Matters of a general nature such as tourism and conventions.

The signs at São Paulo / Guarulhos International Airport are provided in Portuguese, Spanish and English. That is important, in the face of many local and international passengers that use the airport. The voice communication system is also provided in all these three languages. There also are signs on the access roads indicating which curbsides are more adequate to drop passengers, as a function of the airlines check-in counter positions. In addition to the static signs, there are plenty of dynamic monitors to display flight information, including boarding time, gate number, and expected delays.

New technologies have been developed to provide better information systems. Examples being Cathode ray tube (CRT) monitors, Plasma, LCD and LED displays. These are called dynamic displays. BAA (British Airport Authority) uses dynamic display devices in many areas of its airport operations, but specifically for public information, e.g. at Check-in desks, Departure Lounges and Gates, baggage reclaim etc. Some issues of the many dynamic display applications at BAA airports are (International Airport Review, 2002, Issue 3, pp. 41-43):

1. When the new Terminal at Stansted opened in March 1991, CRT monitors were fitted as standard for flight information. Although the screens had an

anti-static and anti-reflective coating, the high ambient light, and in some cases direct sunlight, impaired their performance.

2. LCD display boards were considered for some areas, and have been used at most check-in desks, but although effective, are generally suited to displaying information in text form only.

3. Plasma Displays have an advantage of a relatively large screen size and shallow profile which makes them more versatile for installations, particularly wall mounting.

Calgary International Airport hires some volunteers to work as information personnel. They provide information to users, which cannot be readily obtainable by the signs and monitors. São Paulo / Guarulhos International Airport provides information desks at strategic positions at the terminal, helping users that need additional information.

7.4.4. Departure Lounge

The sizing of the departure lounge must be planned as a function of the number of passengers during the peak period of the design day and the crowding level acceptable by the passengers. The number of passengers in the lounge depends on the number of flights during the peak period, flight passenger load, and the time in advance that passengers arrive in the lounge. This can be determined with the help of arrival distribution charts and micro-simulation models.

It is recommended (De Neufville, 2002) to provide shared use lounges to cope with the fluctuating demand of passengers. By using this procedure, the overall needs of space are greatly reduced. It is not recommended to aggregate international and domestic passenger in the same room, however it is possible to implement reversible rooms that can be used by domestic passengers or international passengers. Such rooms exist at São Paulo / Guarulhos International Airport.

Seating should be provided in the lounges, however this need is inversely proportional to the number of amenities inside the lounge (food areas, shops, toilets, telephones). If there are no such facilities, passengers have no option but to sit and wait for the departing flight.

The ideas discussed on the last section (orientation) should also be applied to the design and management of the departure lounge. Lounges located in pier-finger or satellite terminals usually have long corridors that might confuse the user to find the desired destinations.

7.4.5. Cost-Benefit Evaluation

Many ideas to provide capacity and level of service at an airport passenger terminal have been presented on the last sections. They are recommendations from airport researchers, consultants, and in some cases are just a collection of actions that have been implemented at the surveyed airports or somewhere else. Even though some actions require infrastructure adding or improvements, many non-expensive procedures can be implemented that provide similar benefits. Besides, infrastructure planning is usually expensive, require approvals from many sources, and sometimes degrades the environment (e.g., new terminals, new runways).

All alternatives for capacity expansions should be evaluated as a function of the cost-benefit associated. Airport passenger terminals improvements rarely are without expense. To know whether a particular expenditure is justified, it is necessary to be able to measure the change in LOS resulting from it (Gosling, 1988). One should evaluate not only the change in LOS for the individual facility, but also the change in overall LOS. The models presented in this thesis are able to provide the change in LOS resulting from the different actions implemented. In this case, the models are useful for providing a cost-benefit LOS evaluation.

7.5. Management and Benchmarking

Benchmarking is the process of comparing the performance or capacity of any enterprise, measured in several ways, with that of the best in the industry (de Neufville and Guzman, 1998). Airports Council International – ACI (2000) proposes that measuring level of service should be regarded as part of a whole quality system, which works in a continuous cycle, and should lead to a system of continuous improvement. According to them, the "Quality Chain" which follows is composed of five elements:

- Evaluate customer needs and expectations.
- Implement adequate service.
- Achieve the service.
- Measure quality of service.
- Evaluation of causes and corrective action.

No customer satisfaction research program can be considered complete if it focuses only on the company's own product and service quality. It has to include a probing survey of what the best of the competition is doing. Band (1991) provides the following steps in the benchmark process:

- Determining which functional areas within your operation will benefit most from benchmarking;
- Identifying the key factors and variables with which to measure competitive cost and quality for those functions;
- Selecting the best-in-class companies for each item to be benchmarked. Best-in-class companies can be your direct competitors (domestic or foreign) or even companies from a different industry;

- Measuring your own performance for each benchmark item;
- Measuring the performance of the best-in-class companies for each item, and determining the gap between you and the best-in-class;
- Specifying programs and actions to close the gap;
- Implementing these programs successfully by setting specific improvement targets and deadlines, and by developing a monitoring process to review and update targets over time.

With the method of successive categories it is possible to determine a single scale that represents the level of service of individual components and of the airport passenger terminal as a whole. It is a different approach, because on the last chapters we have treated the subject of level of service standards. With small changes in the methodology we can provide a method that will be useful to assess the actual level of service of the airport as evaluated by its users. In addition to that, the comparison of the LOS of individual airports will be useful for benchmarking purposes.

Table 7.7 presents the frequencies of rating obtained from the surveys applied at São Paulo / Guarulhos International Airport (GR), Rio de Janeiro International Airport (RJ), and São Paulo / Congonhas International Airport (SP).

Table 7.7: Frequencies of Rating for the Surveyed Airports

Component (j)	Frequencies of Rating					
	1	2	3	4	5	Total
GR Curb	0	11	26	67	15	119
GR Check	0	4	18	75	22	119
GR Lou	3	8	34	54	18	117
GR Ov	1	4	22	75	15	117
RJ Curb	0	0	3	19	13	35
RJ Check	0	0	1	11	23	35
RJ Lou	0	0	3	16	16	35
RJ Ov	0	0	5	22	8	35
SP Curb	3	4	4	18	1	30
SP Check	0	0	5	18	7	30
SP Lou	1	2	8	16	3	30
SP Ov	1	2	10	14	3	30

This information is not sufficient to determine how each airport is positioned compared to each other, as a function of the level of service provided. However, application of the methodology proposed in Chapter 3 provided a single scale (μ_j^{LOS}) representing the level of service of each component or airport. In this case the only difference from the previous analyses is that j will represent the components/airports as opposed to the groups of similar stimulus values (waiting time, space available, etc).

Table 7.8 provides the results of the methodology application using data from Table 7.7. The LOS evaluation was obtained comparing the μ_j^{LOS} values with the border between categories (Table 7.9).

Table 7.8: LOS Evaluation for Components/Airports

Component (j)	μ_j^{LOS}	LOS Evaluation
GR Curbside	0.91	Good
RJ Curbside	1.81	Good
SP Curbside	0.40	Fair
GR Check-in	1.35	Good
RJ Check-in	2.38	Excellent
SP Check-in	1.41	Good
GR Lounge	0.89	Good
RJ Lounge	1.85	Good
SP Lounge	0.82	Good
GR Overall	1.23	Good
RJ Overall	1.49	Good
SP Overall	0.78	Good

Table 7.9: Borders between Categories

Category (k)	μ_k^{UB}
5 - Excellent	> + 1.95
4 - Good	+ 0.40 to + 1.95
3 - Fair	- 0.40 to + 0.40
2 - Poor	- 0.94 to - 0.40
1 - Unacceptable	< - 0.94

The chi-square value for this analysis is 44.669, compared to 40.289 (1% signf. - 22 d.f.). Even though the chi-square is higher than the critical value, it is very close to it. A greater sample at São Paulo / Congonhas and Rio de Janeiro Airports would be able to solve this problem.

Table 7.8 indicates that the μ_j^{LOS} values for RJ are always higher than those for SP and GR. That is because a new, big, and modern terminal was recently built for the Rio de

Janeiro International Airport. The comparison between GR and SP always favors GR, except for the check-in analysis where SP has a small advantage. That might be due to the long check-in lines encountered at São Paulo / Guarulhos International Airport. The curbside evaluation at São Paulo / Congonhas is only fair, reflecting the high utilization always present in that area. Even though the μ_j^{LOS} values for RJ components are much higher than those for GR, the overall μ_j^{LOS} values for both airports are very similar. This indicates that the components studied (curbside, check-in counter, and departure lounge) do not have a great importance for Rio de Janeiro users as they have for São Paulo / Guarulhos users. Some of the disadvantages of Rio de Janeiro airport are the high access time, low flight frequencies, and lack of security on the access roads. The overall evaluations for GR are clearly higher than the ones for SP, but still both are situated in the same category (good). The survey done at São Paulo / Congonhas was conducted before the improvement that is under way. After the improvements, the LOS evaluations might be different from the ones formerly presented. The surveys done at Rio de Janeiro were also done before the huge traffic transferring from Rio de Janeiro/Santos Dumont domestic airport. The responses could be different if the surveys were to be performed today.

7.6. Conclusions

A new and effective method for overall airport passenger terminals LOS evaluation has been presented in this chapter. It can be successfully applied at the planning, management, and benchmarking level. Although the methodology has been applied at Sao Paulo / Guarulhos International Airport, it can be transferred to any airport, as long as there are survey data points to validate it. The overall measures provided reflect the perceptions of departing passengers that use the curbside. The measures might be different for departing passengers that use the parking lots, arriving passengers and connecting passengers.

CHAPTER EIGHT: CONCLUSIONS AND RECOMMENDATIONS

8.1. Conclusions

Throughout this work it has been shown that research on LOS of airport passenger terminals is a currently critical need, and despite this fact, most of the researchers have failed to provide a correlation between characteristics of facilities and LOS ratings according to user perceptions. Supplying this critical need, a new approach for LOS evaluation has been proposed, employing the psychometrical scaling theory as a mathematical tool to transform qualitative date into quantitative data, enabling to obtain LOS user perceptions in a quantitative scale. These LOS ratings were supposed to be correlated to performance indexes experienced by passengers, e.g., waiting time, processing time, availability of space, etc. Using the proposed approach, we have been able to obtain the regression equations not only for individual measures, but also for components and the whole airport.

The main hypothesis of this research was that user perceptions of LOS would be correlated to the characteristics of facilities. For instance, if the waiting time at the check-in counter line were very long, then passengers would attribute a low rating and vice-versa. The research has shown that passengers act reasonably concerning this issue, encouraging the LOS evaluation using this approach. Another supposition was that it would be possible to add and combine LOS ratings to get an overall measure for a given component or for the whole terminal. The way to proceed with this addition was obtaining relative importance weightings for individual measures (waiting time, processing time, etc) and for individual components (check-in counter, curbside, etc). Once again, this supposition has been verified, showing that passengers act reasonably according to the importance they assign to individual measures and components.

In face of the existence of multicollinearity between variables, it has not been possible to evaluate some components under a multi-attribute analysis. For instance, the three variables for the curbside (effective curbside utilization, waiting time, and walking distance) have high correlation values between each other. That encouraged us to evaluate the curbside component by the effective curbside utilization alone. This shortcoming also happened between the variables of the departure lounge (number of seats and space available). Finally, for the reasons explained at the Chapter 5, it was more convenient to evaluate the security screening component by the service time alone.

The overall terminal LOS evaluation for departing passengers could be evaluated in function of four components: curbside, check-in counter, departure lounge, and orientation. Some variables were removed from the analysis, because they did not have a high degree of importance for passengers at São Paulo / Guarulhos International Airport according to the study. They are the walking distance, security screening, and concessions. However, these variables could be very representative for airports somewhere. The overall LOS evaluation in function of global indices (total service time, walking distance, and orientation) was successful and provided good results. It is important to mention that the methods for overall terminal LOS evaluation presented in this thesis are very unique. There are no such methods available in the literature.

Considering all the results of this research, we suggest that LOS evaluation at airport passenger terminals be done using the approach provided in this thesis. Most of the previous methods have proven to be ineffective and very limited. On the other hand, our approach is capable of getting passengers perceptions of LOS for most components of the airport and the overall airport as well in a simple and effective way, which application would be affordable to any airport administration.

Future research could be developed to explore the use of other variables that might influence the user perception of LOS. Those include the expectation of level of service. Different passengers may have different expectations of service; accordingly, a given passenger may have different expectations toward specific airports. For instance, a North American traveler might be more demanding when it comes to evaluating Toronto/Pearson International Airport, as opposed to Sao Paulo/Guarulhos International Airport. One alternative to verify this hypothesis is to include a dummy variable, where 0 represents local passengers and 1 represents non-local passengers. Analogously, other socio-economic variables could be included in the analysis to obtain a more complete LOS evaluation, including income, age, nationality, etc; however, the addition of more variables increases the data needs considerably. The research, if extended to a large number of airports, and an increased numbers of variables, could be used to compare and contrast the LOS of airports nationally and internationally.

8.2. Recommendations

We recommend that the methodology for LOS evaluation set forth in this thesis be applied with a number of approximately thirty passenger groups. Only in this case the various LOS ranges will be properly determined. A sample of 300 randomly selected passengers will be able to accomplish that target in most of the cases. It is important to mention that the sample must be distributed across various peak periods of the airport operations. The passenger groups must be as homogeneous as it is practical. Usually, the separation of passengers into groups of similar stimulus values will be able to warrant that assumption, as long as the stimulus interval is not so large. That is why it is important to have the biggest number of passenger groups as possible.

The composite evaluation method proposed must be applied with variables that do not have a high degree of inter-correlation. In this case the selection of variables must be careful planned in advance, and in all cases the correlation values must calculated to check the evidence of multicollinearity. The wording of the questionnaire must be arranged in a way as to present clear sentences and to make sense to the respondent. They should be able to answer the question with certainty; otherwise the analysis will not provide good results. It is also recommended to interview the passenger, as oppose to give them the 'freedom' to fill-out the questionnaire. When the user is interviewed, the interviewer can verify to the user ability to respond and is able to help him with whatever question that arises. It is not convenient to show the respondent the stimulus values previously collected; otherwise they might be biased by this information.

All survey and observation applications must be conducted with approval from many sources. In the case of this research, we had approval from the Ethics Research Committee of the University of Calgary. Approvals were also requested to the administrations of the surveyed airports. In Brazil, a permission request must be sent to Customs and Federal Police in the case of surveys conducted at the international departure lounge and international baggage claim areas. Finally, the user must consent with the survey and observation application. All permissions take considerable processing time and enough time must be planned in advance for this.

It is important to select properly the surveyor team and allow a considerable time to train them. They should be capable of precisely measure dozens of physical characteristics and have good communication capabilities. Eventually they should be able to be bilingual or even trilingual. A great number of passengers in Brazil were not able to speak Portuguese, and the surveyors should carry the surveys in either English or Spanish. The interviewer must not influence the passenger opinion nor interfere in its activities. On the other hand, the user must be observed and properly measured. If a passenger is lost during the observation process, all previous efforts are wasted.

Finally, the analysis will need some software packages to proceed with the calculations. SPSS 13.0 was used for the statistical analysis. MathCAD will be a great help to calculate the Chi-square values to test the normality of responses. In this case, several integrals must be performed and it is too cumbersome to do it by hand or calculators. For the remaining calculations, the Microsoft Excel spreadsheet presented good results.

REFERENCES

1. Aaker, D., Kumar, V. and Day, G. *Marketing Research.* John Wiley & Sons, Inc., 6th Edition (1998)

2. Airports Council International. *Quality of Service at Airports: Standards & Measurements.* ACI World Headquarters, Geneva, Switzerland (2000).

3. Ashford, N. and Wright, P. H. *Airport Engineering.* John Wiley & Sons, 3rd Edition (1992).

4. Ashford, N. et. al. *Airport Operations.* John Willey & Sons, 1st Edition (1984).

5. Ashford, N. et. al. *Passenger Behavior and Design of Airport Terminals.* Transportation Research Record 588, TRB, National Research Council, Washington D.C., pp 18-26 (1976).

6. Ashford, N. *Level of Service Design Concept for Airport Passenger Terminals: A European View.* Transportation Research Record 1199, TRB, National Research Council, Washington D.C., pp 19-32 (1988).

7. Band, W. A. *Creating Value for Customers: Designing and Implementing a Total Corporate Strategy.* John Wiley & Sons, Inc (1991).

8. Bock, R. D. and Jones, L. V. *The Measurement and Prediction of Judgment and Choice.* San Francisco, Holden-Day (1968).

9. Brink, M. and Madison, D. *Identification and Measurement of Capacity Levels of Service of Landside Elements of the Airport.* In Airport Landside Capacity. Special Report 159, Transportation Research Board, Washington, D.C., pp. 92-111 (1975).

10. Caves, R. E. and Gosling, G. D. *Strategic Airport Planning.* Pergamon (1999).

11. Caves, R. E. and Pickard, C. D. *The Satisfaction of Human Needs in Airport Passenger Terminals.* Proceedings of the Institution of Civil Engineers, Transport 147, February Issue I, pp. 9-15 (2001).

12. Condom, P. *Thirty Thousand Passengers State Their Preferences.* Interavia, Vol.11, pp. 1177-1179 (1987).

13. Correia, A. R. *Quantitative Evaluation of Airport Passenger Terminal Configurations.* MSc Dissertation, Aeronautical Institute of Technology (2000).

14. Dada, E. S. and Wirasinghe, S. C. *Development of a New Orientation Index for Airport Terminals.* Transportation Research Record 1662, TRB, National Research Council, Washington D.C., pp 41-47 (1999).

15. Dada, E. S. *Quantitative Measures of Orientation in Airport Terminals.* Doctoral Thesis, Department of Civil Engineering, University of Calgary (1997).

16. Davis, D. G. and Braaksma, J. P. *Level of Service Standards for Platooning Pedestrians in Transportation Terminals.* ITE Journal, pp. 31-35, April (1987).

17. de Barros, A. G. and Wirasinghe, S. C. *Optimal Terminal Configurations for New Large Aircraft Operations.* Transportation Research A, Vol. 37, No. 4, pp. 315-331 (2003).

18. de Barros, A. G. and Wirasinghe, S. C. *Sizing the Baggage Claim Area for the New Large Aircraft.* Journal of Transportation Engineering of ASCE, Vol. 130, Issue 3, pp. 274-279 (2004)

19. de Barros, A. G. *Planning of Airports for the New Large Aircraft.* Ph. D. Dissertation, University of Calgary (2001).

20. de Neufville, R. and Odoni, A. *Airport Systems: Planning Design and Management.* McGraw-Hill Book Company, 1st. Edition (2002).

21. de Neufville, R. and Stafford, J. H. *Systems Analysis for Engineers and Managers.* McGraw-Hill Book Company, 1st Edition (1971).

22. de Neufville, R. *Applied Systems Analysis: Engineering Planning and Technology Management.* McGraw-Hill Book Company, 1st Edition (1990).

23. de Neufville, R. de Barros, A. G. and Belin, S. C. Optimal Configuration of Airport Passenger Buildings for Travelers. Journal of Transportation Engineering of ASCE, Vol. 128, Issue 3, pp. 211-217 (2002).

24. Fernandes, E. and Pacheco, R. R. *Efficient Use of Airport Capacity.* Transportation Research, Part A: General, Vol. 36, No. 3, pp. 225-238 (2002).

25. Forsyth, P. *Price Regulation of Airports: Principles with Australian Applications.* Transportation Research E: Logistics and Transportation Review, Vol. 33, Issue 4, pp. 297-309 (1997).

26. Garcia, J. M. F. *Criterion for Commercial Space Allocation in Airport Passenger Terminals.* AEROSERVICE - Consulting and Design Engineering Ltd., São Paulo - Brazil - Internal Publication (1995).

27. Gillen, D. and Lall, A. *Developing Measures of Airport Productivity and Performance: an Application of Data Envelopment Analysis.* Transportation Research E: Logistics and Transportation Review, Vol. 33, Issue 4, pp. 261-273 (1997).

28. Gosling, G. D. *Airport Landside Planning Techniques: Introduction.* Transportation Research Record 1199, TRB, National Research Council, Washington D.C., pp 1-3 (1988).

29. Green, P. E., Carmone, F. J. and Smith Jr., S. M. *Multidimensional Scaling: Concepts and Applications.* Allyn and Bacon (1989).

30. Greenberg, I. *Encyclopedia of Operations Research and Management Science – Regression Analysis.* Kluwer Academic Publishers, 2nd Edition (2001).

31. Hart, W. *The Airport Passenger Terminal.* John Wiley & Sons, 1st edition (1985).

32. Heathington, K. W. and Jones, D. H.. *Identification of Levels of Service and Capacity of Airport Landside Elements.* In Airport Landside Capacity. Special Report 159, Transportation Research Board, Washington, D.C., pp. 72-92 (1975).

33. Hooper, P. G. and Hensher, D. A. *Measuring Total Factor Productivity of Airports – an Index Number Approach.* Transportation Research E: Logistics and Transportation Review, Vol. 33, Issue 4, pp. 245-247 (1997).

34. Horonjeff, R. and McKelvey, F. X. *Planning and Design of Airports.* McGraw-Hill, 4th Edition (1994).

35. Humphreys, I. and Francis, G. *Traditional Airport Performance Indicators: A Critical Perspective.* Transportation Research Record 1703, TRB, National Research Council, Washington D.C., pp. 24-30 (2000).

36. INFRAERO. Relatorio Infraero 2002 (Infraero Report 2002).

37. Keeney, R. and Raiffa, H. *Decisions with Multiples Objectives.* John Wiley & Sons, Inc., 1st. Edition (1976).

38. Khan, A. M. *Criteria for Evaluation of Airport Airside and Landside Level of Service.* Proceedings, International Conference on Transportation Systems Studies, December 18-22, 1986, Delhi, pp. 27-34.

39. Lemer, A. C. *Measuring Performance of Airport Passenger Terminals.* Transportation Research, Part A: General, Vol. 26, No. 1, pp. 37-45 (1992).

40. Lemer, A.C. *Measuring Airport Landside Capacity.* Transportation Research Record 1199, TRB, National Research Council, Washington D.C., pp. 12-18 (1988).

41. Liu, C. *Total Customer Satisfaction Service System and its Best Practices.* Presented at the APO Symposium on Customer Satisfaction in the Service Sector held in Taipei, Republic of China (1999)

42. Malhotra, N. *Quantitative Data Analysis: Multivariate Techniques.* Handbook of the American Marketing Association & Professional Marketing Research Society (2000).

43. Mandle, P., Whitlock, E. and LaMagna, F. *Airport Curbside Planning and Design.* Transportation Research Record 840, TRB, National Research Council, Washington D.C., pp. 1-6 (1982).

44. Martel, N. and Seneviratne, P.N. *Analysis of Factors Influencing Quality of Service in Passenger Terminal Buildings.* Transportation Research Record, 1273, TRB, National Research Council, Washington D.C. (1990).

45. Miles, J. and Shelvin, M. *Applying Regression and Correlation.* Sage Publications, 1st Edition (2001).

46. Müller, C. *A Framework for Quality of Service Evaluation at Airport Terminals.* PhD Thesis, Institute of Transportation Studies, University of California, Berkeley (1987).

47. Müller, C. and Gosling, G. D. *A Framework for Evaluating Level of Service for Airport Terminals.* Transportation Planning and Technology, Vo. 16, pp 45-61 (1991).

48. Mumayiz, S. A and N. Ashford. *Methodology for Planning and Operations Management of Airport Terminal Facilities.* Transportation Research Record 1094, TRB, National Research Council, Washington D.C., pp 24-35 (1986).

49. Mumayiz, S. A. *Evaluating Performance and Service Measures for the Airport Landside.* Transportation Research Record 1296, TRB, National Research Council, Washington D.C., (1991).

50. Mumayiz, S. A. *Methodology for planning and operations management of airport passenger terminals: a capacity/level of service approach.* Ph.D. thesis, Department of Transport Technology, Loughborough University of Technology, Loughborough, England (1985).

51. Ndoh, N. N. and Ashford, N. *Evaluation of Airport Access Level of Service.* Transportation Research Record 1423, TRB, National Research Council, Washington D.C., pp 34-39 (1993).

52. Ndoh, N. N. and Ashford, N. *Evaluation of Transportation Level of Service Using Fuzzy Sets.* Transportation Research Record 1461, TRB, National Research Council, Washington D.C., pp 31-37 (1994).

53. Novak, E. *Airports and Human Values: An Attempt to Increase the Weight of Ethical Considerations as Design Criteria.* Ph.D. Dissertation, University of California, Berkeley (1978).

54. Omer, K. F. and Khan, A. M. *Airport Landside Level of Service Estimation: Utility Theoretic Approach.* Transportation Research Record 1199, TRB, National Research Council, Washington D.C., pp 33-40 (1988).

55. Omer, K. F. *Passenger Terminal Level of Service Measurement: A Utility Theoretic Approach.* MSc Thesis, Carleton University, Ottawa (1990).

56. Park, Y. A. *A Methodology for Establishing Operational Standards of Airport Passenger Terminals.* Journal of Air Transport Management, Vol. 5, No. 2, pp. 73-80 (1999).

57. Park, Y. H. *An evaluation methodology for the level of service at the airport landside system*. Ph.D. thesis, Department of Transport Technology, Loughborough University of Technology, Loughborough, England (1994).

58. Paul, A. S. *Methodology for Modeling Passenger Evaluations of Airport Terminal Functions and Components*. Ph.D. Dissertation, University of Virginia (1981).

59. Proctor, T. *Essentials of Marketing Research*. Financial Times - Prentice Hall, 2nd Edition (2000).

60. Rand Corporation. *Measurement and Evaluation of Transportation System Effectiveness*. Memorandum RM-5869-DOT (1969).

61. Roads and Transport Association of Canada. *Guide for the Planning of Small Airports*. Ottawa, Ontario (1980).

62. Ross, T. *Fuzzy Logic with Engineering Applications*. McGraw-Hill Company, 1st Edition (1995).

63. Seneviratine, P. N. and Martel, N. *Criteria for Evaluating Quality of Service in Air Terminals*. Transportation Research Record 1461, TRB, National Research Council, Washington D.C., pp 24-30 (1994).

64. Seneviratine, P. N. and Martel, N. *Variables Influencing Performance of Air Terminal Buildings*. Transportation Planning and Technology, Vol. 16, No. 1, pp. 1177-1179 (1991).

65. Siddiqui, M. R. *A Statistical Analysis of the Factors Influencing the Level of Service of Airport Terminal Curbsides*. MSc thesis, Concordia University, Canada (1994).

66. Taha, H. A. *Operations Research – An Introduction*. Prentice Hall, Inc., 6th Edition (1997).

67. Taylor III, B. W. *Introduction to Management Science*. Prentice Hall, 6th Edition (1999).

68. Thurstone, L.L. *The Measurement of Values*. University of Chicago Press, Chicago (1959).

69. Transport Canada. *A Discussion Paper on Level of Service Definition and Methodology for Calculating Airport Capacity.* Report TP 2027 (April 1979).

70. Transportation Research Board. *Special Report 209: Highway Capacity Manual.* TRB, National Research Council, Washington D.C. (1985).

71. Transportation Research Board. *Special Report 215: Measuring Airport Landside Capacity.* TRB, National Research Council, Washington D.C. (1987).

72. Wirasinghe, S. C. and Shehata, M. *Departure Lounge Sizing and Optimal Seating Capacity for a Given Aircraft/Flight Mix - (i) Single Gate, (ii) Several Gates.* Transportation Planning and Technology, Vol. 13, pp. 57-71 (1988).

73. Wright, D. B. *Understanding Statistics: an Introduction to for the Social Sciences.* Sage Publications Ltd., 1st Ed., London (1997).

74. Yen, J.-R. *A New Approach to Measure the Level of Service of Procedures in the Airport Landside.* Transportation Planning Journal, Vol. 24, No. 3, Sept., pp. 323-336 (1995).

75. Yen, J.-R., Teng, C.-R. and Chen, P. S. *Measuring the Level of Service at Airport Passenger Terminals: Comparison of Perceived and Observed Time.* Transportation Research Record 1744, TRB, National Research Council, Washington D.C., pp 17-23 (2001).

76. Zadeh, L. A. *Fuzzy Sets.* Information and Control 8, pp. 338-353 (1965).

Appendix A - Questionnaire Applied at the Final Survey at São Paulo/Guarulhos International Airport

UNIVERSITY OF CALGARY

Civil Engineering Department
2500 University Drive NW
Calgary – AB – Canada

AIRPORT PASSENGER SURVEY – SÃO PAULO INTERNATIONAL AIRPORT

Madam/Sir: I am a Graduate Student from the University of Calgary – Canada, and conducting a survey of the level of service provided at this airport. Could you please complete this questionnaire? Your decision to complete and return this questionnaire will be interpreted as your consent to participate.

1) **Trip Purpose:**
   Business   Non Business   Combined

2) **Flight Type**
   Domestic   International

3) **Gender:**
   Male   Female

4) **Airline:** _____

For the following components, how would you rate the level of service?
Please, use the following scale:
(1) unacceptable   (2) poor   (3) fair   (4) good   (5) excellent

5) **Curbside:**

					For office use:
Space Available for Cars: (1)	(2)	(3)	(4)	(5)	ECU:_____

6) **Check-in counter:**

Waiting Time:	(1)	(2)	(3)	(4)	(5)	WT (min):_____
Processing Time:	(1)	(2)	(3)	(4)	(5)	PT (min):_____
Availability of Space:	(1)	(2)	(3)	(4)	(5)	AS (m²):_____
Overall Check-in:	(1)	(2)	(3)	(4)	(5)	HB: CB: BC: P:

7) Passport Control: (1)   (2)   (3)   (4)   (5) | WT:___PT:___ AS:___

8) Security screening:
Waiting Time: (1)   (2)   (3)   (4)   (5) | WT (min):_____
Processing Time: (1)   (2)   (3)   (4)   (5) | PT (min):_____
Availability of Space: (1)   (2)   (3)   (4)   (5) | AS (m^2):_____
Overall Security Screen.: (1)   (2)   (3)   (4)   (5)

9) Departure Lounge:
Waiting Time: (1)   (2)   (3)   (4)   (5) | WT:___ $T_{ad:}$___ PT:___
Number of Seats: (1)   (2)   (3)   (4)   (5) | NS/P: ____ AVS:____
Area size: (1)   (2)   (3)   (4)   (5) | AS (m^2/P):_____
Overall Dep. Lounge: (1)   (2)   (3)   (4)   (5) | Seated? Yes   No

10) Walking Distance: (1)   (2)   (3)   (4)   (5) | WkD:Min___ Real:___

11) Orientation: (1)   (2)   (3)   (4)   (5) | WkT: Min___ Real:___

12) Total Wait+ProcTime: (1)   (2)   (3)   (4)   (5) | WT___ PT___ OT___

13) Circulation: (1)   (2)   (3)   (4)   (5)

14) Concessions: (1)   (2)   (3)   (4)   (5)

15) Security Environment: (1)   (2)   (3)   (4)   (5)

16) Overall Terminal: (1)   (2)   (3)   (4)   (5)

Thank you for your co-operation!

For office use only: Initials: ____   Date: _____   Hour: _____

Appendix B - Details of the Methodology

B.1 An Approximation for Computing $\hat{Y} = \Phi^{-1}(p)$

Following, we present a procedure to compute the normal deviations $\hat{Y}$, as proposed by Bock and Jones (1968).

Given the value of an area in the right tail under the normal distribution function, it is desired to find the corresponding unit normal deviate $\hat{Y}$ such that:

$$P = \Phi(\hat{Y}) = \frac{1}{\sqrt{2\pi}} \int_{\hat{Y}}^{\infty} \exp\left(-\frac{1}{2}z^2\right) dz \qquad (B.1)$$

A recommended method for machine computation involves the use of one approximate function for $0.02 < p < 0.98$ and a distinct function for p outside that range.

For $0.02 < p < 0.98$, a suitable function is that developed by Tucker (1959). Let $U = p - \frac{1}{2}$. Then the approximation $\hat{Y}$ for Y is given by:

$$\hat{Y} = \frac{U(a_1 - a_2 U^2 + a_3 U^4)}{(1 - a_4 U^2 + a_5 U^4)} \qquad (B.2)$$

where

$$a_1 = 2.5101, \quad a_2 = 12.2043, \quad a_3 = 11.2502$$

The maximum discrepancy ($\hat{Y}$ - Y) is less than 3×10^{-4}.

The sampling variability of normal deviates is large as the parametric deviate approaches either extreme of the normal distribution function. Particularly for sample values of p_{jk} more extreme than 0.01 or 0.99, the sampling variance of y_{jk} is intolerably large. For this reason, it is not recommended that y values be recorded when p exceeds 0.99 or is less than 0.01. For such situations, a y value is estimated as follows. The mean difference between the recorded y_{jk} in two adjacent columns of a Table is found, based upon those rows of a Table in which an y_{jk} is recorded in each of the two columns. This mean difference then is taken as the expected increment in y values in those cases where no entry exists.

B.2 - Estimative of μ_k^{UB}

The estimative of μ_k^{UB}, $\underline{\mu}_k^{UB}$ can be determined by the summation of equation (10) of Chapter 3 over all stimulus j, as follows:

$$\frac{1}{n}\sum_{j=1}^{n}\frac{\mu_k^{UB}-\mu_j^{LOS}}{\underline{\sigma}_j}=\frac{1}{n}\sum_{j=1}^{n}\gamma_{jk} \qquad (B.3)$$

$$\frac{\underline{\mu}_k^{UB}}{n}\sum_{j=1}^{n}\frac{1}{\underline{\sigma}_j}-\frac{1}{n}\sum_{j=1}^{n}\frac{\underline{\mu}_j^{LOS}}{\underline{\sigma}_j}=\frac{1}{n}\sum_{j=1}^{n}\gamma_{jk} \qquad (B.4)$$

Let us fix the location of the scale unit:

$$\sum_{j=1}^{n}\frac{\mu_j^{LOS}}{\sigma_j}=0 \qquad (B.5)$$

and fix the size for the scale unit so that:

$$\sum_{j=1}^{n} \frac{1}{\sigma_j} = n \qquad (B.6)$$

Substituting equations (B.5) and (B.6) into equation (B.4) yields equation (B.7):

$$\underline{\mu}_k^{UB} = \frac{1}{n} \sum_{j=1}^{n} y_{jk} \qquad (B.7)$$

Equation (B.7) indicates that $\underline{\mu}_k^{UB}$ can be determined as the average of the kth value of the standard normal deviates over all passenger groups j.

Appendix C - Complementary Data

This appendix presents the frequencies of ratings, proportion of responses, cumulative proportions and normal deviates for each LOS measure. This information complements the analyses presented in Chapters 5-7.

C.1. Space Available for Cars at the Curbside - São Paulo / Guarulhos

Table C.1: Frequencies of Ratings - Space Available for Cars at the Curbside
São Paulo / Guarulhos

Group (j)	Categories (k)					
	1	2	3	4	5	Total
1	0	0	3	9	1	13
2	0	1	1	12	2	16
3	0	0	0	13	2	15
4	0	2	1	15	5	23
5	0	0	3	9	2	14
6	0	3	5	6	1	15
7	0	2	8	2	2	14
8	0	1	2	1	0	4
9	0	1	2	0	0	3
10	0	1	1	0	0	2
Total	0	11	26	67	15	119

Table C.2: Proportion of Responses - Space Available for Cars at the Curbside
São Paulo / Guarulhos

Group (j)	Categories (k)					
	1	2	3	4	5	Total
1	0.000	0.000	0.231	0.692	0.077	1.000
2	0.000	0.063	0.063	0.750	0.125	1.000
3	0.000	0.000	0.000	0.867	0.133	1.000
4	0.000	0.087	0.043	0.652	0.217	1.000
5	0.000	0.000	0.214	0.643	0.143	1.000
6	0.000	0.200	0.333	0.400	0.067	1.000
7	0.000	0.143	0.571	0.143	0.143	1.000
8	0.000	0.250	0.500	0.250	0.000	1.000
9	0.000	0.333	0.667	0.000	0.000	1.000
10	0.000	0.500	0.500	0.000	0.000	1.000

Table C.3: Cumulative Proportions - Space Available for Cars at the Curbside
São Paulo / Guarulhos

	1	2	3	4	5
1	0.000	0.000	0.231	0.923	1.000
2	0.000	0.063	0.125	0.875	1.000
3	0.000	0.000	0.000	0.867	1.000
4	0.000	0.087	0.130	0.783	1.000
5	0.000	0.000	0.214	0.857	1.000
6	0.000	0.200	0.533	0.933	1.000
7	0.000	0.143	0.714	0.857	1.000
8	0.000	0.250	0.750	1.000	1.000
9	0.000	0.333	1.000	1.000	1.000
10	0.000	0.500	1.000	1.000	1.000

Table C.4: Normal Deviates - Space Available for Cars at the Curbside
São Paulo / Guarulhos

	1	2	3	4	Sum
1	(-3.324)	(-1.641)	-0.736	1.426	-4.276
2	(-3.217)	-1.534	-1.150	1.150	-4.751
3	(-3.168)	(-1.485)	(-0.580)	1.111	-4.123
4	(-3.043)	-1.360	-1.124	0.781	-4.746
5	(-3.380)	(-1.697)	-0.792	1.067	-4.800
6	(-2.524)	-0.841	0.084	1.501	-1.781
7	(-2.750)	-1.067	0.566	1.067	-2.184
8	(-2.357)	-0.674	0.674	(2.365)	0.008
9	(-2.114)	-0.431	(0.474)	(2.165)	0.094
10	(-1.683)	0.000	(0.905)	(2.596)	1.818
Sum	-27.561	-10.731	-1.679	15.230	-24.741
$\underline{\mu}_k^{UB}$	-2.756	-1.073	-0.168	1.523	
	\multicolumn{4}{c}{(-1.073 - 0.168) / 2 = -0.621}	
$\underline{\mu}_k^{UB}$ *(normalized)*	-2.136	-0.453	0.453	2.144	

(*) Cells in parentheses were calculated using the mean difference between adjacent columns

C.2. Waiting Time at the Check-in Counter - São Paulo / Guarulhos

Table C.5: Frequencies of Ratings - Waiting Time at the Check-in Counter
São Paulo / Guarulhos

Group	Categories (k)					
(j)	1	2	3	4	5	Total
1	0	0	1	8	7	16
2	0	0	1	4	4	9
3	0	0	1	0	4	5
4	0	0	2	5	6	13
5	0	0	2	3	1	6
6	0	0	0	4	1	5
7	0	1	2	11	0	14
8	0	1	5	6	2	14
9	0	1	4	9	1	15
10	0	5	5	1	0	11
11	2	4	1	0	0	7
12	3	1	0	0	0	4
Total	5	13	24	51	26	119

Table C.6: Proportion of Responses - Waiting Time at the Check-in Counter
São Paulo / Guarulhos

Group	Categories (k)					
(j)	1	2	3	4	5	Total
1	0.000	0.000	0.063	0.500	0.438	1.000
2	0.000	0.000	0.111	0.444	0.444	1.000
3	0.000	0.000	0.200	0.000	0.800	1.000
4	0.000	0.000	0.154	0.385	0.462	1.000
5	0.000	0.000	0.333	0.500	0.167	1.000
6	0.000	0.000	0.000	0.800	0.200	1.000
7	0.000	0.071	0.143	0.786	0.000	1.000
8	0.000	0.071	0.357	0.429	0.143	1.000
9	0.000	0.067	0.267	0.600	0.067	1.000
10	0.000	0.455	0.455	0.091	0.000	1.000
11	0.286	0.571	0.143	0.000	0.000	1.000
12	0.750	0.250	0.000	0.000	0.000	1.000

233

Table C.7: Cumulative Proportions - Waiting Time at the Check-in Counter
São Paulo / Guarulhos

	1	2	3	4	5
1	0.000	0.000	0.063	0.563	1.000
2	0.000	0.000	0.111	0.556	1.000
3	0.000	0.000	0.200	0.200	1.000
4	0.000	0.000	0.154	0.538	1.000
5	0.000	0.000	0.333	0.833	1.000
6	0.000	0.000	0.000	0.800	1.000
7	0.000	0.071	0.214	1.000	1.000
8	0.000	0.071	0.429	0.857	1.000
9	0.000	0.067	0.333	0.933	1.000
10	0.000	0.455	0.909	1.000	1.000
11	0.286	0.857	1.000	1.000	1.000
12	0.750	1.000	1.000	1.000	1.000

Table C.8: Normal Deviates - Waiting Time at the Check-in Counter
São Paulo / Guarulhos

	1	2	3	4	Sum
1	(-4.287)	(-2.653)	-1.534	0.158	-8.316
2	(-3.974)	(-2.340)	-1.221	0.140	-7.394
3	(-3.594)	(-1.960)	-0.841	-0.841	-7.238
4	(-3.773)	(-2.139)	-1.020	0.097	-6.835
5	(-3.184)	(-1.550)	-0.431	0.967	-4.198
6	(-3.161)	(-1.527)	(-0.408)	0.841	-4.253
7	(-3.099)	-1.465	-0.792	(0.457	-4.898
8	(-3.099)	-1.465	-0.180	1.067	-3.677
9	(-3.135)	-1.501	-0.431	1.501	-3.566
10	(-1.748)	-0.114	1.335	(2.584)	2.057
11	-0.566	1.067	(2.186)	(3.435)	6.123
12	0.674	(2.308)	(3.427)	(4.676)	11.087
Sum	-33.620	-15.647	-3.336	10.407	-42.195
$\underline{\mu}_k^{UB}$	-2.802	-1.304	-0.278	0.867	
	(-1.304 - 0.278) / 2 = -0.791				
$\underline{\mu}_k^{UB}$ (normalized)	-2.011	-0.513	0.513	1.658	

(*) Cells in parentheses were calculated using the mean difference between adjacent columns

234

C.3. Processing Time at the Check-in Counter - São Paulo / Guarulhos

Table C.9: Frequencies of Ratings - Processing Time at the Check-in Counter
São Paulo / Guarulhos

Group	Categories (k)					
(j)	1	2	3	4	5	Total
1	0	0	0	9	5	14
2	0	0	0	13	7	20
3	0	0	2	11	9	22
4	0	0	1	7	4	12
5	0	1	2	11	4	18
6	0	1	2	4	1	8
7	0	1	0	5	1	7
8	0	0	1	1	1	3
9	0	0	1	3	1	5
10	0	0	1	5	1	7
11	2	1	0	0	0	3
Total	2	4	10	69	34	119

Table C.10: Proportion of Responses - Processing Time at the Check-in Counter
São Paulo / Guarulhos

Group	Categories (k)					
(j)	1	2	3	4	5	Total
1	0.000	0.000	0.000	0.643	0.357	1.000
2	0.000	0.000	0.000	0.650	0.350	1.000
3	0.000	0.000	0.091	0.500	0.409	1.000
4	0.000	0.000	0.083	0.583	0.333	1.000
5	0.000	0.056	0.111	0.611	0.222	1.000
6	0.000	0.125	0.250	0.500	0.125	1.000
7	0.000	0.143	0.000	0.714	0.143	1.000
8	0.000	0.000	0.333	0.333	0.333	1.000
9	0.000	0.000	0.200	0.600	0.200	1.000
10	0.000	0.000	0.143	0.714	0.143	1.000
11	0.667	0.333	0.000	0.000	0.000	1.000

Table C.11: Cumulative Proportions - Processing Time at the Check-in Counter
São Paulo / Guarulhos

	1	2	3	4	5
1	0.000	0.000	0.000	0.643	1.000
2	0.000	0.000	0.000	0.650	1.000
3	0.000	0.000	0.091	0.591	1.000
4	0.000	0.000	0.083	0.667	1.000
5	0.000	0.056	0.167	0.778	1.000
6	0.000	0.125	0.375	0.875	1.000
7	0.000	0.143	0.143	0.857	1.000
8	0.000	0.000	0.333	0.667	1.000
9	0.000	0.000	0.200	0.800	1.000
10	0.000	0.000	0.143	0.857	1.000
11	0.667	1.000	1.000	1.000	1.000

Table C.12: Normal Deviates - Processing Time at the Check-in Counter
São Paulo / Guarulhos

	1	2	3	4	Sum
1	(-2.280)	(-1.794)	(-1.308)	0.366	-5.014
2	(-2.260)	(-1.774)	(-1.288)	0.386	-4.938
3	(-2.307)	(-1.821)	-1.335	0.230	-5.233
4	(-2.355)	(-1.869)	-1.383	0.431	-5.176
5	(-2.079)	-1.593	-0.967	0.765	-3.875
6	(-1.636)	-1.150	-0.319	1.150	-1.955
7	(-1.553)	-1.067	-1.067	1.067	-2.621
8	(-1.403)	(-0.917)	-0.431	0.431	-2.320
9	(-1.813)	(-1.327)	-0.841	0.841	-3.141
10	(-2.039)	(-1.553)	-1.067	1.067	-3.593
11	0.431	(2.105)	(3.779)	(5.453)	11.768
Sum	-19.296	-12.762	-6.229	12.188	-26.098
$\underline{\mu}_k^{UB}$	-1.754	-1.160	-0.566	1.108	
$(-1.160 - 0.566) / 2 = -0.863$					
$\underline{\mu}_k^{UB}$ (normalized)	-0.891	-0.297	0.297	1.971	

(*) Cells in parentheses were calculated using the mean difference between adjacent columns

C.4. Availability of Space at the Check-in Counter - São Paulo / Guarulhos

Table C.13: Frequencies of Ratings - Availability of Space at the Check-in Counter
São Paulo / Guarulhos

Group	Categories (k)					
(j)	1	2	3	4	5	Total
1	0	1	1	1	0	3
2	0	0	3	3	0	6
3	0	0	3	5	3	11
4	0	0	4	3	0	7
5	0	0	1	9	5	15
6	0	2	3	18	6	29
7	0	0	2	18	4	24
8	0	0	0	6	1	7
9	0	0	1	5	2	8
10	0	0	0	6	3	9
Total	0	3	18	74	24	119

Table C.14: Proportion of Responses - Availability of Space at the Check-in Counter
São Paulo / Guarulhos

Group	Categories (k)					
(j)	1	2	3	4	5	Total
1	0.000	0.333	0.333	0.333	0.000	1.000
2	0.000	0.000	0.500	0.500	0.000	1.000
3	0.000	0.000	0.273	0.455	0.273	1.000
4	0.000	0.000	0.571	0.429	0.000	1.000
5	0.000	0.000	0.067	0.600	0.333	1.000
6	0.000	0.069	0.103	0.621	0.207	1.000
7	0.000	0.000	0.083	0.750	0.167	1.000
8	0.000	0.000	0.000	0.857	0.143	1.000
9	0.000	0.000	0.125	0.625	0.250	1.000
10	0.000	0.000	0.000	0.667	0.333	1.000

Table C.15: Cumulative Proportions - Availability of Space at the Check-in Counter
São Paulo / Guarulhos

	1	2	3	4	5
1	0.000	0.333	0.667	1.000	1.000
2	0.000	0.000	0.500	1.000	1.000
3	0.000	0.000	0.273	0.727	1.000
4	0.000	0.000	0.571	1.000	1.000
5	0.000	0.000	0.067	0.667	1.000
6	0.000	0.069	0.172	0.793	1.000
7	0.000	0.000	0.083	0.833	1.000
8	0.000	0.000	0.000	0.857	1.000
9	0.000	0.000	0.125	0.750	1.000
10	0.000	0.000	0.000	0.667	1.000

Table C.16: Normal Deviates - Availability of Space at the Check-in Counter
São Paulo / Guarulhos

	1	2	3	4	Sum
1	(-1.131)	-0.431	0.431	(2.247)	1.116
2	(-1.400)	(-0.700)	0.000	(1.816)	-0.284
3	(-2.005)	(-1.305)	-0.605	0.605	-3.309
4	(-1.220)	(-0.520)	0.180	(1.996)	0.437
5	(-2.901)	(-2.201)	-1.501	0.431	-6.172
6	(-2.183)	-1.483	-0.945	0.817	-3.794
7	(-2.783)	(-2.083)	-1.383	0.967	-5.282
8	(-2.149)	(-1.449)	(-0.749)	1.067	-3.278
9	(-2.550)	(-1.850)	-1.150	0.674	-4.876
10	(-2.785)	(-2.085)	(-1.385)	0.431	-5.824
Sum	-21.107	-14.107	-7.106	11.052	-31.267
$\underline{\mu}_k^{UB}$	-2.111	-1.411	-0.711	1.105	
	(-1.411 - 0.711) / 2 = -1.061				
$\underline{\mu}_k^{UB}$ (normalized)	-1.050	-0.350	0.350	2.166	

(*) Cells in parentheses were calculated using the mean difference between adjacent columns

C.5. Waiting Time at the Check-in Counter - Calgary

Table C.17: Frequencies of Ratings - Waiting Time at the Check-in Counter
Calgary International Airport

Group (j)	Categories (k)					
	1	2	3	4	5	Total
1	0	0	0	1	9	10
2	0	0	0	2	6	8
3	0	0	1	8	6	15
4	0	0	6	8	0	14
5	0	2	6	0	0	8
6	0	1	3	3	0	7
Total	0	3	16	22	21	62

Table C.18: Proportion of Responses - Waiting Time at the Check-in Counter
Calgary International Airport

Group (j)	Categories (k)					
	1	2	3	4	5	Total
1	0.000	0.000	0.000	0.100	0.900	1.000
2	0.000	0.000	0.000	0.250	0.750	1.000
3	0.000	0.000	0.067	0.533	0.400	1.000
4	0.000	0.000	0.429	0.571	0.000	1.000
5	0.000	0.250	0.750	0.000	0.000	1.000
6	0.000	0.143	0.429	0.429	0.000	1.000

**Table C.19: Cumulative Proportions - Waiting Time at the Check-in Counter
Calgary International Airport**

	1	2	3	4	5
1	0.000	0.000	0.000	0.100	1.000
2	0.000	0.000	0.000	0.250	1.000
3	0.000	0.000	0.067	0.600	1.000
4	0.000	0.000	0.429	1.000	1.000
5	0.000	0.250	1.000	1.000	1.000
6	0.000	0.143	0.571	1.000	1.000

**Table C.20: Normal Deviates - Waiting Time at the Check-in Counter
Calgary International Airport**

	1	2	3	4	Sum
1	(-5.533)	(-4.285)	(-3.037)	-1.282	-14.135
2	(-4.925)	(-3.677)	(-2.429)	-0.674	-11.707
3	(-3.997)	(-2.749)	-1.501	0.254	-7.993
4	(-2.676)	(-1.428)	-0.180	(1.575)	-2.710
5	(-1.922)	-0.674	(0.574)	(2.329)	0.305
6	(-2.315)	-1.067	0.180	(1.935)	-1.267
Sum	-21.369	-13.881	-6.393	4.136	-37.508
$\underline{\mu}_k^{UB}$	-3.562	-2.314	-1.066	0.689	
	(-2.314 - 1.066) / 2 = -1.690				
$\underline{\mu}_k^{UB}$ *(normalized)*	-1.872	-0.624	0.624	2.379	

(*) Cells in parentheses were calculated using the mean difference between adjacent columns

C.6. Processing Time at the Check-in Counter - Calgary

Table C.21: Frequencies of Ratings - Processing Time at the Check-in Counter
Calgary International Airport

Group (j)	Categories (k)					Total
	1	2	3	4	5	
1	0	0	0	1	3	4
2	0	0	0	7	7	14
3	0	0	0	5	10	15
4	0	0	0	5	12	17
5	0	1	1	5	2	9
6	0	1	0	2	0	3
Total	0	2	1	25	34	62

Table C.22: Proportion of Responses - Processing Time at the Check-in Counter
Calgary International Airport

Group (j)	Categories (k)					Total
	1	2	3	4	5	
1	0.000	0.000	0.000	0.250	0.750	1.000
2	0.000	0.000	0.000	0.500	0.500	1.000
3	0.000	0.000	0.000	0.333	0.667	1.000
4	0.000	0.000	0.000	0.294	0.706	1.000
5	0.000	0.111	0.111	0.556	0.222	1.000
6	0.000	0.333	0.000	0.667	0.000	1.000

Table C.23: Cumulative Proportions - Processing Time at the Check-in Counter Calgary International Airport

	1	2	3	4	5
1	0.000	0.000	0.000	0.250	1.000
2	0.000	0.000	0.000	0.500	1.000
3	0.000	0.000	0.000	0.333	1.000
4	0.000	0.000	0.000	0.294	1.000
5	0.000	0.111	0.222	0.778	1.000
6	0.000	0.333	0.333	1.000	1.000

Table C.24: Normal Deviates - Processing Time at the Check-in Counter Calgary International Airport

	1	2	3	4	Sum
1	(-2.660)	(-2.432)	(-2.204)	-0.674	-7.972
2	(-1.986)	(-1.758)	(-1.530)	0.000	-5.274
3	(-2.417)	(-2.189)	(-1.961)	-0.431	-6.998
4	(-2.528)	(-2.300)	(-2.072)	-0.542	-7.440
5	(-1.449)	-1.221	-0.765	0.765	-2.669
6	(-0.659)	-0.431	-0.431	(1.099)	-0.422
Sum	-11.699	-10.331	-8.963	0.217	-30.775
μ_k^{UB}	-1.950	-1.722	-1.494	0.036	
	(-1.722 - 1.494) / 2 = -1.608				
μ_k^{UB} (normalized)	-0.342	-0.114	0.114	1.644	

(*) Cells in parentheses were calculated using the mean difference between adjacent columns

C.7. Service Time at the Security Screening - São Paulo / Guarulhos

Table C.25: Frequencies of Ratings -Service Time at the Security Screening
São Paulo / Guarulhos International Airport

Group	Categories (k)					
(j)	1	2	3	4	5	Total
1	0	0	1	5	10	16
2	0	0	0	2	9	11
3	0	0	0	13	18	31
4	0	0	0	4	6	10
5	0	0	0	13	8	21
6	0	0	0	12	1	13
7	0	0	1	4	2	7
8	1	1	3	3	1	9
Total	1	1	5	56	55	118

Table C.26: Proportion of Responses - Service Time at the Security Screening
São Paulo / Guarulhos International Airport

Group	Categories (k)					
(j)	1	2	3	4	5	Total
1	0.000	0.000	0.063	0.313	0.625	1.000
2	0.000	0.000	0.000	0.182	0.818	1.000
3	0.000	0.000	0.000	0.419	0.581	1.000
4	0.000	0.000	0.000	0.400	0.600	1.000
5	0.000	0.000	0.000	0.619	0.381	1.000
6	0.000	0.000	0.000	0.923	0.077	1.000
7	0.000	0.000	0.143	0.571	0.286	1.000
8	0.111	0.111	0.333	0.333	0.111	1.000

Table C.27: Cumulative Proportions - Service Time at the Security Screening São Paulo / Guarulhos International Airport

	1	2	3	4	5
1	0.000	0.000	0.063	0.375	1.000
2	0.000	0.000	0.000	0.182	1.000
3	0.000	0.000	0.000	0.419	1.000
4	0.000	0.000	0.000	0.400	1.000
5	0.000	0.000	0.000	0.619	1.000
6	0.000	0.000	0.000	0.923	1.000
7	0.000	0.000	0.143	0.714	1.000
8	0.111	0.222	0.556	0.889	1.000

Table C.28: Normal Deviates - Service Time at the Security Screening São Paulo / Guarulhos International Airport

	1	2	3	4	Sum
1	(-2.894)	(-2.438)	-1.534	-0.319	-7.185
2	(-3.692)	(-3.236)	(-2.332)	-0.908	-10.169
3	(-2.988)	(-2.532)	(-1.628)	-0.204	-7.351
4	(-3.038)	(-2.582)	(-1.678)	-0.254	-7.550
5	(-2.481)	(-2.025)	(-1.121)	0.303	-5.323
6	(-1.358)	(-0.902)	(0.002)	1.426	-0.832
7	(-2.427)	(-1.971)	-1.067	0.566	-4.900
8	-1.221	-0.765	0.140	1.221	-0.625
Sum	-20.098	-16.450	-9.218	1.831	-43.935
$\underline{\mu}_k^{UB}$	-2.512	-2.056	-1.152	0.229	
	\multicolumn{5}{c}{(-2.056 - 1.152) / 2 = -1.604}
$\underline{\mu}_k^{UB}$ (normalized)	-0.908	-0.452	0.452	1.833	

(*) Cells in parentheses were calculated using the mean difference between adjacent columns

C.8. Number of Seats at the Departure Lounge - São Paulo / Guarulhos

Table C.29: Frequencies of Ratings - Number of Seats at Departure Lounge
São Paulo / Guarulhos International Airport

Group	Categories (k)					
(j)	1	2	3	4	5	Total
1	2	4	7	1	1	15
2	0	3	5	4	0	12
3	1	9	6	6	1	23
4	1	2	5	8	2	18
5	1	2	4	3	2	12
6	0	0	0	6	3	9
7	0	1	2	8	3	14
8	0	0	1	1	3	5
9	0	0	0	3	2	5
10	0	0	0	1	3	4
Total	5	21	30	41	20	117

Table C.30: Proportion of Responses - Number of Seats at Departure Lounge
São Paulo / Guarulhos International Airport

Group	Categories (k)					
(j)	1	2	3	4	5	Total
1	0.133	0.267	0.467	0.067	0.067	1.000
2	0.000	0.250	0.417	0.333	0.000	1.000
3	0.043	0.391	0.261	0.261	0.043	1.000
4	0.056	0.111	0.278	0.444	0.111	1.000
5	0.083	0.167	0.333	0.250	0.167	1.000
6	0.000	0.000	0.000	0.667	0.333	1.000
7	0.000	0.071	0.143	0.571	0.214	1.000
8	0.000	0.000	0.200	0.200	0.600	1.000
9	0.000	0.000	0.000	0.600	0.400	1.000
10	0.000	0.000	0.000	0.250	0.750	1.000

Table C.31: Cumulative Proportions - Number of Seats at Departure Lounge
São Paulo / Guarulhos International Airport

	1	2	3	4	5
1	0.133	0.400	0.867	0.933	1.000
2	0.000	0.250	0.667	1.000	1.000
3	0.043	0.435	0.696	0.957	1.000
4	0.056	0.167	0.444	0.889	1.000
5	0.083	0.250	0.583	0.833	1.000
6	0.000	0.000	0.000	0.667	1.000
7	0.000	0.071	0.214	0.786	1.000
8	0.000	0.000	0.200	0.400	1.000
9	0.000	0.000	0.000	0.600	1.000
10	0.000	0.000	0.000	0.250	1.000

Table C.32: Normal Deviates - Number of Seats at Departure Lounge
São Paulo / Guarulhos International Airport

	1	2	3	4	Sum
1	-1.111	-0.254	1.111	1.501	1.247
2	(-1.609)	-0.674	0.431	(1.411)	-0.442
3	-1.711	-0.164	0.512	1.711	0.348
4	-1.593	-0.967	-0.140	1.221	-1.479
5	-1.383	-0.674	0.211	0.967	-0.879
6	(-2.406)	(-1.471)	(-0.549)	0.431	-3.995
7	(-2.400)	-1.465	-0.792	0.792	-3.865
8	(-2.698)	(-1.763)	-0.841	-0.254	-5.557
9	(-2.583)	(-1.648)	(-0.726)	0.254	-4.705
10	(-3.511)	(-2.576)	(-1.654)	-0.674	-8.417
Sum	-21.007	-11.659	-2.438	7.359	-27.745
$\underline{\mu}_k^{UB}$	-2.101	-1.166	-0.244	0.736	
	(-1.166 - 0.244) / 2 = -0.705				
$\underline{\mu}_k^{UB}$ *(normalized)*	-1.396	-0.461	0.461	1.441	

(*) Cells in parentheses were calculated using the mean difference between adjacent columns

C.9. Space Available at the Departure Lounge - São Paulo / Guarulhos

**Table C.33: Frequencies of Ratings - Space Available at Departure Lounge
São Paulo / Guarulhos International Airport**

Group	Categories (k)					
(j)	1	2	3	4	5	Total
1	2	4	12	6	1	25
2	1	2	9	11	3	26
3	0	1	6	14	6	27
4	0	0	3	3	3	9
5	0	0	0	3	1	4
6	0	0	1	3	3	7
7	0	0	0	1	2	3
8	0	0	0	3	3	6
9	0	0	0	3	2	5
10	0	0	0	1	4	5
Total	3	7	31	48	28	117

**Table C.34: Proportion of Responses - Space Available at Departure Lounge
São Paulo / Guarulhos International Airport**

Group	Categories (k)					
(j)	1	2	3	4	5	Total
1	0.080	0.160	0.480	0.240	0.040	1.000
2	0.038	0.077	0.346	0.423	0.115	1.000
3	0.000	0.037	0.222	0.519	0.222	1.000
4	0.000	0.000	0.333	0.333	0.333	1.000
5	0.000	0.000	0.000	0.750	0.250	1.000
6	0.000	0.000	0.143	0.429	0.429	1.000
7	0.000	0.000	0.000	0.333	0.667	1.000
8	0.000	0.000	0.000	0.500	0.500	1.000
9	0.000	0.000	0.000	0.600	0.400	1.000
10	0.000	0.000	0.000	0.200	0.800	1.000

Table C.35: Cumulative Proportions - Space Available at Departure Lounge
São Paulo / Guarulhos International Airport

	1	2	3	4	5
1	0.080	0.240	0.720	0.960	1.000
2	0.038	0.115	0.462	0.885	1.000
3	0.000	0.037	0.259	0.778	1.000
4	0.000	0.000	0.333	0.667	1.000
5	0.000	0.000	0.000	0.750	1.000
6	0.000	0.000	0.143	0.571	1.000
7	0.000	0.000	0.000	0.333	1.000
8	0.000	0.000	0.000	0.500	1.000
9	0.000	0.000	0.000	0.600	1.000
10	0.000	0.000	0.000	0.200	1.000

Table C.36: Normal Deviates - Space Available at Departure Lounge
São Paulo / Guarulhos International Airport

	1	2	3	4	Sum
1	-1.405	-0.706	0.583	1.750	0.222
2	-1.769	-1.198	-0.097	1.198	-1.865
3	(-2.420)	-1.786	-0.646	0.765	-4.087
4	(-2.242)	(-1.608)	-0.431	0.431	-3.850
5	(-2.333)	(-1.699)	(-0.522)	0.674	-3.878
6	(-2.878)	(-2.244)	-1.067	0.180	-6.010
7	(-3.438)	(-2.804)	(-1.627)	-0.431	-8.300
8	(-3.007)	(-2.373)	(-1.196)	0.000	-6.576
9	(-2.753)	(-2.119)	(-0.942)	0.254	-5.562
10	(-3.848)	(-3.214)	(-2.037)	-0.841	-9.942
Sum	-26.093	-19.752	-7.982	3.980	-49.848
$\underline{\mu}_k^{UB}$	-2.609	-1.975	-0.798	0.398	
	(-2.609 - 1.975) / 2 = -1.387				
$\underline{\mu}_k^{UB}$ (normalized)	-1.223	-0.589	0.589	1.785	

(*) Cells in parentheses were calculated using the mean difference between adjacent columns

C.10. Available Seats at the Departure Lounge - São Paulo / Guarulhos

Table C.37: Frequencies of Ratings - Available Seats at the Departure Lounge
São Paulo / Guarulhos International Airport

Group	Categories (k)					
(j)	1	2	3	4	5	Total
1	2	5	7	1	0	15
2	1	5	5	4	1	16
3	0	3	4	4	0	11
4	0	0	1	2	1	4
5	0	0	2	3	1	6
6	0	1	2	2	3	8
7	0	0	0	5	2	7
8	0	1	1	4	4	10
Total	3	15	22	25	12	77

Table C.38: Proportion of Responses - Available Seats at the Departure Lounge
São Paulo / Guarulhos International Airport

Group	Categories (k)					
(j)	1	2	3	4	5	Total
1	0.133	0.333	0.467	0.067	0.000	1.000
2	0.063	0.313	0.313	0.250	0.063	1.000
3	0.000	0.273	0.364	0.364	0.000	1.000
4	0.000	0.000	0.250	0.500	0.250	1.000
5	0.000	0.000	0.333	0.500	0.167	1.000
6	0.000	0.125	0.250	0.250	0.375	1.000
7	0.000	0.000	0.000	0.714	0.286	1.000
8	0.000	0.100	0.100	0.400	0.400	1.000

249

Table C.39: Cumulative Proportions - Available Seats at the Departure Lounge
São Paulo / Guarulhos International Airport

	1	2	3	4	5
1	0.133	0.467	0.933	1.000	1.000
2	0.063	0.375	0.688	0.938	1.000
3	0.000	0.273	0.636	1.000	1.000
4	0.000	0.000	0.250	0.750	1.000
5	0.000	0.000	0.333	0.833	1.000
6	0.000	0.125	0.375	0.625	1.000
7	0.000	0.000	0.000	0.714	1.000
8	0.000	0.100	0.200	0.600	1.000

Table C.40: Normal Deviates - Available Seats at the Departure Lounge
São Paulo / Guarulhos International Airport

	1	2	3	4	Sum
1	-1.111	-0.084	1.501	2.606	2.912
2	-1.534	-0.319	0.489	1.534	0.170
3	-1.726	-0.605	0.349	1.454	-0.527
4	-2.719	-1.598	-0.674	0.674	-4.318
5	-2.476	-1.355	-0.431	0.967	-3.295
6	-2.271	-1.150	-0.319	0.319	-3.422
7	-2.584	-1.463	-0.539	0.566	-4.020
8	-2.403	-1.282	-0.841	0.254	-4.272
Sum	-16.824	-7.856	-0.466	8.374	-16.771
μ_k^{UB}	-2.103	-0.982	-0.058	1.047	
\multicolumn{5}{c}{(-0.982 - 0.058) / 2 = -0.520}				
μ_k^{UB} *(normalized)*	-1.583	-0.462	0.462	1.567	

(*) Cells in parentheses were calculated using the mean difference between adjacent columns

C.11. Claim Frontage at the Baggage Claim - Calgary

**Table C.41: Frequencies of Ratings - Claim Frontage at the Baggage Claim
Calgary International Airport**

Group	Categories (k)					
(j)	1	2	3	4	5	Total
1	0	0	0	15	4	19
2	0	1	1	11	2	15
3	0	0	0	6	4	10
4	0	0	0	2	4	6
5	0	0	0	1	1	2
6	0	0	0	3	4	7
Total	0	1	1	38	19	59

**Table C.42: Proportion of Responses - Claim Frontage at the Baggage Claim
Calgary International Airport**

Group	Categories (k)					
(j)	1	2	3	4	5	Total
1	0.000	0.000	0.000	0.789	0.211	1.000
2	0.000	0.067	0.067	0.733	0.133	1.000
3	0.000	0.000	0.000	0.600	0.400	1.000
4	0.000	0.000	0.000	0.333	0.667	1.000
5	0.000	0.000	0.000	0.500	0.500	1.000
6	0.000	0.000	0.000	0.429	0.571	1.000

Table C.43: Cumulative Proportions - Claim Frontage at the Baggage Claim Calgary International Airport

	1	2	3	4	5
1	0.000	0.000	0.000	0.789	1.000
2	0.000	0.067	0.133	0.867	1.000
3	0.000	0.000	0.000	0.600	1.000
4	0.000	0.000	0.000	0.333	1.000
5	0.000	0.000	0.000	0.500	1.000
6	0.000	0.000	0.000	0.429	1.000

Table C.44: Normal Deviates - Claim Frontage at the Baggage Claim Calgary International Airport

	1	2	3	4	Sum
1	(-2.197)	(-1.807)	(-1.417)	0.804	-4.615
2	(-1.891)	-1.501	-1.111	1.111	-3.392
3	(-2.747)	(-2.357)	(-1.967)	0.254	-6.819
4	(-3.432)	(-3.042)	(-2.652)	-0.431	-9.557
5	(-3.001)	(-2.611)	(-2.221)	0.000	-7.833
6	(-3.181)	(-2.791)	(-2.401)	-0.180	-8.554
Sum	-16.449	-14.109	-11.769	1.558	-40.769
μ_k^{UB}	-2.742	-2.352	-1.961	0.260	
	(-2.352 - 1.961) / 2 = -2.156				
μ_k^{UB} (normalized)	-0.585	-0.195	0.195	2.416	

(*) Cells in parentheses were calculated using the mean difference between adjacent columns

C.12. Processing Time at the Baggage Claim - Calgary

Table C.45: Frequencies of Ratings - Processing Time at the Baggage Claim
Calgary International Airport

Group	Categories (k)					
(j)	1	2	3	4	5	Total
1	0	0	0	4	2	6
2	0	1	1	13	1	16
3	0	0	3	9	5	17
4	0	2	3	1	1	7
5	0	2	1	3	0	6
6	0	3	2	2	0	7
Total	0	8	10	32	9	59

Table C.46: Proportion of Responses - Processing Time at the Baggage Claim
Calgary International Airport

Group	Categories (k)					
(j)	1	2	3	4	5	Total
1	0.000	0.000	0.000	0.667	0.333	1.000
2	0.000	0.063	0.063	0.813	0.063	1.000
3	0.000	0.000	0.176	0.529	0.294	1.000
4	0.000	0.286	0.429	0.143	0.143	1.000
5	0.000	0.333	0.167	0.500	0.000	1.000
6	0.000	0.429	0.286	0.286	0.000	1.000

Table C.47: Cumulative Proportions - Processing Time at the Baggage Claim Calgary International Airport

	1	2	3	4	5
1	0.000	0.000	0.000	0.667	1.000
2	0.000	0.063	0.125	0.938	1.000
3	0.000	0.000	0.176	0.706	1.000
4	0.000	0.286	0.714	0.857	1.000
5	0.000	0.333	0.500	1.000	1.000
6	0.000	0.429	0.714	1.000	1.000

Table C.48: Normal Deviates - Processing Time at the Baggage Claim Calgary International Airport

	1	2	3	4	Sum
1	(-2.467)	(-1.794)	(-1.121)	0.431	-4.951
2	(-2.207)	-1.534	-1.150	1.534	-3.357
3	(-2.275)	-1.602	-0.929	0.542	-4.264
4	(-1.239)	-0.566	0.566	1.067	-0.172
5	(-1.104)	-0.431	0.000	(1.552)	0.017
6	(-0.853)	-0.180	0.566	(2.118)	1.651
Sum	-10.145	-6.107	-2.068	7.244	-11.076
$\underline{\mu}_k^{UB}$	-1.691	-1.018	-0.345	1.207	
$\underline{\mu}_k^{UB}$ (normalized)	-1.010	-0.337	0.337	1.889	

$(-1.018 - 0.345) / 2 = -0.681$

(*) Cells in parentheses were calculated using the mean difference between adjacent columns

C.13. Total Waiting + Processing Time - São Paulo / Guarulhos

**Table C.49: Frequencies of Ratings - Total Waiting + Processing Time
São Paulo / Guarulhos International Airport**

Group	Categories (k)					
(j)	1	2	3	4	5	Total
1	0	0	0	1	4	5
2	0	0	3	11	2	16
3	0	0	2	11	3	16
4	0	0	4	2	1	7
5	0	0	3	7	2	12
6	0	1	3	7	1	12
7	0	1	2	4	0	7
8	0	2	1	0	0	3
Total	0	4	18	43	13	78

**Table C.50: Proportion of Responses - Total Waiting + Processing Time
São Paulo / Guarulhos International Airport**

Group	Categories (k)					
(j)	1	2	3	4	5	Total
1	0.000	0.000	0.000	0.200	0.800	1.000
2	0.000	0.000	0.188	0.688	0.125	1.000
3	0.000	0.000	0.125	0.688	0.188	1.000
4	0.000	0.000	0.571	0.286	0.143	1.000
5	0.000	0.000	0.250	0.583	0.167	1.000
6	0.000	0.083	0.250	0.583	0.083	1.000
7	0.000	0.143	0.286	0.571	0.000	1.000
8	0.000	0.667	0.333	0.000	0.000	1.000

Table C.51: Cumulative Proportions - Total Waiting + Processing Time
São Paulo / Guarulhos International Airport

	1	2	3	4	5
1	0.000	0.000	0.000	0.200	1.000
2	0.000	0.000	0.188	0.875	1.000
3	0.000	0.000	0.125	0.813	1.000
4	0.000	0.000	0.571	0.857	1.000
5	0.000	0.000	0.250	0.833	1.000
6	0.000	0.083	0.333	0.917	1.000
7	0.000	0.143	0.429	1.000	1.000
8	0.000	0.667	1.000	1.000	1.000

Table C.52: Normal Deviates - Total Waiting + Processing Time
São Paulo / Guarulhos International Airport

	1	2	3	4	Sum
1	(-6.049)	(-3.445)	(-2.525)	-0.841	-12.862
2	(-4.411)	(-1.807)	-0.887	1.150	-5.955
3	(-4.674)	(-2.070)	-1.150	0.887	-7.008
4	(-3.344)	(-0.740)	0.180	1.067	-2.836
5	(-4.198)	(-1.594)	-0.674	0.967	-5.500
6	(-3.987)	-1.383	-0.431	1.383	-4.418
7	(-3.671)	-1.067	-0.180	(1.504)	-3.415
8	(-2.173)	0.431	(1.351)	(3.035)	2.644
Sum	-32.508	-11.676	-4.317	9.152	-39.350
μ_k^{UB}	-4.064	-1.460	-0.540	1.144	
$(-1.460 - 0.540) / 2 = -1.000$					
μ_k^{UB} (normalized)	-3.064	-0.460	0.460	2.144	

(*) Cells in parentheses were calculated using the mean difference between adjacent columns

C.14. Real Operational Walking Distance - São Paulo / Guarulhos

Table C.53: Frequencies of Ratings - Real Operational Walking Distance
São Paulo / Guarulhos International Airport

Group	Categories (k)					
(j)	1	2	3	4	5	Total
1	0	0	1	7	1	9
2	0	1	2	9	1	13
3	0	1	5	6	1	13
4	0	3	7	11	2	23
5	0	1	2	3	2	8
6	0	0	3	1	1	5
7	0	3	1	1	1	6
8	0	9	21	38	9	77
Total	0	0	1	7	1	9

Table C.54: Proportion of Responses - Real Operational Walking Distance
São Paulo / Guarulhos International Airport

Group	Categories (k)					
(j)	1	2	3	4	5	Total
1	0.000	0.000	0.111	0.778	0.111	1.000
2	0.000	0.077	0.154	0.692	0.077	1.000
3	0.000	0.077	0.385	0.462	0.077	1.000
4	0.000	0.130	0.304	0.478	0.087	1.000
5	0.000	0.125	0.250	0.375	0.250	1.000
6	0.000	0.000	0.600	0.200	0.200	1.000
7	0.000	0.500	0.167	0.167	0.167	1.000
8	0.000	0.000	0.111	0.778	0.111	1.000

Table C.55: Cumulative Proportions - Real Operational Walking Distance
São Paulo / Guarulhos International Airport

	1	2	3	4	5
1	0.000	0.000	0.111	0.889	1.000
2	0.000	0.077	0.231	0.923	1.000
3	0.000	0.077	0.462	0.923	1.000
4	0.000	0.130	0.435	0.913	1.000
5	0.000	0.125	0.375	0.750	1.000
6	0.000	0.000	0.600	0.800	1.000
7	0.000	0.500	0.667	0.833	1.000
8	0.000	0.000	0.111	0.889	1.000

Table C.56: Normal Deviates - Real Operational Walking Distance
São Paulo / Guarulhos International Airport

	1	2	3	4	Sum
1	-3.615	-2.069	-1.221	1.221	-5.683
2	-2.972	-1.426	-0.736	1.426	-3.708
3	-2.972	-1.426	-0.097	1.426	-3.069
4	-2.670	-1.124	-0.164	1.360	-2.599
5	-2.696	-1.150	-0.319	0.674	-3.491
6	-2.140	-0.594	0.254	0.841	-1.640
7	-1.546	0.000	0.431	0.967	-0.148
8	-18.612	-7.790	-1.852	7.916	-20.338
Sum	-3.615	-2.069	-1.221	1.221	-5.683
$\underline{\mu}_k^{UB}$	-2.659	-1.113	-0.265	1.131	
(-1.113 - 0.265) / 2 = -0.689					
$\underline{\mu}_k^{UB}$ *(normalized)*	-1.970	-0.424	0.424	1.820	

(*) Cells in parentheses were calculated using the mean difference between adjacent columns

C.15. Orientation - Distance - São Paulo / Guarulhos

Table C.57: Frequencies of Ratings - Orientation - Distance
São Paulo / Guarulhos International Airport

Group	Categories (k)					
(j)	1	2	3	4	5	Total
1	0	2	4	19	5	30
2	0	0	1	7	2	10
3	0	1	2	6	3	12
4	0	2	1	5	2	10
5	0	0	2	2	0	4
6	0	1	2	1	0	4
7	1	2	3	1	0	7
Total	1	8	15	41	12	77

Table C.58: Proportion of Responses - Orientation - Distance
São Paulo / Guarulhos International Airport

Group	Categories (k)					
(j)	1	2	3	4	5	Total
1	0.000	0.067	0.133	0.633	0.167	1.000
2	0.000	0.000	0.100	0.700	0.200	1.000
3	0.000	0.083	0.167	0.500	0.250	1.000
4	0.000	0.200	0.100	0.500	0.200	1.000
5	0.000	0.000	0.500	0.500	0.000	1.000
6	0.000	0.250	0.500	0.250	0.000	1.000
7	0.143	0.286	0.429	0.143	0.000	1.000

Table C.59: Cumulative Proportions - Orientation - Distance
São Paulo / Guarulhos International Airport

	1	2	3	4	5
1	0.000	0.067	0.200	0.833	1.000
2	0.000	0.000	0.100	0.800	1.000
3	0.000	0.083	0.250	0.750	1.000
4	0.000	0.200	0.300	0.800	1.000
5	0.000	0.000	0.500	1.000	1.000
6	0.000	0.250	0.750	1.000	1.000
7	0.143	0.429	0.857	1.000	1.000

Table C.60: Normal Deviates - Orientation - Distance
São Paulo / Guarulhos International Airport

	1	2	3	4	Sum
1	(-1.945)	-1.501	-0.841	0.967	-3.320
2	(-2.582)	(-2.138)	-1.282	0.841	-5.159
3	(-2.809)	-1.383	-0.674	0.674	-4.192
4	(-1.285)	-0.841	-0.525	0.841	-1.810
5	(-1.300)	(-0.856)	0.000	(1.662)	-0.494
6	(-1.118)	-0.674	0.674	(2.336)	1.218
7	-1.067	-0.180	1.067	(2.729)	2.549
Sum	-12.107	-7.574	-1.580	10.053	-11.208
$\underline{\mu}_k^{UB}$	-1.730	-1.082	-0.226	1.436	
	(-1.082 - 0.226) / 2 = -0.654				
$\underline{\mu}_k^{UB}$ *(normalized)*	-1.076	-0.428	0.428	2.090	

(*) Cells in parentheses were calculated using the mean difference between adjacent columns

C.16. Tardity Differential - São Paulo / Guarulhos

Table C.61: Frequencies of Ratings - Tardity Differential
São Paulo / Guarulhos International Airport

Group	Categories (k)					
(j)	1	2	3	4	5	Total
1	0	0	1	9	1	11
2	0	0	0	4	7	11
3	0	0	0	6	2	8
4	0	0	1	6	2	9
5	0	1	2	8	1	12
6	0	3	3	5	1	12
7	0	1	3	3	1	8
8	1	2	4	0	0	7
Total	1	7	14	41	15	78

Table C.62: Proportion of Responses - Tardity Differential
São Paulo / Guarulhos International Airport

Group	Categories (k)					
(j)	1	2	3	4	5	Total
1	0.000	0.000	0.091	0.818	0.091	1.000
2	0.000	0.000	0.000	0.364	0.636	1.000
3	0.000	0.000	0.000	0.750	0.250	1.000
4	0.000	0.000	0.111	0.667	0.222	1.000
5	0.000	0.083	0.167	0.667	0.083	1.000
6	0.000	0.250	0.250	0.417	0.083	1.000
7	0.000	0.125	0.375	0.375	0.125	1.000
8	0.143	0.286	0.571	0.000	0.000	1.000

Table C.63: Cumulative Proportions - Tardity Differential
São Paulo / Guarulhos International Airport

	1	2	3	4	5
1	0.000	0.000	0.091	0.909	1.000
2	0.000	0.000	0.000	0.364	1.000
3	0.000	0.000	0.000	0.750	1.000
4	0.000	0.000	0.111	0.778	1.000
5	0.000	0.083	0.250	0.917	1.000
6	0.000	0.250	0.500	0.917	1.000
7	0.000	0.125	0.500	0.875	1.000
8	0.143	0.429	1.000	1.000	1.000

Table C.64: Normal Deviates - Tardity Differential
São Paulo / Guarulhos International Airport

	1	2	3	4	Sum
1	(-3.066)	(-2.179)	-1.335	1.335	-5.245
2	(-3.929)	(-3.042)	(-2.198)	-0.349	-9.518
3	(-2.906)	(-2.019)	(-1.175)	0.674	-5.424
4	(-2.952)	(-2.065)	-1.221	0.765	-5.472
5	(-2.270)	-1.383	-0.674	1.383	-2.944
6	(-1.561)	-0.674	0.000	1.383	-0.853
7	(-2.037)	-1.150	0.000	1.150	-2.037
8	-1.067	-0.180	(0.664)	(2.513)	1.929
Sum	-19.789	-12.692	-5.939	8.854	-29.566
$\underline{\mu}_k^{UB}$	-2.474	-1.587	-0.742	1.107	
$\underline{\mu}_k^{UB}$ *(normalized)*	-1.309	-0.422	0.422	2.271	

(-1.587 - 0.742) / 2 = -1.164

(*) Cells in parentheses were calculated using the mean difference between adjacent columns

C.17. Benchmarking - Three Brazilian Airports

Table C.65: Frequencies of Ratings - Benchmarking - Three Brazilian Airports

Component	Categories (k)					
	1	2	3	4	5	Total
GR Curb	0	11	26	67	15	119
GR Check	0	4	18	75	22	119
GR Lou	3	8	34	54	18	117
GR Ov	1	4	22	75	15	117
RJ Curb	0	0	3	19	13	35
RJ Check	0	0	1	11	23	35
RJ Lou	0	0	3	16	16	35
RJ Ov	0	0	5	22	8	35
SP Curb	3	4	4	18	1	30
SP Check	0	0	5	18	7	30
SP Lou	1	2	8	16	3	30
SP Ov	1	2	10	14	3	30

Table C.66: Proportion of Responses - Benchmarking - Three Brazilian Airports

Component	Categories (k)					
	1	2	3	4	5	Total
GR Curb	0.000	0.092	0.218	0.563	0.126	1.000
GR Check	0.000	0.034	0.151	0.630	0.185	1.000
GR Lou	0.026	0.068	0.291	0.462	0.154	1.000
GR Ov	0.009	0.034	0.188	0.641	0.128	1.000
RJ Curb	0.000	0.000	0.086	0.543	0.371	1.000
RJ Check	0.000	0.000	0.029	0.314	0.657	1.000
RJ Lou	0.000	0.000	0.086	0.457	0.457	1.000
RJ Ov	0.000	0.000	0.143	0.629	0.229	1.000
SP Curb	0.100	0.133	0.133	0.600	0.033	1.000
SP Check	0.000	0.000	0.167	0.600	0.233	1.000
SP Lou	0.033	0.067	0.267	0.533	0.100	1.000
SP Ov	0.033	0.067	0.333	0.467	0.100	1.000

Table C.67: Cumulative Proportions - Benchmarking - Three Brazilian Airports

Component	1	2	3	4	5
GR Curb	0.000	0.092	0.311	0.874	1.000
GR Check	0.000	0.034	0.185	0.815	1.000
GR Lou	0.026	0.094	0.385	0.846	1.000
GR Ov	0.009	0.043	0.231	0.872	1.000
RJ Curb	0.000	0.000	0.086	0.629	1.000
RJ Check	0.000	0.000	0.029	0.343	1.000
RJ Lou	0.000	0.000	0.086	0.543	1.000
RJ Ov	0.000	0.000	0.143	0.771	1.000
SP Curb	0.100	0.233	0.367	0.967	1.000
SP Check	0.000	0.000	0.167	0.767	1.000
SP Lou	0.033	0.100	0.367	0.900	1.000
SP Ov	0.033	0.100	0.433	0.900	1.000

Table C.68: Normal Deviates - Benchmarking - Three Brazilian Airports

Component	1	2	3	4	Sum
GR Curb	(-1.913)	-1.326	-0.493	1.145	-2.587
GR Check	(-2.417)	-1.830	-0.897	0.897	-4.247
GR Lou	-1.949	-1.316	-0.294	1.020	-2.539
GR Ov	-2.363	-1.720	-0.736	1.135	-3.683
RJ Curb	(-2.843)	(-2.256)	-1.368	0.328	-6.137
RJ Check	(-3.377)	(-2.790)	-1.902	-0.405	-8.475
RJ Lou	(-2.843)	(-2.256)	-1.368	0.108	-6.358
RJ Ov	(-2.542)	(-1.955)	-1.067	0.743	-4.822
SP Curb	-1.282	-0.728	-0.341	1.834	-0.517
SP Check	(-2.442)	(-1.855)	-0.967	0.728	-4.537
SP Lou	-1.834	-1.282	-0.341	1.282	-2.175
SP Ov	-1.834	-1.282	-0.168	1.282	-2.002
Sum	-25.804	-19.313	-9.774	8.815	-46.077
$\underline{\mu}_k^{UB}$	-2.150	-1.609	-0.815	0.735	
	(-1.609 - 0.815) / 2 = -1.212				
$\underline{\mu}_k^{UB}$ (normalized)	-0.938	-0.397	0.397	1.947	

(*) Cells in parentheses were calculated using the mean difference between adjacent columns

14780336R00161

Printed in Poland
by Amazon Fulfillment
Poland Sp. z o.o., Wrocław